Robert N. Gunther 1.00

D1433028

Also by Kevin Brownlow

The Parade's Gone By ...
How It Happened Here
The War, the West and the Wilderness
Hollywood—The Pioneers

NAPOLEON

NAPOLEON

ABEL GANCE'S CLASSIC FILM

Kevin Brownlow

Research Collaborators

Bambi Ballard
Veronica Bamfield
Lenny Borger
Bernard Eisenschitz

Alfred A. Knopf   New York   1983

THIS IS A BORZOI BOOK

PUBLISHED BY ALFRED A. KNOPF, INC.

Copyright © 1983 by Kevin Brownlow
All rights reserved under International and Pan-American
Copyright Conventions. Published in the United States by
Alfred A. Knopf, Inc., New York. Distributed by Random
House, Inc., New York. Published in Great Britain by
Jonathan Cape Ltd, London.

Library of Congress Cataloging in Publication Data
Brownlow, Kevin.
Napoleon, Abel Gance's classic film.
1. Napoleon (Motion picture : 1927) I. Title.
PN1997.N3283B77   1983   791.43'72   83-48098
ISBN 0-394-53394-1

Manufactured in the United States of America
First American Edition

For my mother,
who paid for the first two reels ...

Contents

Acknowledgments

Napoleon was a collaborative enterprise; so was this book. I would like to express my heartfelt thanks to my collaborators, listed on the title page, and to the following:

Iwona Barycz, Paul de Bergh, Dagmar Bolin, David Bradley, British Film Institute, Virginia Brownlow, François Caviglioli, Centre National de la Cinématographie, Cinémathèque Française, André Conti, Ian Craig, Carl Davis, André-Marc Delocque-Fourcaud, Jacques Deslandes, Sarah Ellis, Faith Evans, Dr Charles Ford, Rachel Ford, Clarisse Gance, David Gill, Bob Harris, Moya Hassan, Pierre Hodgson, John Holmstrom, Philippe d'Hugues, Roger Icart, Raymond Izard, Pauline Jobson, Nelly Kaplan, Richard Koszarski, Claude Lafaye, Joanna Lambert, M. de la Motte, Ian Lewis, Renée Lichtig, John Lucarotti, Tom Luddy, Sybille de Luze, Shirley McAuley, Tom Maschler, Russell Merritt, Metro-Goldwyn-Mayer Film Co., Peter Miles, Anne Morris, Herbert S. Nusbaum, Markku Salmi, F. Schmitt, Tony Shapps, Deborah Shepherd, Michael Sissons, Michelle Snapes, Liz Sutherland, Rosalie Swedlin, G. Troussier, Thérèse Wright.

I am also extremely grateful to all those connected with *Napoleon* who shared their memories:

Lony Alexandre, Annabella, Robert de Ansorena, Alexander d'Arbeloff, Charly Arnoux, Jean Arroy, Comte de Béarn, Émile Billoré, Raymond Bosc, Robert Braquehaye, Henri Cointe, Marcel David, Albert Dieudonné, Mme Dieudonné, Jean Dréville, Simon Feldman, Gabriel Fornaseri, Simone Genevois, Georges Henin, Arthur Hoerée, Harry-Krimer, A. Malachez, Gina Manès, M. Merle, Severine Mignone, Jean Mitry, Mabel Poulton, Mme Roudenko, Simone Surdieux, V. Tourjansky, Robert Vidalin.

Unless otherwise credited, the interviews with Abel Gance were conducted between 1963 and 1981. Extracts were used in my book *The Parade's Gone By* ... (Alfred A. Knopf, 1968), a paperback edition of which is published by the University of California Press, Berkeley, California. Other extracts

7

Acknowledgments

appeared in my film *The Charm of Dynamite* (1968) which is available from Essential Cinema, 122 Wardour Street, London W1, or from Images Film Archive, 300 Phillips Park Road, Mamaroneck, New York 10543. An interview with Albert Dieudonné was filmed for this same production.

Picture Credits

BBC Hulton Picture Library, p. 39 left

Kevin Brownlow Collection, pp. 13, 18, 21, 29, 33, 38, 59 top right, 62 left, 68, 69 top and bottom, 71, 75, 81, 93, 94, 107, 127, 131, 133, 144, 154-6, 181, 188, 204, 216, 219, 220, 231, 257

Centre National de la Cinématographie, Paris, pp. 27 top and bottom, 50 right, 59 left, 70, 73, 74, 77, 79, 95, 112, 113, 118, 119 top, 128, 157

Madame Dieudonné, p. 60 left and right

Cinémathèque Française, pp. 32, 66 top, 78, 83, 102, 129

Simon Feldman, pp. 76, 84 left and right, 85 left and right, 87 bottom, 89, 134

Simon Feldman-CNC, p. 124

Roger Icart, p. 87 top

Images Film Archive, pp. 111, 145

Nelly Kaplan, pp. 63, 165

Kobal Collection, pp. 106, 114-15, 172

Laurie Lewis, pp. 240-1

Yvonne Martin, pp. 50 left, 141

National Film Archive, pp. 136, 226

Roger-Viollet, pp. 39 right, 59 bottom, 62 right, 103 top and bottom

Madame Roudenko, p. 64

Simone Surdieux, pp. 2, 49, 51, 66 bottom, 72, 82, 86, 88, 91, 98, 105, 109, 119 bottom, 121, 122, 126, 138 top to bottom, 149, 151, 177

Frontispiece *Abel Gance and 'Brienne', a stray adopted during the shooting at Briançon of the Brienne sequences, February 1925*

Preface

Napoléon vu par Abel Gance had a triumphal première at the Opéra in Paris in April 1927. What the audience saw was a shortened version; the *version définitive* was shown privately the following month to an even greater chorus of praise. The film was so far ahead of its time that it seemed set to become the most famous ever made, and to sweep the markets of the world. But then something mysterious happened. The film disappeared. For months there was no sign of it. Other epics, from the United States, won the attention of press and public. When *Napoleon* finally reappeared, it was not the long-awaited *version définitive*. It was the Opéra version again. And four months later, when the supposedly definitive version was unveiled at the Gaumont-Palace, it was a different film. It had suffered a mutation. The crowds no longer stood and cheered. They seemed confused and bored. Within a year, memories of the unrivalled masterpiece had been eclipsed by botched versions. In America, it was a fiasco. It was accorded the status of 'just another movie', and one which was to lose a great deal of money for its backers.

This mystery puzzled me for years. For when I first saw *Napoleon*, I was still at school. I was so impressed that I determined to meet the man who made it. And when I succeeded, I tried to find out what had happened. He gave me his version of the disaster, but he was never able to explain it satisfactorily, perhaps because the facts still hurt. If I couldn't unravel the mystery at that stage, I could attempt to correct the record, and to reinstate the reputation of the film in the history books. I began to write about it, to give talks about it, to show various versions. And soon I found myself trying to piece the film together again. It was a long process, and the result was not ready for several years. Even then, it aroused little interest. No one wanted to show it.

Eventually, the reconstructed *Napoleon* was invited to the least likely film festival imaginable, in the Rocky Mountains of Colorado. What was even more extraordinary was that Abel Gance, aged eighty-nine, travelled from Nice to see it. From that moment, the movement to resurrect *Napoleon* gathered momentum until it burst upon the screens of London and New York, accompanied by full symphony orchestras, accorded the kind of enthusiasm seldom witnessed in the cinema since that triumphal première in Paris in April 1927.

Abel Gance regarded Napoleon as a tragic hero.[1] There was more than a touch of the tragic hero about Abel Gance. He faced death from tuberculosis in his youth; many of his close friends were killed in the First World War; his fiancée succumbed to tuberculosis during the making of his film *La Roue*; he was forced to abandon his epic series of films on Napoleon when only the first had been made. Never again was he given the resources or the conditions to produce the kind of film of which he had shown himself to be the master.

'There are people', said the actor Robert Vidalin, who played in *Napoleon*, 'who go beyond ordinary levels. Abel Gance was a very exceptional person. He was not only a poet, a writer and an actor, he was a magnificent director, and he was to some degree a technical engineer. Yet he had such simplicity. He could embrace several careers at the same time. He was gifted in every way; a great romantic, he was also remarkable in the way he could create a rapport with people and enrich their lives. A man marked by genius. I can never understand why France let him fall as she did. But ingratitude is a trait of the human character.'[2]

If D.W. Griffith gave the cinema its start, Gance grabbed the infant by the hand and gave it a breathless rush through life. Like a benevolent Mephistopheles, he showed it what its future might be. He took the cinema further, technically and aesthetically, than any of his contemporaries. As Welsh and Kramer put it, 'Abel Gance is the epitome of what the cinema might have become, but never did.'[3]

Many film-makers have been inspired by him. Jean Renoir said that Gance's influence was enormous. In Japan, Kurosawa named *La Roue* as the first film that had impressed him. Eisenstein, Dovzhenko, Pudovkin and Ekk thanked Gance for *La Roue*; they had learned their craft, they said, by studying the film at the Moscow Academy. Their appreciation makes Gance's neglect all the more incomprehensible. But the industry, alarmed by his startling ideas and equally startling expenditure, determined to limit his range. And, unfortunately, they succeeded. Gance was forced to dissipate his talents until the flame behind those talents flickered out. Whatever happened to his film-making abilities — and there is no doubt that something did — the power of his intellect remained as acute as ever. Even in his nineties, when physical frailty wore down his mental faculties, he was able to express his ideas so poetically that to listen to him was like being in the presence of Apollinaire or Rimbaud.

In my first book, *The Parade's Gone By ...* , written in 1965–6, I briefly told the story of the making of *Napoleon*, based on what Gance told me, and the little I was able to research from French sources. Since then, a great deal of documentation has come to light, and I have taken advantage of it to expand the story and to correct mistakes and misunderstandings. (I am, however, convinced that there is still much to be learned about how the film was made, and would be immensely grateful for any first-hand information.)

If I admired Gance and his collaborators before I began this book, my researches have increased that admiration a hundredfold. I never fully appreciated the scale of the enterprise, the machinery that had to be set in motion before the creative work could begin, nor the degree of responsibility Gance took upon himself.

Certainly, like Erich von Stroheim, Gance was extravagant. He spent far too much of other people's wealth. And, like von Stroheim, he paid for that extravagance with the rest of his career. He tried to make routine, commercial films, but that was not his strength. He did not, therefore, like so many directors, end up in comfortable retirement. His old age was marked by anxiety and debt. But of course this is the classic fate of great artists. For pioneers make history, not money.

Kevin Brownlow

1·The Fuse Is Lit

I shall never forget my first encounter with Abel Gance's *Napoleon*. I was not one of those fortunate enough to see the film as it was meant to be seen, with the magic of three screens and a vast orchestra. I saw it under the most unpromising circumstances—fragments of the great original, shown on a home projector, twenty-five years after its original release. Yet those fragments changed my life.

I was fifteen, still at school in Hampstead, and already obsessed by the cinema. I was lucky enough to have parents who encouraged my obsession. They had given me a projector for my eleventh birthday, and I had become an avid collector of films. Since the only films available to me were silent films, I found myself immersed in the rarefied atmosphere of a forgotten art. As small boys become experts on stamp collecting or locomotives, so I became an expert on the films of Douglas Fairbanks or the Vitagraph Corporation of America. And I was particularly enamoured of the French cinema.

The films were on 9·5mm, a gauge invented in France purely for the home. A large number of silent films were released on 9·5mm, nearly all heavily abridged so that home movie enthusiasts could afford them. The most interesting had long been withdrawn, so I spent my spare time tramping round London looking for junk shops or old film libraries which might still have a few. Since home movies were being abandoned in favour of television, I found a surprising number of rarities. Among the best were the French silents—de Baroncelli's *Pêcheurs d'Islande* ... Raymond Bernard's *Joueur d'échecs* ... Jacques Feyder's *Visages d'enfants*. I greatly admired the rapid cutting of the dramatic episodes. And there was an atmosphere and an emotional quality about these films which impressed me.

I was so impressed that I set out to make one myself—on 9·5mm— hoping to capture something of the same mood. I chose a story by de Maupassant, and I cast it from people I knew, and from the few Galliclooking people in the neighbourhood. The part of the forester I gave to Liam O'Leary, who was acquisitions officer at the National Film Archive.

Liam had written a book called *Invitation to the Film*. He was in his forties, extremely Irish (which appealed to my Irish father) and he had an infectious enthusiasm for the silent era. He, too, had started with a 9·5mm projector and he shared my admiration for the French silents. I had met him at the British Film Institute, where I did my research. He proved an indispensable guide, suggesting books I might have overlooked, and inviting me to screenings of rare films I would never otherwise have seen.

My admiration for the French silent cinema was subject to the occasional shattering blow. One of these was delivered by a director called Jean Epstein, a revered name of the period. When I was offered a print of his *Lion des Mogols* (1924) I bought it at once. It featured the great Russian émigré actor Ivan Mosjoukine in a story of a Tibetan prince who flees his country, joins a ship at Bombay, and becomes the star of a film being made on board. It sounded fascinating; it proved abysmal, the sort of silent film which parodies the whole period. Depressed, I phoned the film library in Bromley from which I had bought it and asked if they would exchange it. They agreed and suggested I chose an alternative.

I examined their list with care. There was nothing much of interest. One of the 2-reelers was called *Napoleon Bonaparte and the French Revolution*, but who wanted a classroom film, full of textbook titles and static engravings? Nevertheless, the list contained nothing more promising, and not wanting to be stuck with the Epstein film, I sent off for it.

Meanwhile, I telephoned the British Film Institute and asked if they could find a review. They had nothing under the title, which gave me hope; perhaps it wasn't an educational film, but a dramatic epic?

'I know nothing about it,' I said, 'but it might be French, made in the 1920s.'

'There was a silent film of 1927, directed by Abel Gance. Could it be that?'

'It could be … '

And so I heard my first review of *Napoleon* over the telephone. It came from the English trade paper, the *Bioscope*:

'The film cannot be regarded as convincing either in historical accuracy or as a study of character … Here we have a theatrical and sentimental figure strutting about with the futile bombast of a turkey cock. The most convincing aspect is that showing his youth at school … Josephine may have had the faults that historians impute to her, but these faults are out of place in the heroine of romantic drama, and therefore Napoleon's love affairs are entirely lacking in interest … There is far too much use of photographic trickery and mechanical devices. Napoleon's eagle, played alternately by a

15

real bird and a synthetic understudy, is at times nearer the ridiculous than the sublime. There is much fine imagination and many impressive scenes in the production, and judicious and drastic cutting might result in a film of more logical sequence and greatly enhanced interest.'[1]

After that review, I was not optimistic about the film — even if it proved to be the Gance version. But any new film was irresistible — and the moment the parcel arrived, I set up my projector and summoned my parents. On January 18th, 1954, I saw scenes from *Napoléon vu par Abel Gance* for the first time.

The opening title, 'The Three Gods', jolted me to greater attention. The first shot faded in to reveal the leaders of the French Revolution — Marat, Danton, Robespierre. What struck me most (having tried to cast local people as Frenchmen) were the superbly chosen faces. I had no idea that the legendary Artaud was playing Marat. I simply responded to the brilliant casting, and felt the film blaze into life, like a masterly newsreel of the eighteenth century. This was no educational film!

Outside, in the revolutionary Club des Cordeliers, were more extraordinary, expectant faces — all chosen with uncanny skill. Danton orders Rouget de Lisle, a young army officer, to introduce his song La Marseillaise. I was exhilarated by the rapid cutting and the swirling camera movement. What daring, I thought, to make a song the highpoint of a silent film!

The magic of the visuals was especially apparent; the silvery sharpness of the print focused attention on the lighting and the composition. By the time Napoleon had been introduced, in no contrived, theatrical manner, but as an obscure artillery lieutenant on the edge of the crowd, I was in love with the picture. When the action moved to Corsica, and Napoleon was forced to flee, the furious storm at sea intercut with a storm in the Convention made me realise I was watching something exceptional; a film which proved the cinema capable of anything — a film I would have given anything to have made myself.

'That', said my mother, 'is a beautiful film. It's the best one you've got.'

I had only two reels. I gathered that six had originally been released in Britain. I determined to find the remainder. I placed advertisements in *Exchange and Mart*. I continued combing London for junk shops and photographic stores. Every so often, another reel would turn up — to be pronounced by my parents as 'the best yet'.

I knew nothing about Napoleon as a historical figure. My history classes had glossed over his career. I was therefore deeply dismayed, at my O-level exam in history, to be confronted by the question 'Describe the Fall of Napoleon.' I had heard of Waterloo and St Helena, but nothing else. In the hope of transforming defeat into victory, I wrote, 'One cannot understand the fall of Napoleon without knowing of his rise.' And I devoted several pages to a passionate description of the film. Whoever read my paper must have been entertained, if nothing else. But entertained or not, he failed me.

The last episode of *Napoleon* arrived soon afterwards. And when I took it out of its parcel, I was full of misgivings. In only two reels, how could it take the story from the siege of Toulon (1796), where the previous episode had left off, to Waterloo (1815)? The answer, of course, was that it couldn't. The film stopped as Bonaparte's legendary career began — with his campaign to liberate Italy from the Austrian occupation, and to spread the Revolution beyond its frontiers. I was disappointed with the invasion scenes. They were handled in a surprisingly desultory fashion, as though Gance had run out of money and had to finish the film in a hurry. Shot after shot of marching men retained the newsreel effect, but now it was rather a dull newsreel.

My favourite library book, Bardèche and Brasillach's *The History of the Film*, explained the reason; the film was to have included the Emperor's entire career, but Gance had, indeed, run out of money. However, far from sloughing off the final scenes, he had presented them with astonishing spectacle and imagination across three screens, a process later called Polyvision. The ordinary screen suddenly became a vast fresco, three times the normal size:

'Sometimes he used it simply to enlarge his image, to show the vast panorama of the Armée d'Italie being harangued by its leader. Sometimes he used it as a triptych, as in the unforgettable episode of the descent into Italy, where the central screen showed the front ranks of superb, ragged soldiers with women hanging about their necks as they bawl "Auprès de ma blonde" while the two side screens showed long shots of the great column of the army on the march. Never had the very incarnation of an epic been so magnificently transferred to the screen.'[2]

How maddening that I would never be able to project this part of the film as it was intended to be shown! I considered mounting three projectors in a row, but the 9·5mm version included mere scraps of the triptychs, loosely cut together, giving no impression of the power and excitement suggested by Bardèche and Brasillach.

How would I ever be able to see *Napoleon* in Polyvision? I was particularly interested because a new invention had recently reached London: Cinerama. I went to see it, and was as exhilarated as everyone else by the roller-coaster ride. But a short history of the cinema which preceded it contained no mention of Gance. And as far as I could judge, the system was simply a revival of Gance's idea. It employed three projectors and three screens — just like Polyvision.

With Abel Gance as the fountainhead of so much modern technique, it seemed criminal that he was so little known. I couldn't even find out if he was alive, although since the film was only twenty-seven years old, there was a good chance that he was.

I felt it was up to me to do what little I could to revive Gance's reputation, and that of *Napoleon*. But all I could think of doing was to show my modest 'rediscovered' version, of about 90 minutes, to as many people as possible. I set up twin turntables, selected a range of 78 rpm gramophone records, and presented the film with full orchestral accompaniment, the thunder of which was equal to any Napoleonic cannonade. My audiences were always stunned.

I produced my own film magazine, its circulation limited to visitors to my home cinema. In one issue, I devoted a long article to *Napoleon*, pointing out that Gance's career appeared to have ended with *Le Capitaine Fracasse* (1942).

'Since then, little has been heard from Gance. Why cannot prints be made from the copy of *Napoleon* lying in the Cinematique Francais [*sic*]? *Napoleon* has not dated at all, and it would be bound to draw the crowds,

My father designed this programme for my first proper show of Napoleon

even if they came out of mere curiosity to see the beginnings of CinemaScope. The triptych could be shown on a CinemaScope screen, and *Napoleon* might be supported by a CinemaScope sub-feature, which would show how little we have advanced in the last thirty years!'

I discussed with Liam O'Leary the possibility of giving a show to the staff of the British Film Institute. Liam spoke to the curator of the National Film Archive, Ernest Lindgren, and reported back that he had turned down the idea.

By coincidence, Lindgren had just returned from a film festival in Brazil, where he had actually met Abel Gance and seen a version of *Napoleon*. He told Liam that he hardly thought it worthy of the name of a film.

When I met Lindgren, I was unlikely to be prejudiced in his favour. I found him an ice-cold individual, with a tortured face and a manner familiar to me from unsympathetic schoolmasters. It was hard to associate him with so pleasurable an activity as preserving film; he seemed as puritanical as our seventeenth-century Lord Protector, Oliver Cromwell, who had closed the theatres. At the top of Lindgren's list for immediate execution were film collectors. He refused to deal with them in any way, thus gaining for the Archive a reputation for incorruptibility which was to prove so valuable to the industry, and so disastrous with collectors. (Many priceless items, in private hands, were lost for ever.)

For all his failings, he deserves the highest praise for starting the Archive in the first place, in company with Harold Brown. And without his single-minded determination, it might never have survived, for the industry disliked collectors (of any sort) as much as he did. But he never overcame his distaste for *Napoleon*, and years later, when the film was being reconstructed on Archive premises, the job had to be done without his knowledge.

Lindgren's attitude towards the film was shared by Paul Rotha in his *Film Till Now*, the film enthusiast's Bible of those days: 'Abel Gance is the *grand maître* of the French cinema, theoretically the apotheosis of great directors, but in practice always out-of-date with ideas. He spent five years on the production of *Napoleon*, a theme so vast that it defeated its own, Abel Gance's and everybody else's purpose. It was filled with imaginative technical devices and ramifications of complicated scenario work, needing three screens on which to exhibit its lumbering bulk. It was tediously cumbersome and hopelessly overweighted with symbolic references.'[3]

How could I change this attitude? Denied the opportunity to see the film itself, film enthusiasts could only derive opinions from those who had. So the best way was to find someone to write positively about it. I did not consider myself a candidate — after all, I was still at school. However, I had just seen my name in print for the first time, at the foot of a letter in *Amateur Cine World* describing my film, and one evening I received a visit from the assistant editor of the magazine.

Derek Hill proved to be a catalyst. He was the antithesis of Lindgren, short, young, with dark curly hair, a hilarious sense of humour and a perpetually worried expression. A brilliant raconteur, he was an equally brilliant writer, and his work ranged from film criticism to short stories in literary quarterlies.

He was so enthusiastic about *Napoleon* that on his next visit he brought a friend, another film critic called David Robinson, who was equally impressed. Gradually, word spread, and to my delight, several members of the staff of the British Film Institute came to see it. The praise that greeted it thrilled me as much as if I'd made the film myself.

Derek Hill urged me to write an article for *ACW* — a suggestion which would prove a turning point in my career. The editor commissioned a piece of 2,000 words, and dragging those words from my brain was like pulling teeth. In misery, I carried the article over to Derek Hill, and he patched it up and made it flow. He taught me the basic skills of journalism, enabling me eventually to spread my own propaganda about *Napoleon*.

He also took me to press shows, and at one of them introduced me to a critic called Dr Francis Koval, a Central European with a lugubrious expression, but a kind and encouraging manner. He turned out to be a friend and admirer of Gance. Yes, Gance was still alive, and he had recently visited him in Paris. I invited Koval to see the film, and he brought a signed photograph. It showed Gance at sixty-five, still an astonishingly handsome man.

I wrote an effusive fan letter, but did not expect an answer. Few people bothered to answer letters from a schoolboy. But this one *was* answered — a brief paragraph, typed in French, but contact at last with the man who, for me, represented the best qualities of the cinema:

July 23rd, 1954

I was very touched by your letter of June 4, 1954, the sincerity of which struck me keenly.

I thank you for the interest which you take in my efforts.

I will soon make some films in Polyvision which will create, I think, an international upheaval in the cinema world.

The Polyvision referred to so optimistically was the three-screen process of *Napoleon* revived, sadly, too late to hold its own against the much more heavily financed processes from America, Cinerama and CinemaScope.

Koval told me that Gance had acquired a new ally from an unexpected quarter. A girl called Nelly Kaplan had seen Gance's films, including *Napoleon*, when she was a child in Buenos Aires. At the age of twenty, she

The photograph lent me by Francis Koval which led directly to my first meeting with Abel Gance. (It was signed to Koval, but when I used it to illustrate an article in Amateur Cine World, *the printers removed the signature. I was appalled, but eventually had Gance sign it again.)*

came to Paris and had recently met Gance. Amazed that this young girl from a distant country knew his films so well, he invited her to work on his next project. She came at just the right time, giving him the spur of encouragement he so desperately needed. He had been unable to find the money to make a film for twelve years. Now he was about to begin work on *La Tour de Nesle*, a Dumas romance.

That same year, an extraordinary coincidence occurred that enabled me to realise my ambition and to meet Abel Gance myself.

It was March 1955. I was still at school, and the prospect of another year stretched before me. I was not the academic type, and the chances of moving on to a university were remote. I searched for excuses to leave. I could find none, and I was soon enmeshed in preparations for A-level examinations.

One day, I was undergoing a mock exam in German when the headmaster's secretary appeared at the door. 'Could Brownlow take a telephone call?' Only an appalling emergency would have caused me to be pulled out of an exam, albeit a trial exam. I was escorted to the headmaster's study. A telephone was thrust into my hand, and I heard my mother trying her best to sound calm.

'Liam's just rung to say Abel Gance is going to be at the NFT. Can you get there as soon as possible?'

I was allowed to leave without a word of explanation. I rushed home, grabbed some stills and a copy of the scenario (published in 1927, which I had just bought, brand new, from a French bookshop in Regent Street). I arrived at the National Film Theatre before anyone else, and I waited impatiently in the foyer.

Apparently, Abel Gance, unknown and unannounced, had flown to London to see the presentation of Cinerama at the Casino Theatre. Emerging from the theatre, Gance was strolling down Shaftesbury Avenue when he saw a nameplate at no. 164: BRITISH FILM INSTITUTE. He entered the building and found himself in the reception area.

By coincidence, Liam O'Leary walked into reception and saw a man with a mane of white hair and a familiar face. He had seen it before—in Dr Francis Koval's photograph.

Gance was both surprised and flattered at being recognised.

Liam reported to the director of the Institute, Denis Forman, who arranged a small reception at the NFT that afternoon, since Gance was flying back that evening. Liam was tied up at a meeting. Forman asked him if he knew anyone familiar with Gance's work, and Liam mentioned my name. Forman asked him to invite me.

Among the others at the reception were Karel Reisz, then employed by the BFI and now the well-known director, Basil Wright, the celebrated documentary film-maker, and Michael Balcon, the famous head of Ealing Studios.

At last a taxi drew up, and the unmistakable figure of Abel Gance stepped out. He was smaller than I expected, but far less elderly. Having tried to translate some of his writing, I feared that his personality might match his rhetoric—a sort of de Gaulle of the film industry. Instead, he fulfilled all my youthful ideals. His aquiline nose gave him the look of a poet, his hair, swept arrogantly back, suggested a medieval saint. His diabolically mischievous grin, however, dispelled all illusions of sanctity.

He had one major drawback, however—he spoke no English. I cursed the years I had spent 'learning' French; I had passed my exams, yet I could hardly speak a coherent sentence. I tried to put a few words together to convey my feelings about his work, but they wilted as some linguistic expert rattled away beside me. Gance was swept off to the bar to meet the establishment figures, and I sat forlornly, nursing a glass of cider, trying to forget my grammar and remember my French.

After half an hour, we were ushered into the theatre and Gance was shown an example of experimental English cinema — *London to Brighton in 4 minutes*, a speeded-up train journey. I have never been able to fathom why that was chosen; I assume it had something to do with the fact that Gance had once made a film about railways. A Norman MacLaren followed, and Gance said he had adapted one of MacLaren's cartoons to Polyvision.

My opportunity came when we returned to the bar, and the linguists ran out of conversation. I moved in. Enthusiasm can cross any kind of barrier, and that is the only explanation I can think of for the long conversation I had with Gance. I'm sure someone interpreted. But I monopolised Gance for as long as I could, and I was quite enchanted by him. One could not have imagined a more eloquent, amiable or amusing character.

He had refused a drink since his arrival, but he suddenly emptied my glass, and, now that the room was almost deserted, he went round the bar emptying everyone else's.

'I thought you didn't drink,' someone said.

'Only at times like these,' said Gance.

When I asked him how he got the idea for the three screens, he answered, 'I had so many extras at Nice that I couldn't fit them all into one frame.'

Despite his mischievous humour, he was not in the least patronising. And to a shy seventeen-year-old, who looked about twelve, that was a notable rarity. He expressed surprise that someone so young had ever heard of his work, let alone seen it. And he was sympathetic to my naive enthusiasm. He told me of the harsh times he had experienced in the French film industry, and warned me against starting a career in the cinema. It was then that I heard that before *La Tour de Nesle* he had not worked for twelve years, except to make a film about his little girl. 'I enjoyed making that film more than any other,' he said.

I asked him what he thought of Cinerama.

'It's exactly the same as my idea. They haven't even solved the problem of the joins between the screens!'

He signed a still of *Napoleon*: 'Avec toute ma sympathie pour le jeune enthousiasme de Kevin Brownlow' — 'With all my appreciation for the youthful enthusiasm of Kevin Brownlow.' At least, that is what I thought it said — his writing was not too clear — but now I realise the inscription was more typical of Gance: ' ... pour les yeux enthousiastes' — 'for the enthusiastic eyes ... '

As he was leaving, he delivered some professional advice: 'Keep your eyes straight ahead.' Then he checked himself, and making the gesture of someone looking at both ends of a wide screen, he said, 'Non! Les yeux Polyvision!'

2·Chasseur d'images

I set out to discover all the facts I could about this remarkable man, but it was hard to find anything. Bardèche and Brasillach described him as 'unquestionably the most famous of all the directors of this period',[1] but when they detailed his career, the detail was not always very kind.

As for his early life, I depended on the fragments and rumour I found in obscure French publications at the British Film Institute's library. For the full story, I had to wait for a book by Roger Icart, *Abel Gance.*[2] According to this, Gance was born in Paris on October 25th, 1889. His father, a doctor, was ambitious for his son to become a lawyer, and he was sent to the Chaptal college. Here he developed a deep love for literature and philosophy, but he found school discipline too constricting. To assuage his unhappiness he turned to the world of poetry. Once he had passed his Baccalauréat, his father arranged for him to enter a solicitor's office as an articled clerk — assigned to divorce cases. He found this even more depressing than school, and once again sought escape into the world of great authors at the Bibliothèque Nationale.

None of this seemed to me remotely unlikely, and I accepted it without question. What I did not realise was that Roger Icart was dissatisfied with his book, and being even more obsessive than I was, he embarked on further research. The research continued year upon year; just before I completed this book he revealed some of his results. He had found documents which proved that Gance had invented his bourgeois background.

This is the first of many links with another great director, Erich von Stroheim, also renowned for overlong masterpieces, and for his battles with producers. Von Stroheim invented a background of nobility and military grandeur; he was actually the son of a Jewish hat manufacturer. According to Icart, Gance's father *was* a doctor, but he was not married to his mother. The possibility of Jewish origin caused Gance problems during the Occupation. Abel lived in Commentry, Nivernais, until he was eight, when his mother married Adolphe Gance, a chauffeur-mechanic, who died in Neuilly in 1922. Gance passed no examinations — let alone the Baccalauréat — and he left school at fourteen. He was thus partly self-educated, which perhaps helps to explain his obsession with the great authors, and his insistence on referring to them at every opportunity.

Why should he seek to hide his humble origins? One can only guess. Today, his achievement would be hailed as a miracle of class mobility. But the world was a very different place in the early years of the century. French class consciousness, Revolution or not, persisted as strongly as in England, and one's background was of supreme importance to one's future.

As soon as his career in the theatre had begun, Gance stopped inventing a past. At the age of eighteen, he was engaged for a season by the Théâtre du Parc in Brussels where he made friends with Blaise Cendrars, the poet, and Victor Francen, the actor. When he returned to Paris, he found it hard to find work and his friends often had to help him. He joined a circle of artists which included Léger, Apollinaire, Chagall, Canudo, Séverin-Mars, Magnier ... In 1909, he found a job acting the role of Molière in a film directed by Léonce Perret. And he began writing scenarios.

Gance's driving ambition, like D.W. Griffith's, was to become a great playwright. Scenario writing was no substitute; it merely paid the rent. The cinema was hardly a rival to the stage and the early efforts of the moving picture did not impress Gance. 'I thought they were infantile and stupid,' he said, 'much like travelling shows. They were a mere amusement, and of no artistic value.'

In 1910, Gance learned that he was suffering from tuberculosis, for which there was then no cure. He demonstrated the remarkable will-power which was to overcome so many obstacles on *Napoleon*; he went to the country and in the pure air, with intensive exercising, he managed to overcome the disease — for a while. But he was wretchedly poor. Since moving pictures paid well, he returned to Paris and in 1911 directed *La Digue, ou pour sauver la Hollande* which introduced Pierre Renoir. With typical optimism, he formed a film company, but with typical bad luck it went bankrupt after four films.

He was still determined to become a great playwright, and he began writing a play for the dancer Ida Rubenstein, *La Victoire de Samothrace*. It was submitted, however, to Sarah Bernhardt, who was far too old for the part, but who praised it highly and would have appeared in it had the outbreak of war in 1914 not closed theatres and shattered Gance's hopes. It was the first profound disappointment in a career soon to be punctuated with them like milestones.

In August 1914, Gance, helping out as a civilian stretcher-bearer, was confronted by the full horrors of war. When the war began, he resolved not to worry about it—he had too many problems of his own. Now his letters from the war zone were full of anguish. Because of his TB, Gance was at that stage in no danger of being called up. He returned to the cinema, to the very kind of ephemeral entertainment he had scorned. When he attempted something bolder—a film shot through distorting mirrors to depict the world of a madman, *La Folie du Dr Tube* (1915)—his employer, Louis Nalpas, refused to release it. The ban discouraged Gance more than ever.

He wrote in his diary that he was now making films for concierges. 'The cinema, this alphabet for eyes tired of thinking, wastefully devours my most precious possession.'[3] He may have held the commercial cinema in contempt, but he could not resist attempting the occasional technical innovation. As he did so, and as they passed the scrutiny of his employers, so his faith in the cinema was rekindled: 'Little by little, I made progress with my understanding of camera-work. My understanding of optics kept pace with the technical advances in cinematography. The quality of the photographic image was getting better and better ... I realised the insanity of the sort of thing I was making. I pulled myself up short and said, "Why are people making films which are nothing but events, when they have at their disposal such a marvellous medium for psychological stories? They go on making films about people chasing each other, killing each other or trying to commit suicide, but why not films which show feelings instead of merely action?"'

Gance used his powers of persuasion on his producers, and began, in a small way, to combine the thriller with psychological elements. *Le Droit à la vie* was so successful he was given an increased budget to make another. And so began Gance's *grande époque*—*Mater Dolorosa* (1917), *La Dixième Symphonie* (1918) and then *J'accuse* (1919)—all melodramas, in the style of the time, their solemnity relieved by the beauty of the imagery. Gance was now in love with cinema, and his passion was evident in every shot.

Which is not to under-estimate the contribution of his cameraman, Léonce-Henry Burel, one of the finest cinematographers Europe has ever known. Between them, they created some remarkable films, the most memorable of which was *J'accuse*, the first film courageous enough to question the war.

The film was made for Charles Pathé; Burel recalled that when they left Nalpas, with a flamboyant stroke of his pen their former employer cancelled all their debts. 'We had been good little boys and our last two films had brought in a considerable amount of money.'[4] This was the only period in Gance's career when his high ideals found a fervent public response.

Burel claimed that *J'accuse* began life as a recruiting film, and Gance was thus able to secure the co-operation of the army. 'With his assistant Blaise Cendrars, who had lost an arm in the war, he set to work. The film was nearly finished when suddenly the war was over. Pathé and Gance were at a

Les Cadavres Allemands après la bataille | The German bodies after the battle

In October 1914, Gance sent this postcard to his friend t'Serstevens with the comment, 'A specimen of modern civilisation.' Below, in 1919 came Gance's powerful comment from the screen: J'accuse.

loss to know what to do with a propaganda film with no war to go with it. Abel changed the titles around and turned it into the famous anti-war film we all know.'[5]

I had heard the rumour long before I read this interview with Burel, and the cynicism shocked me. I put the allegation directly to Gance, who denied it equally directly. 'Why would I call it *J'accuse?*' he said. Well, Gance's life is full of contradictions, and he might have entitled it *J'accuse* when the war was safely over. But letters and diary entries survive which support his assertion that he was opposed to the war. (Although as to what he produced for official consumption, one can only hazard a guess.) In 1916, he wrote: 'How I wish that all those killed in the war would rise up one night and return to their countries, their homes, to see if their sacrifice was worth anything at all. The war would stop of its own accord, horrified by its own awfulness. Until 1914, I suffered only for myself, but for the last two years I have suffered for everyone else ... Oh, to walk naked between the two trenches and make each side hesitate to fire for fear of killing one of their own. Because what one shoots at in war is not men, but uniforms.'[6]

Many of Gance's friends were killed in the trenches. He had a recurrence of his TB and was operated on several times. Nevertheless, he was drafted into the army and assigned to the cinematographic section. 'I had a feeling of frenzy,' he said, 'to use this medium to show the world the stupidity of war. At this time a book came out called *Le Feu* by Henri Barbusse. It made a great impression on me as it was very energetic in its opposition to the war. So I was wondering what subject I could take to demonstrate the futility of war. And one day, when I was crossing the Boulevard du Château, still mobilised, I had this idea which I'd had long before, that if all the dead from the war—and they were uncountable—came back, the war would stop at once. I told myself that I must give the public this message—and so the idea came to me from one pavement to the other. All I had to do was to make the film, getting the co-operation of the army, which was extraordinary. I had a great friend, the poet Blaise Cendrars, who was my assistant, and I started to write the scenario and I finished it very quickly.

'We made the film under very moving circumstances, because the men you see in the film who play the Dead Returned were men from the front, from Verdun. They came on eight days' leave. I had those 2,000 soldiers who knew they'd never survive that hell. They had seen it all, and now they played the dead knowing they would probably die themselves. This drama, the source of the psychological impact, stems from the acting of those dead men on leave. In a few weeks or months, eighty per cent of them would disappear. I knew it and so did they. This was the atmosphere in which the film was shot, and it gave me the courage to make the film, which may be melodramatic, but intrinsically it is based on a very moving situation. It had a shattering effect on everyone who saw it, especially in England. My agent at Pathé telegrammed that people were fainting in the theatre in London. The same thing happened in other towns, too — women fainted because they were so affected at the idea of the dead coming back to find out if their deaths had done any good.'

The success of *J'accuse* made Gance one of the most important directors in Europe. He was twenty-nine years old.

His next film, *La Roue*, was also a tragedy. It was again influenced by the semi-documentary quality of a book, Pierre Hamp's *Le Rail*. Gance treated *La Roue* like a symphony, a black symphony of the railways followed by a white symphony in the mountains. He interwove Greek tragedy and high melodrama in the story of Sisif, an engine driver, who rescues a small girl orphaned by a crash. She is English. Her name is Norma. He adopts her, but when she reaches adolescence, he falls in love with her, as does his son, Élie. Sisif's attraction leads to an overwhelming passion. He even names his locomotive Norma. When Norma goes away to be married to a middle-aged engineer, Sisif decides to destroy both Normas — both the things he loves. An accident is averted, but the family is torn apart. Norma's marriage fails; Sisif loses his eyesight and he is sacked by the railway company. He retreats to the mountains, where Élie becomes involved in a fight with Norma's

The set for the engineer's house in La Roue *was built among the tracks so that real trains could be seen through the windows*

husband and is killed. Sisif is reunited with Norma, with whom he finds serenity. Eventually, peacefully, he dies.

'This gloomy tale,' wrote Bardèche and Brasillach, 'redolent of Zola and his *Bête Humaine*, of Hugo and a dozen other romantic writers, would have been laughed off the screen had not everything else been effaced by its technical mastery and a very genuine and even nobly poetic quality which this technique served to express.'[7]

The story of the making of the film was as much of a tragedy as the film itself. 'I started on the film with a young woman [Ida Danis] who was perhaps the greatest love of my life,' said Gance. 'I had hardly written two pages when the doctors told me that she was so ill with TB that she would not live. I didn't tell her. But the whole time I was shooting *La Roue*, over a year, she was terribly ill. I looked after her, which was why *La Roue* took so long. She had to have operations, and she was sometimes in agony, so the film had to fit in with her illness. I travelled wherever it was necessary for her and the film went too. It was not the film that made the changes necessary, it was her state of health.'

The doctors advised Ida to stay in the warm climate of the South, so Gance shot the first part of *La Roue* in the marshalling yards at Nice.

'While she was so ill, my friend Blaise Cendrars, the poet, was often her nurse. He looked after her while I had to go and shoot and was really an enormous help.'

Ida's condition deteriorated and the doctors suggested she should be moved to the mountains. But not even the pure air could save her. 'She fell ill the day I started the scenario, and she died the day I finished editing the film. I was so affected by her death, and the terrible drama of her illness, that I couldn't even go to her funeral. It was then that I went to America, to get away from it all.'

And it was in America that he decided to make an even greater film, a film about Napoleon Bonaparte.

3 · Pictures in the Fire

The place where Abel Gance conceived the idea for the film about Napoleon was hardly appropriate. And yet it proved prophetic. He was walking with a friend, the comedian Max Linder, down Broadway in New York, a city he had never visited before, when he made the fateful decision. It was 1921, exactly a hundred years since Napoleon's death. It would be sixty more before the film would return, to be shown as it was meant to be shown. It would take the city by storm.

Many films had been made with Napoleon as a character, and many film-makers had considered a film on the Emperor's career. The logistics had always defeated them.

Gance, who besides being the most inventive director in France was also the most ambitious, determined to film all these events, in all the original locations. It was a project even D.W. Griffith might balk at.

D.W. Griffith was Gance's god. Regarded as the greatest director in the world, Griffith had, against great odds, produced two epics, *The Birth of a Nation* (1915) and *Intolerance* (1916); the first had influenced the American film-makers, the second had influenced the Europeans.

Gance had come to America to help to exploit *J'accuse*, and D.W. Griffith had agreed to attend the première.

The American film industry had won world markets after the war; it was none the less experiencing a slump. War films, which had been huge money-makers, were now avoided by a public which sought escapism. The Americans in any case had an innate dislike of foreign films, which their reviewers tended to dismiss as 'weird' and 'over-acted'. The outlook for *J'accuse* was not bright — even though a special version had been prepared for the United States.

'The film was shown to a very snobbish audience,' said Gance, 'in the ballroom of the Ritz-Carlton Hotel. About four hundred people. But only one opinion mattered to me and that was Griffith's. If he liked it, then it was a good film and I had done well. If he didn't like it, then it was a bad film. So I saw this priest-like man, who for me was the greatest the cinema had, watch my film without a single muscle of his face moving. At the end, he went away with his companions, the Gish sisters, without a word to anyone. I waited for a word from him, but nothing came. So I said to myself, that means he didn't like the film, and it was a terrible disappointment.

'The next day, D.W. Griffith telephoned. He said he had been so moved that he had given his crew the day off. He and the Gish sisters had felt unable to work after seeing *J'accuse*.'

Griffith invited Gance to the studio, at Mamaroneck, New York. Gance was startled to see sets of Paris at the time of the Revolution,[1] even an elegant guillotine. These were images from his own thoughts. Was Griffith already working on *his* version of *Napoleon*?

Griffith greeted him warmly, and explained he was making a version of *The Two Orphans* which would encompass the French Revolution. Yes, he had been considering a film on Napoleon, but he felt it his duty to bow out before the creator of *J'accuse*.[2]

Where the idea to make Napoleon *first occurred to Gance: Broadway at Times Square and 44th Street, 1921. In the background, Loew's, New York, where* Napoleon *was shown in January 1929.*

D. W. Griffith congratulates Abel Gance after the New York première of J'accuse. *Mamaroneck, N.Y., 1921.*

Gance watched Griffith at work, noting that his chief cameraman, Billy Bitzer, worked faster than his own, Burel. There were two cameras, the second in the charge of Henrik Sartov. His Bell & Howell was turned by motor, a fact Gance found unusual, since most cameramen preferred the reliable method of hand-cranking.[3]

'Griffith asked me if I wanted to sell my film to United Artists,' said Gance. 'It was fantastic luck for me. Three days later, I signed a contract. So if I hadn't had this drama of Ida in my life, perhaps I would not have gone to New York. But nothing could efface my unhappiness. And soon I came home.'[4]

Gance returned to work on *La Roue*, and completely recut it. The job took months. When he had finished it, he launched it as a film of episodes. The première, at the Gaumont-Palace in Paris in December 1922, was such a triumph that at the end the audience refused to leave and Gance had to show the last reel again, as an encore.[5] 'There is the cinema before and after *La Roue*,' said Jean Cocteau, 'as there is painting before and after Picasso.'[6]

The critics might acclaim it as the greatest film ever made, but *La Roue* had taken nearly three years to make, it had cost 2·6 million francs, it ran to 36 reels and it had to be released in episodes. It had been boycotted by a number of distributors.

Gance took criticism seriously. There were many who complained of the *longueurs* in *La Roue*, of the doom-laden misery of it all, so he decided to attempt something totally different. In 1923 he made a skittish comedy with Max Linder set in a haunted house. He shot *Au Secours!* in a week, just to prove he could do it. (Alas, it was not released.) Then, after one of the shortest schedules, he embarked on what was to prove perhaps the longest when he travelled to his retreat in the Midi and began work on the scenario for *Napoleon*.

'I have recovered what I thought was lost for good,' wrote Gance, 'Health, or rather vitality, without which there is no work of genius. The flow of my blood is returning.'[7]

This young man, often prostrated for weeks by illness, now found an astonishing capacity for work, which he would be able to sustain for four years. When necessary, he would sleep only two hours a night.

Unlike most directors, Gance decided to do the research for the film himself. Had he wanted a superficial authenticity, he could have hired a couple of experts as technical advisers, as directors usually do. Instead, Gance immersed himself thoroughly in the subject. 'With Napoleon,' he wrote, 'I take on the greatest drama of all time. I am held, by this very fact, to a rigorous historical accuracy and I must sacrifice nothing to this immortal truth.'[8]

He read several hundred books. His bibliography alone listed more than eighty works, consisting of 250 volumes, and his pictorial reference library contained 3,000 pictures.[9] His closest collaborator at this stage was William Delafontaine, a documentary film-maker who was to work throughout the picture. His job was to locate books and illustrations; Gance's was to absorb them, compare them, challenge them.

Jean Arroy found one of these research books at the studio — *La Jeunesse de Napoléon*, vol. iii, by Arthur Chuquet. 'The margins were black with notes. On p. 161 I discovered the words: "All this is too small. He must be made as large as the imagination of the crowds that understand the *Chanson de Roland*."' For Arroy, this was a vital clue to the whole work: 'Magnify the epic to fit the imagination of the crowd.'[10]

Gance's approach was thus paradoxical. On the one hand, he expressed a firm commitment to authenticity with a scenario whose margins were peppered with references, many of which would appear on the subtitles of the final film. On the other, he wrote long sequences involving fictitious characters. They were intended to give the audience relief from the torrent of battles, riots and political upheavals. But they would eventually detract from the film's reputation as a historical document.

Emotion was all-important, and the transfer of emotion from the screen to the audience was worth any sacrifice. In 1928, Gance wrote that a major fault of *Napoleon* was its 'abuse of documentation'.[11] Gance felt that he had lost emotion by forcing his narrative to follow the facts.

Actually Gance was no more a historian than D.W. Griffith. He was a poet, unable to shackle his story to a slavish recital of facts. He preferred to use the facts as a springboard for his imagination — elaborating an incident like Bonaparte's escape from Corsica into a flamboyant verse from an epic poem.

Gance had much in common with Victor Hugo. Dagmar Bolin, who worked as his assistant on many later productions, saw such a close similarity that she went so far as to equate it with reincarnation. 'He was certainly Victor Hugo,' she said. 'I always told him that. In the last year of his life, he was saying it, too. He had all the same qualities, all the same faults — he made things too long, too many little flowers, and he had the same versatility in political matters.'[12]

One of the strongest influences on *Napoleon* was Hugo's *Ninety-Three*. Describing the Convention, Victor Hugo wrote, 'At the same time that it threw off revolution, this Assembly produced civilisation. Furnace, but forge, too. In this cauldron where terror bubbled, progress fermented.'[13] Gance would fashion this metaphor into a sequence of astonishing power — when Danton tells the crowd, gathered in a blacksmith's forge, how totally they have destroyed the monarchy. The characterisations of Danton, Marat, Robespierre and Saint-Just were drawn from Victor Hugo and Gance was to be both praised and criticised for being 'Hugoesque'.

Gance did not intend his portrayal of Napoleon to remain that of a romantic hero. An indication of how it would change was contained in an interview he gave to *Paris-Soir*:

'After a great deal of reading and research, I conceive of a Napoleon who did not altogether detest warfare, but who was forced into it by an irresistible process which he was always trying vainly to halt — for war was the black cloud on his horizon. From the battle of Marengo on, war is his fate. He does all he can to avoid it, but he must submit to it. That is his tragedy.

'Napoleon represents the perpetual conflict between the great revolutionary who wanted the Revolution and peace, and a man of war, fighting in the mistaken belief that the war would bring peace for ever. He was a man whose arms were not long enough to encompass something greater than himself: the Revolution. An admirable human will. But the brain is greater than the heart. His worst mistake was to turn his relatives into royalty. He loved them, but with too small a heart, and Napoleon perverted his destiny partly by being the chief of his tribe, when he was born to be the great man of the Revolution.

'It will now be easier to understand why I have come to create Napoleon, because he was a paroxysm in his time, which was a paroxysm in history. General Bonaparte lies at the edge of a maelstrom, a lucid observer, whereas the Emperor lies in the whirlpool, is dragged into it and loses his self-control.

'Bonaparte is not dragged off by this current. He watches and observes; he is master of his fate. He can halt it should he wish to. Napoleon cannot. He has neither the time nor the means to do so. He must go where fate leads him; that is his tragedy, the one I shall try to compose with the music of light.'[14]

Gance initially sketched a plan to follow Napoleon's career in six films — these were later expanded to eight, then returned to six. The first, *Arcole* (1782–98), began with a prologue at the Royal Military Acadamy of Brienne where Napoleon was a cadet; the main film opened at the height of the Revolution, and the two attacks on the Tuileries. Napoleon is shown in his first experience under fire in Sardinia, and in his flight from Corsica, when the island allies itself with England. In France, Napoleon has grim experience of civil war, and writes of it in a pamphlet, *Le Souper de Beaucaire*. He distinguishes himself at the siege of Toulon, expelling foreign armies from French soil, but suffers arrest and imprisonment during the Terror. A period of disgrace follows, when he refuses a command, and he is attached to the topographical office. Here he plans the invasion of Italy. His success at Toulon is remembered, and he is called upon to crush a royalist uprising. He is so successful he becomes the hero of the day. He meets Joséphine and marries her, leaving forty-eight hours later to take up his new command, the Army of Italy. Without food and without discipline, the Army is in a state defying the imagination. Morale soars, thanks to the new general, who leads it to victory in Italy. After the triumphs at Montenotte, Arcola and Rivoli, Napoleon liberates Italy of the Austrian occupier, then follows up his success by pursuing the enemy to the gates of Vienna. The film would finish with the Treaty of Campo Formio, when Austria is forced to make peace after five years of war against France.

The second film, *18 Brumaire* (1798–1800), was to have started with the campaign in Egypt, by which Napoleon hoped to strike at England's richest possession, India. Napoleon insists that the French go to Egypt in order to teach and learn, and he takes scientists, artists and archaeologists. Much valuable work is done apart from fighting, although the film would cover the Battle of the Pyramids, Napoleon's victory against the rulers of Egypt, the Mamelukes, the siege of Acre, defeat, and the French army struck by the

Black Death. After victory at Aboukir, Napoleon returns to France and sets out to win political power. He becomes First Consul and introduces a new constitution, drafts the civil code, revolutionises education and revitalises France. The war with England drags on, and Napoleon closes continental ports to English ships. When the Pope refuses to close his ports, Napoleon occupies Rome and the Papal States, in a second Italian campaign. The film would end with the decisive battle of Marengo.

The third episode, entitled *Austerlitz* (1804–8), was to have dealt with the creation of the Empire. Napoleon, shaken by an assassination attempt, realises that such attempts will not cease until he creates himself Emperor, with a hereditary line. As a royalist agent says of Napoleon, 'He has only his sword, and it is a sceptre that one hands on.' Napoleon crowns himself Emperor in the Roman sense, on behalf of the people and the Republic. He faces the hostility of the crowned heads of Europe and disaster at Trafalgar. When Austria attacks his ally Bavaria, Napoleon leads his troops on a fourteen-day campaign which results in the Battle of Austerlitz, the era's most crushing victory. By 1808, Napoleon rules over half of Europe, and has made kings of his brothers, upon whose loyalty he can count. The film was to end with the Treaty of Tilsit.

The fourth sketch, *Retreat from Moscow* (1809–13), began with the campaign in Spain. It showed Napoleon's attempt to win the friendship of the Russian Tsar, Alexander, and Alexander's treachery in ordering French troops out of territories Napoleon had guaranteed. Reluctantly Napoleon goes to war with Russia; he is met by a scorched earth policy, and decides to retreat from Moscow. There follows the most appalling route march in military history. Napoleon rallies at Lützen and Bautzen, but when Austria declares war, he is crushed at Leipzig.

The fifth film was to follow Napoleon's campaign through France, the surrender of Paris and his departure for Elba. It was called *Waterloo* (1814–15) and would show Napoleon's escape from Elba, his landing at Cannes, and the triumphant hundred days, which ended with his defeat at Waterloo and abdication.

The sixth film, *St Helena* (1815–21), would begin with the occupation of Paris by Allied troops, and deal with the drama of Napoleon's battle against his English jailer, Hudson Lowe, until his death on May 5th, 1821. There was to be an epilogue entitled *Champs-Élysées*, presumably to take place at the Arc de Triomphe.[15]

Since he could not type, Gance had to write everything in his often indecipherable handwriting. It was then typed by his secretary Simone Surdieux: 'I was mad about the cinema. When Gance took me on as his secretary, I lived in a dream. I spent six years with him, being completely enchanted.

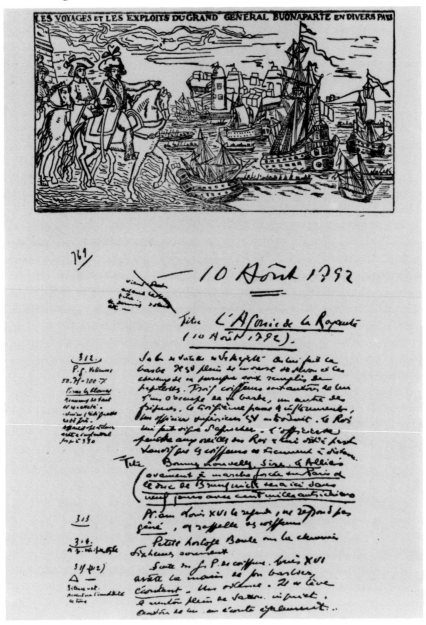

A page of Gance's scenario. The notepaper was specially printed for the production, and displays the original title. In the margin, Gance notes the lens he wants—'Vollensec' for Wollensak—with precise details of its focal length.

Left, *'Ninety-Three'* — *Danton, Robespierre and Marat in the wine-shop, drawn by H. Herkomer, from Gance's library of pictorial reference.* Right, *the setting transferred to the convent of Les Cordeliers. Antonin Artaud as Marat, Alexandre Koubitzky as Danton and Edmond van Daële as Robespierre.*

'He had a beautiful study at his home on the Avenue Kléber which was in the style of the Middle Ages. There were stained glass windows, and the Hermaphrodite from the Louvre, lifesize, by the fireplace. Once he started work on the scenario, although people came to see him, he seldom went out. He wrote very fast and gave me the sheets as he completed them. I had my own room to work in, and a piano was there if I wanted it.

'Later on, Georges d'Esparbès, the curator of the Palais National de Fontainebleau, placed part of his château — the Aumôniers wing — at Gance's disposal. This enabled him to work in peace and quiet, far from the noise of the capital and the intrusion of visitors. I had a room in this wing to type the scenario. We were really the proprietors of the château!'[16]

When Gance had completed the first scenario, he submitted all 600 pages to the critical scrutiny of d'Esparbès, who was a novelist and historian of the Napoleonic era:[17]

'I'll confess', he wrote to Gance, 'that I felt certain misgivings during the preparation of your work, at the sight of the large quantity of books and pamphlets piled up on your desk. I had the uncomfortable impression that your work would be crushed, or at least dangerously compressed, by the wealth of material.

'The result is amazing. If you continue in the same way you will have created a picture of Napoleon that will permit no one to change a single characteristic. I get the impression of something monumental but perfectly balanced ... This is the opinion of a man who has lived with the image of Napoleon before his eyes for thirty years of his life.'[18]

4 · The Sum of Recollection

In France, Gance was regarded as a sort of home-grown Griffith, but no one had the intention of supporting him with anything more substantial than fine speeches and shallow promises—no one, that is, other than his friend and producer, Charles Pathé, the founder of France's most important film company.

The relationship between Pathé and Gance was an unusual one. Neither in Europe nor in America did the creative people mix easily with the money men. But Pathé had shown his faith in the most direct fashion possible—by putting vast sums behind Gance's ideas. He had backed *J'accuse* and *La Roue*.

According to Pathé's daughter, Maud, while Pathé liked Gance and was sensitive to his enthusiasm, he could not always follow him along the road of his more grandiose ambitions, 'a road that led him beyond the limits of reality. He supported him to the utmost, however, and not without risk.'[1]

Pathé Frères had undergone several convulsions since the war; the original company had become Pathé Cinema and Pathé Consortium, both of which were concerned with distribution, not with production. After a disagreement, Charles Pathé walked out of the organisation, which, after more convulsive changes, embarked on production again. Pathé had interceded with Pathé Consortium to finance *La Roue*; could he do the same for *Napoleon* now that *La Roue* was in trouble?

Gance was not the kind of director who made the occasional *succès d'estime* and consistently lost money. He had a solid commercial record:

Le Droit à la vie (1917)	320%
La Zone de la mort (1917)	400%
Mater Dolorosa (1917)	425%
La Dixième Symphonie (1918)	544%
J'accuse (1919)	668%

Admittedly, these were his own figures,[2] released with the proposed *Napoleon* budget, but even allowing for exaggeration there is no reason to doubt a steadily increasing percentage of profit.

Despite this record, Gance was no businessman. He threw himself into the money side with his usual enthusiasm, but he did not understand it. He was hurt and bewildered when financiers failed to respond to his ideas. His financial administrator, Édouard de Bersaucourt (whom he had met in the cinematographic section of the army in 1918), did what he could to take some of the load from his shoulders, and to couch his enthusiasm in more conventional business language.

In 1923 Gance formulated his first budget, announcing *Napoleon* as 'the greatest film of modern times ... the Imperial Era in five [later eight, then six] super-films of 1700 metres each, a total of approximately 10,000 metres being reduced to 3500m for the American market.'[3]

Before revealing what he intended to spend, Gance, like Napoleon leading his army into Italy, speculated on the riches to come. Europe would yield 25,900,000 francs, the USA 20,000,000 francs and the rest of the world 29,700,000 francs: a grand total of 75,600,000 francs ($4,422,600) for an outlay of 7,238,000 francs ($423,423).

He compounded this optimistic forecast by adding that the six films could be shot in six months. The figure of seven million francs could even be reduced by operating economies on each of the episodes. But in case he overspent his budget — and this demonstrates how endearingly naive he was in terms of business — he undertook to find the rest of the money himself. He was to be given absolute creative control, and his share of the profits was to be 45 per cent with a guarantee of 500,000 francs and daily expenses of 250 francs.

Realising that potential financiers would be shaken by this vast outlay, Gance included details of the cost of a film called *Foolish Wives*, recently made in Hollywood by Erich von Stroheim. Universal Pictures had been so amazed by the skyrocketing expenditure that they used the figures in their advertising, and Gance quoted the budget as $1,103,736·38 (around 19 million francs). He pointed out that *Foolish Wives* had few of the elements of success of *Napoleon*, and was only one film, whereas *Napoleon* would be six.

'A film about Napoleon was the greatest project of Griffith,' continued Gance, with pardonable exaggeration. 'He had abandoned it because of the immense difficulties he would have had to film it in America. The budget for this film was already above two million dollars (34m francs).'[4]

The budget went out in September 1923, together with a résumé of the films, to potential backers. Yet the following month, he sent a further list of seventeen films to Signor Barattolo, of Unione Cinematografica Italiana, Rome — a list which included *Jeanne d'Arc* with Lillian Gish! Signor

Barattolo, who had produced *Au secours!*, had been the first to whom he had
sent a proposal for *Napoleon* — an early version of 6,000 metres. But the tone
of Gance's latest letter was calculated to infuriate: 'My instinct is never
wrong, my artistic conscience too great just for you to make money and
expand your reputation.'[5] There was a row, which left Gance disillusioned
and angry. A strange letter survives which shows how deeply Gance's pride
had been hurt: 'You did not perceive the kind of man I was, nor the kind of
man I am going to become in this vicious world of the cinema. It is not
difficult to become king in a kingdom of dwarfs, and the time is approaching
when regrets will be of no use. Too bad. In a few years, I shall become
redoubtable — be fully aware of the power of this word … I am carefully
preserving a copy of this letter in order to read it again in a few years' time
after I have, with the help of a few understanding and critical friends, put
order into European cinema, for it is high time it was done.'[6]

His anger turned to dismay when financier after financier turned the
project down. As for the French, their industrialists had never looked upon
their national cinema with anything more than condescension. French
films, unlike German films, had failed to make an impact on the American
market, and only through the American and to a lesser extent the British
market could impressive profits be made.

The French apathy was such a bitter blow to Gance he seriously
considered abandoning the project and setting up another series of films
with Charles Pathé. For Pathé did not desert him, although *Napoleon*
needed more than he was able to invest.

But early in 1924, a copy of the résumé was acquired by a White Russian
operating from Berlin, Wladimir Wengeroff.

A businessman who traded in coal, steel, locomotives and pharma-
ceutical supplies as well as films, Wengeroff made deals between Russia,
Germany and France. Gance told me that Wengeroff went to talk, early one
morning, to one of the biggest German industrialists, Hugo Stinnes, about a
sale of coal. He took the synopsis in his brief-case. Stinnes was unenthusiastic
about the coal, but Wengeroff accidentally dropped the résumé of *Napoleon*.
When they met again, Stinnes told him, 'I'm not interested in the coal deal,
but the other day you dropped a sheaf of papers as you left. Now that *does*
interest me.'

And so, to his delight, Gance received a letter from Wengeroff which
talked of *Napoleon* in terms which matched his own enthusiasm. 'I am
absolutely convinced *Napoleon* will be an enormous success. Your project
interests us greatly, especially because we intend to adapt for the screen
War and Peace … Would you be interested in directing this after *Napoleon*?
We are ready to buy all the films you are going to make, and import them to
Russia, Poland, Germany, Romania, the Far East and China, with the help

of Hugo-Stinnes-Linien-Film, which has asked us to install cinemas aboard those of its ships which go to these countries, to allow theatre owners in these far-off places the chance of seeing the films before they buy them.'[7]

Gance was only too happy to accept Wengeroff's offer, but he did not want him to know the wretched response he had received from the French financiers. He inflated hopes into guarantees, saying he had found two-thirds of the finance in France: Pathé had guaranteed two million, Gaumont 1·2 million, and he listed the subsidiary investors.'[8]

Wengeroff was delighted at this state of affairs, because he did not want Stinnes controlling the project. He wanted to use him only as a banker.

Hugo Stinnes was no newcomer to the picture business. In 1921, on the advice of General Ludendorff, he had invested millions of marks in the German film industry, which proved one of the few businesses to thrive during the inflationary period.

Born in 1870, the son of coal baron Mathias Stinnes, Hugo first worked for his father, then founded a rival firm at the age of twenty-three. The Great War brought him fortune and notoriety. The Armistice and peace terms dealt heavy blows to his interests. He was accused of being a prime mover in the systematic destruction of French and Belgian industrial concerns in the occupied areas. His recovery astonished the Allies, and he was described as one of the greatest financial geniuses of his age.

Stinnes did not want to be merely a banker. He was attracted by the notion of a European alliance to help combat the flood of American motion pictures—an idea Gance had also toyed with. Together with Wengeroff, he formed the Consortium Wengeroff-Stinnes; in customary German style, the name was abbreviated to Westi. Since neither man could devote much time to their film activities, they appointed Dr Rudolph Becker, a Russian lawyer living in Berlin, to be their representative. Becker was passionately interested in the cinema, and co-operated eagerly with Gance.

The machinery of negotiation was being carefully oiled by each party when the French press threw a monumental spanner into the works. They became aware of the German connection. Considering what Stinnes had been accused of, their reaction was understandable. The French might have won the war, but the experience had embittered the nation as severely as a defeat. German recovery was a spectre equated in the French press with German rearmament. And German rearmament meant another war. The previous year, French troops had moved into the Rhineland as security against German reparations. Any French organisation doing business with the Germans was asking for trouble.

The confused state of post-war politics was camouflaged by a veneer of nationalism. Napoleon was a shining reminder of former glory, and the thought of the Germans tampering with his memory enraged many Frenchmen. The newspapers tried to fan the rumour into a blaze of scandal, but they got the story wrong. They wrote that France could only find a million francs for its national film, that the Germans were investing nine million and that Gance was being forced to make the film under German supervision in Berlin. The underlying message was that Gance was a traitor and that the Prussians would pollute the glory of the National Hero.

De Bersaucourt rushed out a statement on behalf of Gance's company, Les Films Abel Gance, to counter the 'thousands of rumours and fantasies':

'M. Gance sees no reason why he should not go about his business without informing the public or the press. However, the gossip has become so ill-informed and malicious that it is on the point of sabotaging the project.

'Everyone recognises that *Napoleon* is *the* international subject. Today a Frenchman takes on this responsibility, and what happens? It is from France that the first attacks come—and, what is worse, the first malicious insinuations. 'As for the so-called German contribution, why shouldn't they be included in this international enterprise to the glory of the greatest French genius? But why see white as black? Why can it not be believed that M. Wengeroff, a Russian, in consideration of an option on world distribution rights, has put up what he had earmarked for *War and Peace*, a Russian film of the Napoleonic era? Is it going to be claimed that just because capital is invested in dollars, there must be an American involvement? Don't start this foolish jealousy and intolerance again. And in particular, don't waste our energy with underhand arguments. Only the truth counts.'[9]

The French press retracted nothing, and the campaign succeeded in unsettling the leading French investor, Charles Pathé. As the deadline approached for signing the contract, cables flew back and forth to Berlin; would Pathé sign? At the last minute, he decided against. In desperation, Gance sent instructions that the money lost from Pathé would have to be raised from banks, to be reimbursed from the first French receipts. But Pathé was persuaded to change his mind—no documents survive to prove how—and the deal was rescued. A contract was signed in May 1924.[10]

It revealed that Gance's earlier line-up of investors had been optimistic, to put it mildly. Gaumont did not now appear. Pathé's two million was now $1\frac{1}{2}$ million francs, half to be in the form of supplies. Svensk Filmindustri was down from one million to 500,000 francs. But at last he was within sight of his seven million:

Investors	Shares	Investment in francs
Pathé	30	1,500,000
Westi/Wengeroff	70	3,500,000

Investors	Shares	Investment in francs
Vilaseca y Ledesma (Spain)	10	500,000
Kanturek (Prague)	7	350,000
Wilton (Voorburg)	6	300,000
Svensk Filmindustri (Stockholm)	10	500,000

A further 350,000 francs remained to be found within three months.

Gance retained absolute control. He accepted responsibility to produce the first film by December 31st, 1924, and the complete series of six by March 31st, 1926.[11]

The contract was signed just in time. In the spring of 1924, the government of Raymond Poincaré was defeated by what was known as the Cartel des Gauches, supported by the Socialists. At this period, Socialists were seen as only one step from Bolshevism. The campaign against them by the right caused financial disaster. The franc slumped and prices soared, bringing renewed inflation and increasing the feeling of xenophobia.

Gance wanted to avoid this feeling in his film at all costs. He planned different versions for different countries—which was why he went to the lengths of including extra scenes with Washington, Cromwell, even Simon Bolivar, in his scenario. It was in this spirit that he travelled to Italy where he was granted an audience with Mussolini in Rome. This resulted in a letter authorising him to film on the original locations of the Italian Campaign.[12]

The French press sprang back into action on his return. 'Heart-breaking news,' reported *Éclair*, 'denied for a long time was confirmed today from Germany … It is repugnant to think that the Germans are going to make money out of one of our greatest national glories. Who will be naive enough to imagine that our neighbour will make a production to galvanise the patriotic spirit of the French? Berlin will carry out its task with the method and mastery we all know so well.'[13]

Had they known the next turn of events, their anger would have turned to vindictive glee.

5·Unsung Heroes

In the 1920s, Abel Gance's reputation was at its zenith. *La Roue* was the equivalent of *Citizen Kane* for the film-makers of France — the most daring film ever made. This gave him a unique standing among his colleagues. Who else would have asked fully-fledged directors to work on his film as assistants — and who else would have succeeded? Gance surrounded himself with men he liked and whose work he respected. Needing an atmosphere of frank collaboration to create freely and to find new ideas, he selected his associates as Napoleon selected his marshals.

One of the most important was the veteran Henry Krauss. An actor who had appeared with Bernhardt, he entered films in the early days. He played Jean Valjean in Albert Capellani's *Les Misérables* (1912), a film which was considered a classic, and his performance made him a much-loved figure in the French cinema. In 1917 he began directing, although he continued to act, and besides using him as a chief collaborator, Gance gave him the part of the grizzled old soldier Moustache. Part of Krauss's job was to rehearse the players.

Krauss had appeared in a Pathé epic directed by Henri Andréani, *The Siege of Calais*, made in 1910. It was a spectacle in the currently fashionable Italian manner, capably handled by Andréani, who was himself Corsican. He had started as Charles Pathé's secretary, and then joined the company as an actor. He became one of the leading directors of the early years. By the time he worked on *Napoleon* he was fifty-three years old and had lost some of his prominence, although he had recently co-directed a serial based on *The Three Musketeers*.

Mario Nalpas was a younger director, although he had assisted Gance since 1915 and was a cousin of his former employer, the Armenian Louis Nalpas. His directing career stopped in 1924 and started again in 1927, indicating the amount of time he devoted to *Napoleon*.

Pierre Danis, whose full name was Danis-Voogd, was the brother of Ida

Danis, whose tragic illness had coincided with the production of *La Roue*. After her death Gance had married her sister Marguerite. Pierre Danis, handsome, energetic and reliable, was perhaps the most indispensable of all the assistant directors.

Supporting these men were the *stagiaires*, or trainees. One of these was Jean Mitry, who became a celebrated film historian. A young artist and writer, he was so enamoured of the cinema that his artistic ability was channelled into film posters, his writing into articles for movie magazines. He had been overwhelmed by *La Roue* — 'the great revelation' — and when he heard that Gance was starting on *Napoleon* he was only too eager to work with him. Gance replied, 'I can't take a beginner as assistant. My assistants are Andréani, Krauss, Volkoff ... but I could take you as a trainee.'

'We were all fascinated and enthralled,' said Mitry, 'and we were with Gance all the time. We discussed things, we asked him questions, talked over problems. He was always very approachable, kind and charming. I adored Gance. I had a profound admiration for him.'[1]

Mitry had a friend, the journalist Jean (he also signed himself Juan) Arroy, who was taken on in the same capacity. He became one of Gance's most ardent disciples.

'Arroy was a boy who saw very clearly,' said Gance. 'Much more clearly than most. He had a sensibility that I understood, and he understood me very well. And when I made too many concessions, he did not say it outright, but he seemed to imply, "Don't lower yourself, M. Gance." And I would say to him, "But Juan, can't you see that I'm obliged to do that?" "No," he would say, "don't do it." He frequently prevented me from bowing to circumstance, albeit very discreetly. He had a good eye and a strong devotion for me.' Arroy proved this devotion by writing a short book about the making of the film.[2]

Another *stagiaire* was a Belgian poet called Sacher Purnal. These trainees served as the assistants' assistants. They worked with the makeup and the costume people and had responsibility for a group of twenty extras. 'We were like lieutenants in the army,' said Mitry.

Because they were uncredited, it is hard to confirm the presence of such directors as Jean Epstein, but Mitry and one or two others remember him working for a short period. Others recall Germaine Dulac and Blaise Cendrars. Anatole Litvak worked on the film for a short time. Also uncredited, but playing a small part, was René Jeanne, another journalist, who was the husband of Suzanne Bianchetti (Marie-Antoinette). Later, he too became an important film historian.

Jean Arroy, René Jeanne and Jean Mitry were the chief chroniclers of the film, together with a mysterious writer who published surprisingly well-informed articles in *Mon Ciné* and *La Wallonie*: Stéphane Vernes. This turns out to be a pseudonym for Gance's secretary and script girl, Simone Surdieux: 'Gance never knew I wrote articles!'

Gance rented space at Billancourt studios—49, quai du Point-du-Jour, Billancourt, just outside Paris. The studios were owned by Cinéfrance Film, which was headed by the Russian Noë Bloch, who joined de Bersaucourt as chief administrator.

The Russian names on the credits were a mere fraction of the number of White Russians who contributed to the film. It is intriguing that men uprooted by one revolution should invest so much dedication and skill to re-create another. And when one thinks of the reputation of Napoleon in Russia, their enthusiasm is quite bewildering. However, the reason is simple. When Gance took the studio, he inherited most of this Russian 'family'.

Gance liked using Russians, because they were so reliable. 'I really like Russians in general,' said Gance, 'because they don't have the frivolity of the French. But', he added, 'they lack wings!'

A group of Russian stage and film people, led by producer Joseph Ermolieff and including actor Ivan Mosjoukine, director Alexander Volkoff, designer Lochakoff and cameraman Bourgassoff—all of whom were to be connected with *Napoleon*—abandoned their Moscow studio after the February revolution and fled south to Yalta, in the Crimea. The October revolution quickly caught up with them and they retreated across the Black Sea to Constantinople, smuggling out a small amount of gold hidden in the heels of their shoes.

In August 1920 they arrived in Paris and completed their film, appropriately entitled *Une Angoissante Aventure* (*An Alarming Adventure*), at an old studio at Montreuil-sous-bois. It is no exaggeration to say that they changed the face of the French cinema. Strangely, no one has fully chronicled their remarkable story, nor has sufficient tribute been paid to their achievements.

Two directors already well established in Russia became even more celebrated in France and joined Gance on *Napoleon*—Viacheslav Tourjansky and Alexander Volkoff. I sought out Tourjansky when I paid a visit to Paris in 1967 because I had been so impressed by his *Michael Strogoff* (he told me it had been made in the same studio and at the same time as *Napoleon*, with many of the same people). He recounted how he had left Russia, separately from the Ermolieff group, by bribing the captain of a boat with a bottle of vodka. He established himself in France very quickly, first in the theatre, then with a series of highly praised films.

'Abel Gance asked me to help him on *Napoleon* by directing certain sections. I would not have done this for anyone else. I shot small sections of Toulon and the Convention—no complete scenes. I also did the editing of

Outside Billancourt studios, 1925: the staff of Cinéfrance Film and Les Films Abel Gance. Front row, from the left: Simon Schiffrin, production manager, Cinéfrance; Lochakoff, art director; seated foreground on camera box, Viacheslav Tourjansky, director of Michael Strogoff *and assistant director to Gance; behind him, with moustache, Noë Bloch, producer for both companies; Nathalie Kovanko (Mme Tourjansky); Abel Gance; Mme Gance; Koline; Édouard de Bersaucourt, business manager for Gance. Art director Pierre Schildknecht is standing, extreme right, and Simon Feldman's brother Michel, who ran the studios at Billancourt, is standing sixth from left. The baby is a mystery!*

those sections I had directed. It was all a great rush, because I had to work day and night — these were the last days before I left for America. And I *had* to leave.'[3]

In Russia, Alexander Volkoff had been a commercial traveller for a distribution company, a translator of subtitles, a scenario writer, actor and director. As an officer during the war, he had been wounded during the invasion of East Prussia, and once he had recovered and been invalided out, he was free to make films. He made six in 1916.

He directed one of the most highly acclaimed French films of 1924, *Kean, ou désordre et génie*, with Ivan Mosjoukine (who enjoyed a tremendous vogue in France) as the great English actor Edmund Kean, and another Russian, Nicolas Koline, as his devoted friend Salomon the prompter.

Gance appears to have been fascinated by *Kean*. I ran the picture recently to discover why. It is a handsome, rather long but powerful film with one exceptional sequence — the dance in the Coal Hole Inn.[4] This is shot and edited in the style Gance had pioneered in *La Roue*, but Volkoff had taken it one stage further still and heightened the rhythm to a frenzy. Since Gance intended to take the technique as far as it would go in the first scene of *Napoleon*, the Brienne snowball fight, he enlisted Volkoff's help, together with that of his art director Lochakoff (who did not stay) and his cameramen Mundviller and Bourgassoff. He also hired Nicolas Koline to play Tristan Fleuri, the scullion who befriended the young Napoleon at Brienne. Koline, a Stanislavsky veteran, was a gifted comedian, much loved by the Russians, who recalled his playing a complete act of *Midsummer Night's Dream* entirely on his own at a Moscow theatre. The French compared him to Chaplin.[5]

With so many Russians employed at Billancourt in January 1925, Ciné-france Film celebrated the Russian Christmas with a lavish party. A theatre set, built for Germaine Dulac's *Ame d'artiste*, was cleared of seats and lined with long tables. Vodka flowed, and with it the characteristically Russian good humour. Many of the guests were to start work on *Napoleon* in a few days, and Abel Gance was asked to address them.

Alexander Volkoff

Nicolas Koline as Tristan Fleuri

Celebration of the Russian Christmas, Billancourt studios, January 6th, 1925

He had scribbled a few words, he said, as an excuse for not making a speech. 'I will make one next year, in Russian,' he said. 'But this evening that is impossible. How I would like to have seen you coming along snow-covered paths with little lanterns, as in your great country. But destiny has decided otherwise. It is, however, with strange satisfaction that I see you celebrate your Christmas in one of the churches of our new art. For, my friends, this studio will, through our common effort, become a temple where the beauty I aim for will often come to seek refuge. It is also the Christmas of the cinema; we are all a bit like shadows come from the far corners of the world to watch its birth in its cradle of light. It will grow — smile at it! And now, drink, sing, laugh — for joy is the cheapest coin in existence, but the one that enriches us the most.'[6]

6·Anything Possible

Gance thought the cinema could become a universal language, transforming mankind and making war impossible by instilling the finest qualities of the human spirit. He saw it as a pantheon of all the arts and because of his almost religious attitude, he was able to call upon hidden reserves of strength, and an invincible confidence. He was determined that *Napoleon* should reflect the greatness of its subject.

To achieve this exalted standard, he rejected the straightforward tableau approach of most historical films. He felt intense technical experimentation was essential to achieve a style stirring enough to shake the audience. An engineer was therefore attached to the production.

On a film full of unsung heroes, Simon Feldman deserves a special place, for it was he who made of Gance's inspirations practical reality. In doing so, he came up with inspirations of his own and proved himself a genius in his own right.

Feldman was born at Odessa in 1890. During the war he served as an engineer officer in an army motor-cycle maintenance shop, which proved ideal training. Afterwards he became an automobile engineer. His brother Michel (who was studio manager during *Napoleon*) went to Paris in 1905, the year of revolution. Simon left Odessa in January 1920, under fire from the Bolsheviks, and spent six months at the Fiat factory in Sofia, Bulgaria, before joining his brother in Paris. He was hired as a technician at Billancourt to start on *Napoleon*.

'But Gance was not ready, as always,' said Feldman, 'so first we made another film, with Tourjansky – *Le Prince Charmant*. Then I was asked to be Chief Technical Director for the studio to work on the technical scenario of Gance. I had to envision all the technical possibilities, especially *le travelling* – the moving camera.' Feldman enjoyed the challenge. 'Very seldom can a technician have worked so freely. I had no chief. I worked for ten directors and I had only technical problems, and I was glad to have them. I had three first-class mechanics and we had a little workshop at the studio.

'Gance was a brilliant man, but once he had the idea, he expected immediate results. I was not always ready. Sometimes, I did not know what to do. Because one has not only to understand, but to build. And I had not only Gance, I had the rest of the studio on my back—workmen and electricians—the staff of 120.'[1]

On the later stages of the film, Gance's former cameraman, Léonce-Henry Burel, joined the production as technical assistant and he and Feldman worked together.

Another vital contribution was the camera pioneer André Debrie. 'He was a marvellous man,' said Marcel David, in charge of Debrie's commercial department. 'Very clever, at the same time very hard. But he was a genius. During his career he took out nearly 100 patents.'[2]

Debrie was a friend of Gance, and he did the work more for the sheer pleasure of it than for the money. According to someone who knew him in his later years, he was the last of the nineteenth-century industrial heroes. 'He was like Henry Ford. He talked in a way that suggested industry was poetry.'[3]

Debrie had become an inventor of motion picture equipment at a surprisingly early age. His father, Joseph Debrie, was a manufacturer of laboratory apparatus. In 1908, an Englishman going on safari ordered some of his equipment and then wanted a camera as well. Joseph asked André, then aged seventeen, if he could do it. André, having no preconceived ideas about moving picture cameras, produced the Parvo, a camera which was so well designed it could truthfully be advertised as the smallest, lightest and strongest camera on the market. It was an instant success throughout the world, and was to become the workhorse of the camera department on *Napoleon*.

The chief cameraman was Jean-Paul Mundviller, a French operator who had worked in Russia. Jules Kruger supported him, together with Émile Pierre and Roger Hubert. But after a disagreement Mundviller was replaced, six months into production, by Kruger.[4]

A former press photographer, Kruger was by all accounts a testy and rather short-tempered man, but a cameraman of surpassing brilliance. Jean Arroy called him 'one of the most remarkable technicians I have ever come across'. Kruger had not worked with Gance before, but had photographed two important productions for Henry-Roussell, *Les Opprimés* (1923) and *Violettes Impériales* (1924), both starring Raquel Meller.

On the evidence of these films, it is not difficult to see why Gance selected him. They were historical productions, beautifully lit, and *Violettes Impériales* contained brief moments of mobile camerawork, including a rapid track down an alley which Gance would repeat in Corsica. The climax took place at night in pouring rain, an effect Gance needed for the siege of Toulon.

The photographic equipment organised for *Napoleon* was more complex than for any film before or since. As Alexander Volkoff wrote, 'Gance is obsessed by the idea of doing better and better, of surpassing himself—and everyone else. He is constantly seeking cinematic innovations, bringing together all the new technical systems. With his unique technical experience, he does not waste time with tried and tested techniques. In preparing the production, I was astonished by the number of important technical questions which preoccupied Gance, and by the huge order for technical equipment— lighting, lenses, cameras, accessories. Anything which seemed a new possibility he immediately passed on to the workshop. Because he spent so much of his creative resources in researching new techniques, he needed a great deal of time, but it was time invested in the future of the cinema.'[5]

An important influence on Gance were the photographic effects in Griffith's films. He carefully listed the visual devices used even in so inferior a Griffith film as *America* (1924)—and he placed a similar emphasis on lenses. The film involved the use of more long-focus lenses than any film before it. Gance and Kruger considered it a fundamental error to photograph faces with landscape lenses like the 35mm or 50mm. They introduced a system of photographing closeups with long lenses—some as long as 275mm—at the same time as the looser close shots and mid shots were being filmed by other cameras. The long lenses were also used to pluck from the crowd vivid vignettes which would otherwise be lost.

But Gance needed extreme wide-angle lenses, too—and since he could find none, he invented one. Manufactured by the Société Optis, it was called the Brachyscope, and was an attachment designed to be placed in front of a 50mm lens, converting the field of view to the equivalent of a 20mm. 'It was a simple thing to invent,' said Gance, 'but no one had bothered to do it until I came along. It was like a telescope used the wrong way round.' The Brachyscope later became a proper lens.

Another lens Gance valued highly was the Wollensak soft-focus lens, *objectif flou*, which gave the iridescent shimmer to scenes at the Hôtel Chantereine and the Bal des Victimes.

In his earlier films, working with Burel, Gance had already shown his fascination for vignetting devices and masks. He outdid himself in *Napoleon*. He favoured masks because they made trick effects simpler.

'They mould the visual surface,' said Gance. 'It was I who devised the white mask—an effect contrived by using very thin, transparent ivory.' In the scenes which fade to white, such as the snowball scene at Brienne, the iris itself was made from slivers of ivory.[6]

Throughout the writing of the scenario, Gance had flashes of inspiration which he scribbled down on his carnets—scraps of paper he carefully preserved until he needed them, and some of which he despatched to his collaborators. A piece of film showing horses in a stable (probably from *L'Atre*, a film Gance produced) was attached to a note: 'Burel—we must obtain photography with the quality of these blacks and whites—they are *pure*.' Another was sent to Feldman: 'M. Simon—my Sept camera in a rubber ball.' They reveal the involvement of unexpected people: 'See M. Man Ray's tests of friend of Roché's! *Very important*. Tell Mundviller to see them.'[7] They show that he was considering stereoscopy: 'Important—only use the plastigrams and shadows in stereoscopy (ombres en relief) in Marengo after Desaix's arrival.' (Plastigrams were an American three-dimensional process.) The most significant ideas were marked 'Primordial', and many of these concerned camera movement: 'Primordial—make a series of scenes *entirely* on the move, without one static shot. Closeups will be made on horizontal or vertical rails—the camera rising or descending. Battles will be taken thus in perpetual movement.'

Gance made his first priority clear in a letter to Mundviller: 'I ask you to devote all your care to the question of the movement of the cameras—rapid and easily manageable movement. It is the most important problem we have to resolve.'[8]

Nowadays, when camera movement is so overdone, it is hard to appreciate Gance's vision. But even when I entered the industry, the effort involved in moving the camera was laborious and time-consuming. In 1924, the stationary camera was accepted practice. Of course, movement had always been possible, but it was difficult and it was felt that it tended to attract attention to the technique. The aim was to maintain the illusion for the audience, so when the camera moved, it was very discreet. Cameramen anguished at unsteady shots and editors would discard them. Gance changed all that.

'The spectator has so far been passive,' he told *Paris-Soir*. 'I want to make an actor of him. He must no longer watch, he must participate in the action and then his critical powers will be stifled in favour of his emotions.'[9]

To give the camera something of the mobility of the human eye, Mundviller recommended a device called the photo gun—*Fusil viseur*[10]—which Debrie had attached to his high speed cameras. 'It was difficult to make a hand-cranked camera mobile enough to film fast-moving objects,' said Marcel David, 'so instead of moving the camera, we moved this optical system, which was basically a mirror.'[11]

'It was designed to photograph planes passing at great speed,' said Gance. 'You find the image on a mirror. You follow with the mirror everything that is happening. The mirror reflects into the lens whatever picture it captures. It was very interesting, but rather complicated to handle.'

It is clear in hindsight that what Gance needed was a hand-held camera —
a simple concept for us but a great deal less simple in 1924, when virtually
all cameras were cranked by hand, and when the idea of divorcing a camera
from its tripod seemed positively perverse.[12]

Ironically, several firms were working on hand-held cameras, including a
company called Bourdereau, who tried to produce one especially for *Napoleon*
(the Ad Hoc) but who completed their work too late.

The most portable camera was Debrie's Photociné Sept.[13] This contained
five metres of 35mm film, and could operate either as a miniature still
camera or it could shoot short bursts of moving pictures. It was designed for
press photographers and amateurs, but was seldom used by professional
film-makers. Gance had ambitious plans for it, ever since his scribbled note
to Feldman to pack one in a football and hurl it about. It would be an idea
the critics would never let him forget.

'The camera had, at great cost, been put in a football so it could become a
snowball,' wrote historian Jacques Brunius. 'Why should anyone be asked
to watch a flying snowball?' Gance, he admitted, certainly had a sense of
movement; what a pity he didn't have a sense of what was worth moving.[14]

But Brunius was relying on hearsay, not on the evidence of his eyes. For
no such shot appears in *Napoleon*, for the simple reason that Gance never
carried out the idea. Simon Feldman made some experiments and found the
camera, small as it was, too heavy. Also the short roll of film would not
permit the camera to be left running for any length of time. So the idea of
putting the Sept in a football was abandoned.[15] However, the camera was
used from time to time, and it was particularly useful to grab brief shots of
the company in action for a film about the film — *Autour de Napoléon*.
Attempts at the flying snowballs were made with the *Fusil viseur*.

On the back of a letter about the *Fusil viseur* I found a scribble in Gance's
handwriting which I could not decipher. Nor could anyone else. But it was
marked 'Debrie', and I felt it might be of significance, so one evening I
pored over it with a magnifying glass, and suddenly it sprang to life, as clear
as a headline: 'What I want above all is a mobile, portable camera which can
be carried by a harness around the neck.' Debrie's chief engineer Maurice
Dalotel duly produced this camera *cuirasse* and this one inspired idea solved
almost all Gance's problems of mobility.

It was tested by Marcel David, who remembered that Debrie's original
wooden Parvo was chosen because it was lighter than the later, metal-
bodied models L and K. It was equipped with a short focal length lens —
35mm — for working in confined spaces, like Napoleon's snow fortress at
Brienne, or among the crowd in the Convention, when Rouget de Lisle
inspires them with his Marseillaise. Once again, an idea of Gance's had been
translated into practical reality; it would prove the saving of *Napoleon*, for

no other method at that time could offer such swift and simple movements.[16]

Camera mobility made it hard for cameramen to crank by hand, so emphasis was placed on motors. This gave Feldman another monumental headache. How could they shoot in remote rural areas without electricity? The sole source of power for location work was the vast generator truck, which would be no use on difficult terrain. Feldman therefore stripped down a French cycle car, a Sima Violet, and transformed it into a portable generator, the power coming from an American Homelite dynamo.

Because of all the unique technical requirements, there were two versions of the scenario. The *découpage littéraire* contained the continuity of the film (it was so readable that Librarie Plon published an abridged edition of it in 1927). The *découpage technique* contained instructions written in an equally vivid style: 'The camera becomes a snowball ... Camera K [for Kruger] defends itself as if it were Bonaparte himself. It is in the fortress and fights back. It clambers on the wall of snow and jumps down, as if it were human. A punch in the lens. Arms at the side of camera as if the camera itself had arms. Camera K falls on the ground, struggles, gets up.'[17]

No one who glanced at the first scenarios could fail to be impressed. No one who read them could fail to realise that were they shot as excitingly as they were written, a masterpiece of cinema would result. Since Gance had surrounded himself with some of the most talented men in the industry, his chances of success were immensely strengthened. The morale of the company was thus extremely high.

To appreciate what Gance and his collaborators were about to do, it is important to realise when they were doing it. Of all the films usually compared with *Napoleon* for their technical virtuosity — *The Last Laugh*, *Variety*, *Metropolis* and *Battleship Potemkin* — only *The Last Laugh* had been released. In the eyes of everyone connected with it, *Napoleon* was to be a pioneering work of the first magnitude.

'Gance has in front of him a staggering undertaking,' wrote Alexander Volkoff. 'One must have confidence in him. Victory to the man with the strongest nerves.'[18]

7·The Search for Napoleon

Gance intended using no fewer than four actors to play Napoleon across the six episodes. First the cadet—then the young artillery officer, who was surprisingly slim considering the amount of weight he put on as First Consul. The second player would last until the Coronation and the next actor would play the Emperor throughout the Spanish and Russian campaigns. Another would be required for the portly exile on St Helena.

For his casting director, Gance had secured the invaluable help of Louis Osmont, a stout, middle-aged man who resembled not so much the Emperor as Edward VII. He had directed successful comedies, and he had a close relationship with Marguerite Beaugé, the film's editor. Over the years, Osmont had built up files on virtually every player in theatre or cinema, and he made this splendid array of photographs available for Gance's benefit.

Gance based his vision of the young Bonaparte on the portrait by Gros, 'Napoleon at the Bridge of Arcola'.

To find an actor to match the portrait needed more than Osmont's filing system. Wengeroff, being Russian, favoured Ivan Mosjoukine. A brilliant actor, very popular in France, he carried an air of authority; he had been, albeit briefly, an officer in the First World War. While his face was more hawk than eagle, his eyes had something of the hypnotic, piercing quality so often referred to in descriptions of Napoleon. The fact that he was Russian rather than French was a drawback, but there was a strong precedent for a foreigner; Napoleon was a Corsican of Italian descent. Mosjoukine was ten years too old, and he looked his age. Nevertheless, he was the front runner.

He had just finished *Le Lion des Mogols* when two outstanding parts were offered him—that of Napoleon and that of Michael Strogoff, in a film for Tourjansky. He was extremely anxious to work with Gance, whom he admired extravagantly, but the prospect of playing Napoleon for perhaps two years made him demand a salary consistent with the investment of time and effort.

This forced Gance to hesitate. He tested a whole range of men of Napoleonic appearance, including René Fauchois,[1] a playwright; Pierre Bonardi, a Corsican writer and friend of Gance who became the film's production manager in Corsica; Jean Bastia, a singer; Edmond van Daële, an actor of Polish origin who was eventually given the part of Robespierre; the Romanian-born Lupu Pick, an actor and film director in Germany, and, for the older Napoleon, the Prefect of Paris police, Jean Chiappe.[2] One of his carnets says, 'Make serious test of Vanel [Charles Vanel, the French film star].' Another says, 'Do not forget Léon-Paul Fargue [the poet], Werner Krauss [the German actor] or Sacha Guitry [the playwright].'

It may seem strange for Gance to have placed so much more importance on physical appearance than on acting ability. But this was true of other

Left, *Lupu Pick, the celebrated director of German films, in a test*
Right, above, *the original choice for Napoleon: the Russian actor Ivan Mosjoukine*
Right, below, *tested for the older Napoleon: police chief Jean Chiappe.*

Amateur snapshot of the two friends, Albert Dieudonné and Gance

Albert Dieudonné aged four, already enmeshed in the Napoleonic legend

great silent directors, from Chaplin and Eisenstein to De Sica, who were so confident of their skill at drawing out performances that they frequently employed non-professionals. The right faces were as integral a part of their visuals as the right art direction.

Gance also tested a rank outsider, his old friend Albert Dieudonné, who wanted the part more than anyone. He had worked with him on several films, although recently Dieudonné had become a director as well as an actor.[3] Gance did not seriously consider him for the role.

'Frankly,' he told me, 'when I did the test, I didn't find him much good. His makeup was poor, and when he put on a wig he looked rather like an old woman.'

Dieudonné realised the poor impression he had made. Like Mosjoukine, at thirty-five he was ten years too old. Worse still, he had put on far too much weight to play the young Bonaparte. But unlike the other candidates, he had been fascinated by Napoleon since childhood. At school, when he and his friends played soldiers, he was always chosen to play Napoleon.

Dieudonné's real name was Sorré, and he had been born in Paris the same year as Gance, 1889. His grandfather, Alphonse Dieudonné, had been a celebrated actor, especially popular in Russia, where the French arts were fashionable among the upper classes. Albert entered the Conservatoire in 1907, in the class of Paul Mounet, and made his debut at nineteen at the Théâtre des Arts. In repertory, he toured France, Belgium, England and Ireland. His roles, however numerous, were not stimulating enough for his creative ambitions, and in 1912–13 he began to write plays. He played the role of Napoleon as First Consul in *Le Chevalier au Masque*, in Brussels in 1913. When war broke out, he served in the transport corps as a corporal.

It was during the war that he first began to be drawn to the cinema. He played in some of Gance's first films, including *La Folie du Dr Tube* (1915). On the stage, he played opposite the great Réjane, yet the cinema claimed more and more of his attention. He began to write scenarios.

Since he often talked about Napoleon, it is likely that he unconsciously influenced Gance in his final choice. But he knew he would never get the part unless he did something drastic.

Gance warned him that he was obliged to take Mosjoukine, although he had not yet tested him. If for some reason Mosjoukine did not take the role, he would consider Dieudonné and do another test — 'but by eye … no camera'. The situation was not very encouraging.

Dieudonné went on an intensive slimming course, surviving on *haricots verts*. Gance was now working on the scenario at Fontainebleau. By a useful coincidence, Dieudonné's mother had a villa near the palace.

Gance's version of what happened next conflicts with Dieudonné's; since there is no way of checking, I present them both.

'One evening,' said Gance, 'I met him at Pathé and he told me he would come down to Fontainebleau for an audition and would read Napoleon's address to the troops of the Army of Italy. I said he could come if he wished.

'The caretaker, who was at the gate, saw Dieudonné arrive. It was eight o'clock and already dark. He called out, "Who's there?"

'Dieudonné called back, "Don't you know Bonaparte, you fool?" The caretaker was dumbfounded. Dieudonné was in full uniform, and completely convincing.

'"It can't be," the caretaker mumbled.

'"Are you asleep, are you dreaming or something, that you can't see me?" Dieudonné went on. The caretaker took to his heels and came rushing up to d'Esparbès, the curator. D'Esparbès was just getting into bed. He was just a little man, but very, very intelligent and obsessed by the story of Napoleon.

'"Bonaparte is at the g-g-gate," stuttered the caretaker.

'D'Esparbès went to investigate. The caretaker's story had impressed him to some extent, and when he got to the gate he was stunned. He was positive for just a few moments that it really was Bonaparte. He just stood there.

'Then Dieudonné called out, "D'Esparbès, what's the matter? Aren't you going to let me in?" Then he realised what was happening. But he had been so taken in, this man who loved Bonaparte so much, that his eyes were full of tears.

'Dieudonné was taken to the great hall, the Salle des Glaces, where I suddenly came upon him. He was lit by candlelight and he looked absolutely perfect.

'He launched into his address: "Soldiers, you are naked and ill-fed. The Government owes you much, but has nothing to give you … " and so on. He spoke with such power and conviction that d'Esparbès and I were amazed. Afterwards, I went up to him and told him that he had got the part.'

Dieudonné related his version of how he got the role: 'When I saw Gance at Fontainebleau, he was astounded. If I hadn't recaptured the youthfulness of ten years ago, I had at least regained my slim figure. "Ah," said Gance, "we can now get on with it. The part didn't entirely suit Mosjoukine and I've been talking about you to the directors [of Westi]. They'll give you the part, I think. Mind you, I shall want you to make some tests here in the palace before doing some more in the studio."

'He ordered a uniform for me, to be made by Grenier, the theatrical costumier, and one night, when the palace was closed, we arranged to make a test.'

The incident with the caretaker was a practical joke, as Dieudonné remembered it:

'D'Esparbès was a charming man, and we had many a good laugh together. He said to me one day, "There is a nightwatchman here in the

Left, *Albert Dieudonné aged twenty-four, as Napoleon in the stage play* Le Chevalier au masque, *Brussels, December 1913.* Right, *Dieudonné's test, 1924.* 'When he put on a wig,' said Gance, 'he looked rather like an old woman.' Opposite, *the final transformation.*

palace, a young man of eighty or so, who claims to see Napoleon every night. I think he's slightly dotty, but it would be marvellous if you 'appeared'."

'The old man was sleeping on a bench in a small room. I flung open the door and said, "What? Asleep on guard duty, Mathard?" I was wearing my uniform, of course. The poor fellow woke up, completely bewildered. He rubbed his eyes and stared at me. Then I went away. Next day, he told d'Esparbès about it. He admitted that in the past he had made the stories up. He had just been joking. But this time he really *had* seen Napoleon. Unfortunately, the poor fellow died a week later. Was I one of the causes? Who knows. But at least he had fulfilled his life's ambition to see Napoleon — as I fulfilled mine acting in this film.'[4]

Gance finally turned down Mosjoukine on the basis of his salary demand, and Mosjoukine accepted the role of Michael Strogoff. He sent Gance an anguished letter, which showed how much the role would have meant to him: 'I express to you once again all the grateful feelings of a Russian artist, to whom the greatest cinematographer of your land offered the chance of playing the world's greatest hero, and it is with tormented sorrow that I abandon this dream.'[5]

In an inspired piece of casting, Gance gave the part of Napoleon as a boy to Nicolas Roudenko (known professionally as Wladimir Roudenko). He is so poignant, and so powerful in the role, that it is tempting to attribute his playing to bitter experiences in the Russian Revolution and Civil War. Jean Arroy did just this (in his book on the making of the film), as did several other journalists.

The Roudenkos had actually come to France before the Revolution, and had settled in Nice where Nicolas was born in 1909. His parents separated, and his mother continued her career as a nurse. When the family moved to Paris, Nicolas played truant from school and haunted the studios. His headmaster wrote to protest that the boy had not been seen for a month. He never took a single exam. He worked as an extra in the occasional picture, always being cast much younger than his actual age, for he was small and thin — 'to his great despair' as his sister remembers.

Nicolas was a solitary child. When he was ten, he told his sister that he had been in a cinema when the place caught fire and the spectators panicked. He flattened himself against a wall while the audience rushed past him to the exits. With this Napoleonic piece of self-control he proved to himself that he could remain calm in a crisis, and he was able to walk out without being burned.

'He had a very hard childhood,' said his sister. 'He was eleven years older than me, and he knew much more poverty than I did. There were two sides to his character, a very agreeable side, and a very closed-in side. Curiously enough, he would never talk about the film.'

Alexandre Benois's design for Tristan Fleuri's garret at Brienne, where Napoleon keeps his eagle

A picture posed to mark the filming of the first scene, January 1925. The set is Fleuri's garret. Gance stands with Roudenko, while behind them the trainer peers anxiously into the cage at the eagle. Set musicians stand at left. Behind the cameras: Pierre (Bell & Howell), Kruger (Debrie) and Mundviller (Éclair).

8 · 'On tourne!'

In the original contract with Westi, Gance had agreed to produce the first film by December 31st, 1924. December came and went, and the only shots to be taken were tests. Setting up a vast epic was infinitely more complicated than anyone had imagined, and Westi were obliged to accept the delays.

The first time a camera turned in earnest was in January 1925 at Billancourt studios. It was an occasion of such importance that, according to Arroy, it was broadcast over the radio.[1]

Gance posed with Roudenko, the cameramen and musicians for a commemorative photograph on the first set. This set showed a garret at the school in Brienne where Napoleon kept his pet eagle. It was the work of Alexandre Benois, who designed for Diaghilev's *Ballets russes*. His paintings and sketches were executed by Pierre Schildknecht, a former pupil of the Russian Academy of Art, who had worked with Benois in the theatre.[2] He was assisted by Jacouty and Meinhardt.[3]

The cry of 'On tourne!' silenced the visitors and technicians, the three cameramen began cranking their machines, and the set musicians played mood music. The first shot was a closeup of the young Napoleon conversing with his pet eagle. Named Michel, the eagle came from the Hagenbeck menagerie in Hamburg. 'His troubles were only just beginning,' wrote Arroy. 'As he appears so often, superimposed over other scenes, and over subtitles, we had to disturb his rest time and again, taking him from his cage to make him work. The poor eagle did not enjoy his work very much. Blinded by the arc lamps — blinded and burned — he had to be sacrificed to Art to earn his reputation as a film star.'

Gance was struck by the affinity between the boy and the bird. Apart from his trainer, the young eagle allowed only Roudenko to touch him, and the boy spent his spare moments talking to it.

The next scenes were interiors in the dormitory of Brienne. Here, Gance instructed a spare camera to film shots for his auxiliary film, *Autour de*

The first shot taken on Napoleon: *Roudenko and Michel, the eagle*

Napoléon. There had been a one-reel documentary about the making of *La Roue*, which Blaise Cendrars had compiled from the odd scene of the filming, shot home-movie style over the months. Jean Arroy was eventually given charge of *Autour de Napoléon*, but it was a casually made affair, shots being taken when the equipment was available and somebody felt like using it. Now, of course, these fragments are priceless, for they allow us to see exactly how this historic production was filmed. And they are historic in themselves, for no one at that period considered such a record worthwhile.[4]

In the dormitory scene, one can see the camera mounted on a dolly, or moving platform. Gance starts the scene in unconventional manner by firing a revolver. (It belonged to Simon Feldman.) The camera sweeps back the entire length of the set as the two bullies, Phélipeaux and Peccaduc, scamper back to their beds after releasing Napoleon's eagle into the night air.

Then the portable camera makes its first appearance, to film the boys in their cubicle beds from the point of view of the angry Napoleon, pacing the dormitory in search of the culprits. The cameraman, Mundviller, looks so peculiar being pushed along by Simon Feldman on a platform resembling a skateboard, the camera mounted on his chest, that one can see the crew

Benois's first idea for the Brienne dormitory, which was rejected

Benois's final design for the Brienne dormitory, as it appears in the film

laughing. A grinning Pierre Danis runs up at the end of the shot and places a prop beneath the camera to relieve the weight.

But even an inspired record like this has frustrating gaps. There is no footage, for instance, of the shooting of the pillow fight — that memorable scene which demanded such an enormous sacrifice of down-filled pillows. One of the boys who took part, Emile Billoré, recalled that it was a 'splendid brawl'. As stagehands in the gantries threw down handfuls of feathers, the boys were ordered to attack Napoleon with pillows. At one point, a wig flew into the air. 'I heard M. Gance shout "Stop! This animal has a badly fitted wig." (The boy was Louis Decloedt, who lived near me.) Gance made everyone collect all the feathers and put them back into the eiderdowns and pillowcases and restart the scene. This lasted for three days. Then we had to go back to school — our teacher sent a school-fellow to bring us back.'

The battle took a long time to shoot because it had to be repeated over and over again for what Gance described as the checkerboard effect, consisting of first four, then nine separate images. Except for the minute area being photographed, the whole frame was matted out by a system of tiny shutters. Then the film was wound back and the next image exposed. And when the

The set for the portico, where Napoleon is thrown out into the snow

A frame enlargement from the multiscreen section of the pillow fight. Gance said that this represented the first appearance in the film of Polyvision.

effect had been achieved, and dozens of separate images amassed, it had to be done all over again for foreign negatives.

'We used the Éclair for this,' said Simon Feldman. 'The camera was so well finished that there was not a scratch on the negative after the film had gone through nine times.'[5]

The multiscreen checkerboard effect is followed by whirling super-impositions. These could be equally complex, and were based on careful calculations made on charts. In later scenes, there were as many as sixteen images superimposed at once. 'The audience saw the first and the third,' admitted Gance, 'but the others got mixed up in their mind. However, it was like an orchestra playing. You cannot recognise each instrument, but the audience understands because they are playing the same theme. Of course, it was a terrible responsibility for the cameraman. Everything had to be done in the camera. One magazine would be marked "Go back to 32", another "Go back to 16". It was terribly complicated, and if he made one mistake, the whole effect would be ruined.'

When Napoleon is dragged down the stairs after the pillow fight, *Autour de Napoléon* reveals another of its myriad of surprises. The shot could hardly be more simple; just a closeup of the struggling boy. But to achieve that simplicity, Simon Feldman had to construct an elaborate platform

The trainer trying to dislodge the eagle
Opposite, *the conclusion of the Brienne sequence*

which could move up and down the stairs on wooden rails. (Gance also covered the scene with the portable cuirass camera.) It is a tribute to Gance's direction, and to his enlightened attitude towards technique, that the audience remains unaware of artifice, being conscious only of the angry face, and feeling the emotion Gance wants them to feel.

Out on the portico, Napoleon slumps miserably on the limber of a cannon. His friend Tristan Fleuri (Koline) brings out his hat and coat. Napoleon weeps as he thinks of the loss of his eagle. Suddenly, a movement in a tree attracts his eye. The eagle has returned! It swoops from a branch on to the muzzle of the cannon. Napoleon smiles through his tears.

'I always had music on the set,' said Gance, who employed an organist, a violinist and a cellist, 'not only to give the mood, but to keep everyone quiet. You can capture their attention more easily by the use of music. In the scene where the young Napoleon lies on the cannon … he had to cry in that scene. He couldn't, until the musicians played Beethoven's *Moonlight Sonata*.'

The snowball sequence owed much to de Bourrienne's *Memoirs of Napoleon Bonaparte*. De Bourrienne was the same age as Napoleon and had been at Brienne with him:

'During the winter of 1783–4, so memorable for heavy falls of snow, Napoleon was greatly at a loss for those retired walks and outdoor recreations in which he used to take much delight. He had no alternative but to mingle with his comrades, and, for exercise, to walk with them up and down a

73

Abel Gance and frozen extra

spacious hall. Napoleon, weary of this monotonous promenade, told his comrades that he thought they might amuse themselves better with the snow, in the great courtyard, if they would get shovels and make hornworks, dig trenches, raise parapets, cavaliers etc. "This being done," said he, "we may divide ourselves into sections, form a siege, and I will undertake to direct the attacks." The proposal, which was received with enthusiasm, was immediately put into execution. This little sham war was carried on for the space of a fortnight, and did not cease until a quantity of gravel and small stones having got mixed with the snow of which we made our bullets, many of the combatants, besiegers as well as besieged, were seriously wounded.'[6]

Gance had planned to start with this sequence. He had found the location, and had arranged for local children to be released from school for a day or so. But he could hardly shoot a snowball fight without snow. And so far that winter there had been no sign of it. Artificial snow was adequate for confined areas, but Gance wanted the camera to perform earthbound aerobatics to transform a childish game into an epic symbol of future combat.

Since most films were shot out of sequence, Gance continued in the studio filming interiors until a telegram arrived saying, simply, 'SNOW HAS FALLEN'.

In February 1925, the company set off for Briançon in the Hautes-Alpes. Nothing remained of old Brienne, while the fortifications of Briançon had been built by the seventeenth-century military architect Vauban. It was here that the battle of the snowballs was to be staged.

'This first expedition', wrote Arroy, 'was like setting off across a desert with a caravan. Sixty people travelled with thirty-five cases of equipment. Whenever this troupe stopped anywhere, whole camps had to be organised, because no hotel could cope.'[7]

The mobile camera in action at Briançon: left to right, Simon Feldman, Jules Kruger, Alexander Volkoff, Gance. The Debrie camera is motor-driven.

The Making

At Briançon, Simon Feldman's engineering skill was displayed in all its glory. The portable camera came into its own; mounted on a sledge, it could move unobtrusively round the action, or speed pell-mell through the middle of it. *Autour de Napoléon* shows a sledge, with camera, being pushed off the top of a hill and hurtling towards a crowd of boys, scattering them. It also shows the camera Gance had asked Feldman to adapt so that it would pan in a circle all by itself. Feldman constructed the complex mechanism, buried the cables in the snow and operated it by remote control.

Gance also wanted the audience — via the camera — to be punched on the nose and pelted with snowballs. The lens of Kruger's portable camera was encircled with a huge sponge, so that the boys attacking it would not be hurt; the sponge also cushioned the impact for the camera.

Most of the other innovations were tried out here, too, — the *Fusil viseur* and the *ascenseur de prise de vues*, a sort of primitive crane, mounted on a sledge, which took its inspiration from the guillotine. The camera was hauled up in place of the blade, the sledge was pushed towards the action, and the camera descended on a rope.

To direct the sequence, Gance made use of what would now be called a public address system, but which was then, for a film director, a rare and expensive luxury. But *Autour de Napoléon* also shows him directing in a far more energetic way, almost participating in the action himself. Kruger, the portable camera strapped to his chest, can be seen scampering after Roudenko,

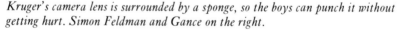

Kruger's camera lens is surrounded by a sponge, so the boys can punch it without getting hurt. Simon Feldman and Gance on the right.

The combatants pose by a camera designed to pan in a circle by itself. The designer, Feldman, stands on left of camera, with Andréani on his left; Gance is right of camera, and Volkoff on his right; Kruger behind Gance, his hand on the camera; Roudenko right, with folded arms. (The child at centre, with Gance's hand on shoulder, is a girl.)

doggedly cranking while darting about in the thick of the battle, one moment on the parapet and the next in among the boys, who are punching each other as well as hurling snowballs — finally ending up on his rear end, still cranking. Assistants hurl snowballs from behind the camera, and Gance is expending as much energy as any of the boys, pounding the air with his arms and yelling encouragement.

For a week at Briançon, there was no school. 'We were enchanted,' said one of the extras, Henri Cointe. 'Our wages consisted of a glass of hot wine every evening, which made us feel very happy, and one bar of Reveillon chocolate, the old-fashioned kind you don't see now, very hard and sandy. At that time, chocolate was a luxury.'[8]

The battle took place on a large field. 'We were armed with snowballs of cotton wool,' said Gabriel Fornaseri. 'They were so light we couldn't throw them very far. One of the boys made one out of real snow, very hard, and threw it at Roudenko, making his nose bleed and wounding him slightly on the forehead. He began to cry and there was a great hullabaloo with all the cameramen and directors shouting at him to carry on, as they didn't want the sequence interrupted.'[9]

Meal break on camera platform for Phélipeaux (Vidal), Peccaduc (Roblin) and Pavlov, a Russian assistant

The accident followed the script precisely — Bonaparte was due to be struck on the forehead by a snowball surreptitiously loaded with a stone.

'A lot of the boys had their clothes torn. Everything was damaged, especially our shoes.' Henri Cointe remembered these as black lacquer shoes, with a metal buckle and cardboard soles which were instantly soaked through. 'The result for me was a severe sore throat which shortened my activity as an extra.'[10]

The children were warm enough in the heat of battle, recalled the critic René Jeanne, who accompanied the unit, but between takes they froze. A lot of them had to go to bed, and the parents sent a delegation to ask for their boys back before they caught flu or bronchitis. 'I only have a few more scenes to shoot. It will be over soon,' promised Gance, with his most angelic smile. And having got everyone together again, he yelled, 'On tourne!'

'The next day, needless to say, they hadn't finished,' wrote Jeanne, 'and the parents came over to see if the promise was going to be kept. But Gance had assembled a band from the garrison, and the battle began again, more furious than ever, to the beating of drums and the call of bugles. And this time the parents joined the boys in shouting "Vive Abel Gance!" For three more days, the young combatants continued throwing snowballs and delightedly falling about in the snow, with their thin jackets and open shoes. The charm of dynamite!'[11]

Filming is over. The boys with their master, M. Secly. Some of them still hold their bars of chocolate. Two on the extreme left adopt a Napoleonic pose.

9·The Enchanted Isle

The fact that Napoleon was born in Corsica is the island's main claim to fame. What is less well known is that Napoleon and his family were forced to flee the island, and were almost killed in the process. Pasquale Paoli, who had driven out the occupying Genoese, was Corsica's national hero, and he had paid for his heroism with exile. He had given the island a democratic constitution and had ruled so wisely that he was much admired, especially by the Bonapartes. But in 1793 Paoli allied Corsica with the English. Napoleon as representative of the French became an enemy, and an order was issued for his capture, dead or alive. Paoli's militia pursued Napoleon while Paoli supporters ransacked his mother's house, Les Milelli, and set it alight. On June 10th, 1793, with no money and no possessions, the Bonapartes sailed for France.

In March 1925, an advance guard consisting of two Corsicans, Pierre Bonardi and Henri Andréani, sailed from Marseilles to obtain official co-operation for the company to film on the island. It was not easy, for they stepped ashore into the turmoil of election fever. The question preoccupying the citizens of Ajaccio was, appropriately enough, whether the Bonapartists would win back the town after being in eclipse for four years.

The republican mayor of Ajaccio, Jérôme Péri, was dismayed when asked for his official blessing. 'You want to parade a Bonaparte through the streets of Ajaccio? Do you want me killed? Emotions are already at fever pitch. We'll have a riot. Come back after the elections.'[1]

Bonardi appealed to the mayor as a Corsican, and pointed out that the film would be shown throughout the world — 'even in Polynesia!' The mayor made the connection; he realised what the film could mean in economic terms for the underprivileged island. The crew would fill the hotels, crowd scenes would provide much-needed employment and the film would stimulate tourism. He agreed — and that agreement took courage for it spelled his almost certain defeat in the elections. The presence of a film company making a picture about Napoleon would hardly help the anti-Bonapartist cause.

The main party arrived in April 1925 to an enthusiastic welcome. The leader of the Bonapartist party asked Gance if they could borrow Dieudonné to lead a parade down the rue Fesch. 'Flowers will be thrown by the people. That will be an unforgettable moment for him. And for you, what publicity!' But the Prefect of Corsica had asked the company to remain on the sidelines, and the parade went ahead without Dieudonné.

Whenever the film people appeared there was all the excitement of a parade. In cafés and shops, the locals insisted on paying for the cast and crew. When Dieudonné walked the streets in uniform, old ladies would clasp his hand and kiss it, as if he were the Emperor reincarnated. The Corsicans called him 'Nabuleo', the Bonaparte family's pet name.

'There was always a tumult on the square as people gathered to watch our departure,' said Simone Surdieux. 'Everyone was in ecstasy over Dieudonné's resemblance to Napoleon. Gance was followed by crowds who were totally unconcerned about the trouble they caused him.'[2]

The Gance troupe in the rue Forcioli-Conti, Ajaccio

Lunch break in Corsica

Outside the city, the company set itself up wherever it had to film, no matter how primitive the conditions. Old barns or abandoned cabins became offices and dressing rooms. 'Most of the time,' said Simone Surdieux, 'everything happened in the middle of the wind. But Gance always let his gaiety burst forth to overcome the tiredness we felt.

'The lunch hour provided the greatest enjoyment each day. One of our production managers, Pironet, became chief cook. He pretended not to understand the word diet, and got upset if you failed to eat his leftovers.' Pironet made bouillabaisse in a huge kettle, and transported it to the company by horse and cart.

Among the first sequences to be photographed was the chase of Napoleon by Paoli's gendarmes. Dieudonné, like Bonaparte himself, disliked riding, although his horsemanship was adequate. For the long shots, he was provided with a double, Pierre de Canolle, who became one of the chief stunt men on the film. The closer scenes, however, Dieudonné had to do himself.

His horse was called Bijou, and was found in the stables of a brothel. The inmates were evidently very fond of him. Not so Dieudonné. The horse was thoroughly perverse. He would do rehearsals correctly, at a walk or a trot, but he tended to break into a furious gallop as soon as he heard the cameras turning. On one occasion, having passed beneath an olive tree at walking pace for the run-through, he shied and charged full tilt at it on the take. Dieudonné had time to duck, but he struck his arm, and was out of action for eight days.

The company brought with them a group of *dzhigit* Cossacks—acrobatic riders—and they played Paoli's gendarmes. To boost their ranks, Pierre Danis was added, and the financial secretary, de Bersaucourt, doubled as an officer, dealing with administrative mail between gallops.

There were a couple of serious accidents to the horses, and one involving the riders. Dieudonné accidentally led them full tilt into a wood. Before they could check their speed, some of them followed and crashed into trees. Danis's helmet was crushed, although he escaped serious injury. Chakatouny, playing Pozzo di Borgo, had no helmet for protection and was injured badly enough to bring production to a halt.

The epic chase began at the Auberge Stephanopoli,[3] near Ajaccio, which stood in for the Moulin du Roy, Bocognano. In true Western style, de Canolle, doubling for Dieudonné, leaped from the roof on to the back of Bijou and galloped off like Tom Mix, pursued by a posse of gendarmes. A

Chakatouny injured during a chase sequence when he hit a tree. In the foreground, the armourer, Lemirt.

reporter who watched the scene wrote, 'The Corsican horses, whose qualities on the racecourse are famous, performed miracles. This pursuit by the cavalry will be comparable to the American chases.'[4]

It was never Gance's intention to produce a sequence which was comparable to anything else; it had to outdo it. And this chase, inspired by the Ride of the Klan in *The Birth of a Nation*, was shot in a more complex and exciting way than any similar scene, involving extreme long shots across undulating hills, pit shots with the camera buried in a hole,[5] and rapid travelling shots from camera cars. These *travellings*, as the French called them, were enhanced by the use of wide angle lenses which gave an exhilarating sense of the grace and movement of the horses.

'They were filmed from an open passenger car,' said Feldman, 'with three cameras. Two on tripods, one facing back, one sideways, the third fixed to the running board by means of a special clamp made by Debrie. This filmed the legs of the horses. The dynamo was fixed beside the driver and I stood up, operating the switchboard.'

And, naturally, Gance asked Feldman to put a camera on the back of a horse. 'You couldn't use a battery,' said Feldman, 'because you can't put an accumulator on a horse. So I had an idea. I used two steel bottles of compressed air either side of the saddle. The camera was a Debrie Parvo but the motor was special. It was a motor for a steam engine, but I used the

Left, *how the chase was filmed, with cameras mounted on a car. Feldman standing, left.* Right, *Simon Feldman (right) checks the compressed air cylinders which power the camera on the saddle. Jules Kruger and Pierre Danis (left) are in gendarmes' uniform.*

Left, *Jules Kruger rode alongside the camera-horse so that he could turn the cylinders on and off. In case he appeared in shot, he wore uniform, although in this photograph he has replaced the heavy helmet with his soft hat.* **Right,** *Simon Feldman in his stripped-down Sima Violet car, which carried the Homelite dynamo — the silver object by the steering wheel — and cable drum.*

compressed air instead of steam. We had two horses; on one was the saddle, with the camera, on the other was Kruger, who had to open and close the valves on the cylinders to make the motor work.'[6]

The main location for the ride was the flat ground of the Campo dell'Oro, now Ajaccio airport, and it came to an end at the Capitello Tower. In reality, Napoleon was holed up at the tower for three days, besieged by Paoli's forces. Since this would have brought the sequence to a grinding halt, Gance merely acknowledged the historic spot with a title 'Surrounded at the Capitello Tower'. The action then moved to the beach beneath the tower.

If Bonaparte disliked riding, he detested swimming, and Dieudonné was the same. As if to fulfil his worst fears, he nearly drowned. Two reports survive of this incident. The first, by Arroy, has him rescued by Pierre de Canolle, who administered a sharp blow to prevent Dieudonné dragging them both to a watery grave. But Arroy did not accompany the crew to Corsica. The reporter for *Lectures pour tous*, Pierre Scize, did. He got the story direct from Dieudonné, and he made the incident more of an accident: 'When he had finished the scene, the cameramen turned their backs and went to lunch, leaving Bonaparte in the waves. Soaked to the skin, he tried to get back to shore. He climbed over the edge of the boat, fell into the water — and disappeared.

"'If I fall into the water," Dieudonné had told Gance, "I warn you that I

85

A Corsican landmark, the Capitello Tower, from where Napoleon sets out to sea. Simone Surdieux keeps script, foreground.

shan't move. I'll wait till you come and look for me." This time it looked as though he was going to have a long wait.

'"I hadn't lost consciousness," he told me later. "But my legs were caught up in my coat. And I swallowed a lot of water."

'A fisherman who owned the boat, but had not witnessed the drama, walked into the sea to get back to his boat. By chance he bumped into the unfortunate Dieudonné, who was splashing about. "Good heavens," he thought, "the dummy." He took Dieudonné for the dummy of a gendarme which they had thrown into the sea the night before, and he was going to pass it by if the dummy had not grabbed him firmly by the leg as he passed. It was thus that Bonaparte, like Moses, was rescued from the waters.'[7]

During the chase, Napoleon gallops to Paoli's headquarters and tears down the French tricolor, which still floats from the flagpole even though Corsica had declared war on the French. 'I am taking it away,' he tells the astonished politicians. 'It is too great for you!'

He wraps it around his waist and rides into the *maquis*, where the chase resumes more furiously than ever. His last resort is the sea — his only hope a

Gance and Dieudonné in Ajaccio harbour. Judging by Dieudonné's expression, he's either just come back, or he's having to face going out again.

Napoleon escapes from Pozzo di Borgo's gendarmes on the beach below the Capitello Tower

'A future Emperor, three kings and a queen, on a few metres between the sea and the sky.'

small dinghy. He clambers aboard, slashes the mooring line with his sabre, and turns to put up the sail. There is neither sail nor oars. So he hoists the tricolor, and as the new sail fills in the wind, he calls to Paoli's henchmen, 'I shall bring it back to you!'

Out at sea, two torpedo boats of the United States Navy were preparing to enter Ajaccio harbour. The sailors were lined up as the colours were hoisted, as part of the traditional ceremonial. Suddenly, a small dinghy, with Napoleon Bonaparte at the tiller, hove into view. The Americans knew at once what was going on. 'Hip, hip, hooray for the movies!' they shouted. A fishing smack with three cameramen on board passed by, and the cameramen acknowledged the cheers.

Once the chases and the scenes aboard ship had been shot, Gance turned to the scenes involving the citizens of Ajaccio. He incurred their goodwill by the warmth of his remarks, quoted in the press: 'The eminent artist has found in the population of Ajaccio an enthusiasm and a co-operation which have infinitely touched him.'[8] Through the newspapers, Gance appealed for extras of distinctive Corsican appearance—'men preferably bearded'.

Constantin Geftman of the production staff would receive volunteers at the Villa Palmieri, cours Grandval. There was a mad rush, and Geftman had as many as he needed within half an hour. Payment was at the standard rate for extras of 25 francs a day.

As *Lectures pour tous* pointed out, what they were being offered was no sinecure; starting at six in the morning, wearing old clothes which were far too hot in the blazing sun—goat-skin capes, sheepskins, wigs—rehearsing again and again, being shouted at by assistant directors, being made to run and jump over rocks, shout, gesticulate and generally exhaust themselves ... They had to snatch a bite to eat whenever they could, often returning to Ajaccio after nightfall, and be ready to set out next day at dawn.

But the eagerness of the extras was beyond praise. The only reluctance occurred when they were supposed to oppose Bonaparte, Gance instructed one crowd to shout 'Death to Napoleon Bonaparte!' and they refused to do so.

One old man who offered himself as an extra turned out to be the grand-

Kruger, on the ladder, is about to switch on the camera. It has been mounted on a cable by Simon Feldman, at right, operating the dynamo. The camera will follow the Bonaparte family through the maquis.

son of the shepherd from Bocagnano who had rescued Bonaparte at the Moulin du Roy. At seventy-four he was too old to play the same role—the part was given to Henri Baudin—but he appears in the same scenes, and can be recognised by his magnificent white beard. He scrambled over rocks and ran through the *maquis* helping the Bonaparte family to escape. His name was Félix Guglielmi, and he enjoyed film-making so much that he willingly agreed to return to Paris for interiors; sadly he died before the picture was completed.

The escape of the family took place across wretchedly hard terrain. They had to struggle through the *maquis* and wade through rivers. It was a standing joke on the film that whenever Gance saw water, he made sure that the Imperial family were thrown into it. When the troupe was caught by a thunderstorm, near the Îles Sanguinaires, Gance was charmed. He needed a storm to add to the sequence. 'A hundred extras pattered through the rain after the outlawed family,' said Simone Surdieux. 'I assure you it wasn't pretence. We had to suffer a terrible deluge. It was no fun running through water in clothes three times heavier than one was used to—and when you scrambled down the rocks into the sea, there was even a risk of drowning. When we returned to town, people were wearing swimming costumes, they were wrapped in sheets or they were barefoot. Abel Gance was a most elegant figure, padding barefoot through the streets with his boots in his hands.'[9]

The return to town each evening became a ritual. 'As soon as they saw the first cars, the excitement of the people reached a peak. What shouting! What singing! And when, sitting prosaically in an open tourer, Albert Dieudonné came back without makeup and with both his wig and his hat taken off, you should have heard the Ajaccians begging as he passed, "Your hat, Nabuleo, put on your hat!" Because Napoleon without his hat is no longer Napoleon, is he? But Dieudonné remained totally detached as he went on his way, inexorable and hatless, and the shouting of the crowd did not alter a single muscle in "that mighty brow, that head made in the mould of the Imperial globe".'[10]

Part of Corsica's charm at this period was that it seemed to be frozen in time. If this applied to the look of the place, it applied equally to the prevailing attitudes, especially towards a craft as mysterious as the cinema. Acting was still synonymous with sin. When Pierre Bonardi issued an appeal for an ingénue, the local papers suddenly felt a need to express an opinion.

'The young girls have replied with embarrassment, and the parents have trembled,' reported *La Jeune Corse*. 'The actress in the theatre, flirtatious when not already somebody's pet, is quite unlike the actress in the cinema,

Violine Fleuri, Tristan's daughter, a young girl who worships Napoleon from afar. The role was played by Suzanne Charpentier, whom Gance clearly regarded as his 'Lillian Gish'. He renamed her Annabella after a poem by Edgar Allan Poe, 'Annabel Lee'.

'My father was a director of a magazine,' said Annabella, who later became an important star in British and American pictures. 'He spent all his time with writers and painters, and he was a keen photographer. One evening he was showing off his pictures of his children to a writer, t'Serstevens, a close friend of Gance. He knew he was looking for a dopey little girl who would make a god out of that strange general. That's how I got in, although first I was supposed to play a sister of Napoleon.

'They knew I was crazy about the movies. I always talked about movies. When I was twelve, I wrote STUDIO on the chicken house in the back garden and I was the director, cameraman, actor, everything ... I was selling my children's books to buy Cinémagazines! My father was an angel, but perhaps he thought it would be such hard work that it would be the end for me and the movies!'

who has to express her talents far from the audience, and thus renders herself inaccessible to the professional seducers.'[11] The unintentional irony would have amused would-be seducers, professional and amateur, among the crew.

The part for which the ingénue was required was never revealed, but presumably it was one of Napoleon's sisters. Suzanne Charpentier had been brought out to play the role, but she was now returning to Paris. She had originally been spotted by Gance's friend t'Serstevens, who recommended her for the part of Violine, the daughter of Tristan Fleuri, who plays a half-mystical role in the film. But Gance, who renamed Suzanne Annabella (after the poem 'Annabel Lee' by Edgar Allan Poe), cast her for the lesser part.

'I did nothing in Corsica, except a few tests,' said Annabella. 'I went to Napoleon's house in Ajaccio, but more as a tourist. I didn't feel I was an actress, and at first, when that little part was taken away from me, I thought I was too bad and looked awful. They told me I would get another part, even a better one, but I was sent back to Paris. I thought it was the end.'[12]

The role of Violine had been assigned to an English actress, Mabel Poulton, who was awaiting the company's return and working at Billancourt in another film, *Ame d'artiste*. But Gance was coming under pressure, from t'Serstevens and Westi, to cast the role with a French girl, particularly since Violine was at one point to be linked to Joan of Arc.

The part of Napoleon's sister was given to Yvette Dieudonné, who had accompanied her husband to the location, and Annabella eventually won the coveted role of Violine.

The Corsican sequences are among the most beautiful in the picture. They were photographed in the spring, the ideal season, before the island becomes baked and brown. The introductory sequence is a lyrical series of shots of the most picturesque scenery imaginable; superimposed are images of Napoleon walking then riding through the land of his birth.

'One day,' said Dieudonné, 'Gance told me I wouldn't be needed for that day's shooting, so I stayed in the hotel. Before long, however, a messenger arrived to say that arrangements had been changed and I would be needed after all. So I got into my uniform, and as all the taxis were already on location I went there on horseback, accompanied by a cavalry escort of two extras. For some reason, these extras rode a long way behind me, and I rode alone into the *maquis*. Rounding a corner, I came upon a shepherd, an extraordinary shepherd. His gun must have dated from the time of Henri IV! At the sound of my horse's hoofs he turned, and stood petrified. He took off his hat, and just stood, staring. I gave him a friendly wave and rode on. I turned round and there he was, still petrified, still hat in hand.

Like the night watchman, he must always have been convinced he saw Napoleon, but this time, riding in the *maquis*.'

The Corsicans were mostly poor, and some of their historic sites were in a bad state of repair. Having secured permission to film in all the places associated with Napoleon, Gance was horrified to find that Les Milelli, Napoleon's mother's house in the hills above Ajaccio, was 'like a pigsty'. The company had to spend valuable time cleaning it out and clearing the undergrowth around it before shooting could begin. However, the lack of maintenance had one advantage — it meant Simon Feldman could set light to Les Milelli with a controlled blaze, re-creating what happened when Paoli's mob attacked it in 1792.

Feldman had to do it without damaging the building. The interior blaze was easy, as it could be suggested with smoke grenades. For the exterior, he replaced hinges of the shutters with petrol-soaked string. As the smoke poured out of the window, he set light to the string and the shutters flared up and fell to the ground. 'I had no right to do any more,' said Feldman, 'because it was, after all, *un monument historique*.'

At Les Milelli, a curious and uncanny incident took place. It was local legend that whenever Napoleon visited the house, a swarm of bees would hover around him. When Dieudonné was filmed at the door, the bees made their appearance again. They can clearly be seen on the film.[13]

One night, the company was relaxing at the Grand Hotel when they heard shouting and firing from the street, as if Paoli's men were on the rampage. They rushed to the windows and were confronted by the sight of

Benois's design for the interior of Les Milelli

two thousand people taking part in a torchlight procession to the grotto at Casone. Outside the hotel, which is on the route to Casone, they halted and a roar went up for Napoleon. Dieudonné hastily put on his uniform and appeared on the balcony. The crowd reached such heights of enthusiasm that Dieudonné had no option but to accompany them. The procession moved off to the accompaniment of the 'Ajaccienne', and the celebration lasted until two in the morning.

It is impossible to visit Corsica and remain unaware of its politics and its legends. The controversy between supporters of Napoleon and those of Paoli can still be strong enough to set even visitors arguing with passion; in 1925, with the company re-creating those events, feelings must have been at boiling point. Amidst all the excitement, another celebrated Corsican figure — who had nothing to do with either party — decided it was time he was given the spotlight.

'There was still a traditional bandit in Corsica,' said Dieudonné. 'A man called Romanetti. He was a very courageous man, often in conflict with the police, whose accusations against him were not always justified, but which caused him to go into hiding. He was quite the modern bandit; he owned all the taxis in Ajaccio, as well as many farms in the country, and he had a great many girlfriends. In fact, he knew how to live!

'One day, Gance said to Pierre Bonardi, "I don't believe this fellow Romanetti really exists. I think it's all a bit of a romance."

'Romance? Two or three days later we were travelling through the *maquis* in a carriage when five bandits appeared from nowhere. They all had guns.

On location near Ajaccio: Eugénie Buffet, Felix Guglielmi, Yvette Dieudonné, Simone Surdieux, Albert Dieudonné, Abel Gance, Émile Pierre, Annabella, Marguerite Gance, Rauzena, Morlas

Abel Gance wrote on the back of this picture: 'The most celebrated Corsican bandit, Romanetti, and Abel Gance, who succeeded in interviewing him in the maquis *in 1926 [sic] and shot some film of the meeting, thanks to the novelist Pierre Bonardi, who knew Romanetti before he took up his job. Romanetti, who escaped from thousands of gendarmes, was killed in an ambush a few months after this picture was taken.' Behind Gance, Mme Chiappe, wife of the Paris police chief.*

"Monsieur Gance? Monsieur Dieudonné? Follow us." We both had our wives with us, and Gance was uneasy, but I noticed the smile on Bonardi's face, and as I knew him to be fond of a joke, I suspected he had arranged all this. We were taken to a farm where we were introduced to Romanetti, who had arranged a splendid lunch to which he had invited Mme Chiappe, whose husband was at that time Prefect of the Paris police.[14] They were on exercises in Corsica, and it was amusing to see the great bandit and the wife of the Prefect lunching together side-by-side with Romanetti's personal bodyguard.' Gance even managed to obtain some film of the meeting.[15]

The elections were over. The Bonapartists were back. Poor Jérôme Péri, the mayor, was defeated, as he had known he would be. Now Dieudonné could ride at the head of the victory procession without risk of affecting the result. He was also made an honorary citizen of Ajaccio.

Towards the end of June, the company packed up to return to Paris.

'Their departure leaves us feeling rather lonely,' said *Petit Bastia*, 'accustomed as we were to their displays and exhibitions. With them disappear the beautiful horses, the handsome costumes and ... the beautiful women.'[16]

10 · Entr'acte

Even before the departure from Corsica, rumours had reached the company. No one took them seriously, yet a cloud of misfortune had been relentlessly building up since the sudden death of Hugo Stinnes the previous April. His elder son, Egmund, who had inherited the business, assured Wengeroff that he intended to continue as before. But Egmund was full of ideas to revolutionise his father's organisation, such as making his workers his associates, which smacked of socialism to the banks and industrialists upon whom he depended for support. They began to exert pressure. Egmund was compelled to examine very carefully how his money was being spent. The *Napoleon* project was not satisfactory; by now it was spring 1925, and less than a third of the initial production had been shot. Egmund conveyed his displeasure to Rudolph Becker, and Becker tried to alert Gance to the danger ahead. He warned that Egmund Stinnes would probably prefer to accept a severe loss, even if it came to millions, rather than pursue the kind of project *Napoleon* seemed to be turning into, which consumed money ceaselessly.

Becker also warned Gance that Stinnes had demanded an indication of how much profit he might expect that year. 'Here', wrote Becker, 'I have my doubts because so far there has been no accuracy in your predictions, nor in your budget estimates. You have told me you will stay within limits. Can I trust you? I don't doubt your goodwill, but you have not been able to keep yourself within the limits of the sums set by yourself for your personal needs, where we must admit estimates are rather easier than in the matter of art.'

Becker had now been given responsibility by Stinnes for the entire affair. He did not want to cut down on costs that might affect the quality of the film. 'The only way is for you to accept that the whole future rests entirely with you.' He begged Gance to consider his heartfelt advice: 'Do not try to put all your beautiful ideas and innovations into the same film, or you will never finish.'[1]

Gance replied humbly, agreeing with almost all Becker said. 'I will make every effort in the direction you have indicated. I do it without difficulty because my guiding law is to finish my film by reconciling in the best possible way all the requirements, beginning with those of the investors ... Work is going well. I have never been so certain of success, despite the enormous difficulties we have to overcome. I ask you to have absolute faith in us.'[2]

Egmund's experiments brought him into open conflict with his brother, Hugo, and the great finance houses moved against him. They were willing to refloat Stinne's banks and metal factories, deeming them essential to the national economy, but they refused further credit for activities outside Germany – in particular, Westi, which they classed as a luxury business.

In a sinister and prophetic phrase, a journalist wrote: 'At this emergency, the Stinnes heirs laid all the sins of Israel on M. Becker.'[3] Becker was forced to resign from Westi and he went over to the great production company of UFA.

According to *Le Courrier cinématographique*,[4] Egmund did his best to defend Westi, but in the light of Becker's revelations to Gance it seems more likely that he did nothing of the kind. Westi had irritated the industrialists with the enormous publicity it had attracted, and it served as everyone's scapegoat. Westi withdrew from *Napoleon* on June 21st, 1925. Gance was saddled with immense debts, such as the rent of Billancourt studios – at 2,000 francs a day – and the smaller Boulogne studios, at 700 francs.

In a confidential memo, Gance explained why expenses had soared so far above the original budget; it had been agreed to set up everything for the first three films, and the cost of materials, initially so high, would prove much cheaper when spread across the three films. But due to the price of this material, the installations at the studio and the numerous props and accessories, the total cost of the first film had risen to nine million. Almost five million had been spent.[5] Westi would lose two million on their investment of 3·7 million. A future participant would therefore be required to invest four million.[6]

Neither Pathé nor the other investors deserted the film, but French financiers were no more eager to back it than before. '*Napoleon* frightens the French,' wrote Gance, 'who prefer *Phi-Phi*, *Tire-au-flanc* or *The Girl from the Metro*.' He felt the cinema was not ready for such a vast subject. And his self-righteous idealism did not appeal to the money men. 'I feel that cupidity and avarice are lighting a fire around me which is so bright that I can understand better the behaviour of the scorpion.'[7]

Westi's liquidation was placed in the hands of Noë Bloch. Gance kept the staff on for eight more weeks, in the hope of a rescue bid. He even managed to shoot one or two sequences. On August 29th he made out the dismissal notes, assuring them that he would recall them as soon as circumstances permitted. He gave them all a month's notice. 'My actors and technicians said they would somehow be ready when I got the money,' recalled Gance. 'They said, "The film is too important to be abandoned. It absolutely must be finished."'

The weeks passed, and there was no sign of a rescue. The financiers all had perfectly good reasons why they could not help. One who put his argument into print was François Coty, an industrialist best known for his manufacture of perfume, who also owned *Le Figaro*. He admitted that as a Corsican he was passionately interested in Napoleon. But he found it significant that the 'Prussian' Stinnes should have been the first to back the project: 'One of the most dangerous arguments exploited in the United States by hostile propaganda over the matter of our war debts is the one which says "France would be able to pay if she did not ruin herself through military spending. But her imperialism and her militarism are incurable. The French cannot or will not honour their signature because they are so bellicose." One cannot explain the reasons which led the Grand Army into the capitals of Europe; the conspiracy of the old powers against the spirit of the new — the alternative for France being destruction. And so such people say hastily and mendaciously, "War without respite is always France's aim. The hero of France is Napoleon, warmonger. La France ... Napoleon ... it's war forever." The visual impression will simply consolidate this slander. I do not want to participate.'[8]

It was a curious irony that Coty should accuse Gance of planning a nationalistic and bellicose film, for Coty was moving towards the extreme right wing in his political views. He saw, however, that Gance's film,

Napoleon captured at the Moulin du Roy by Pozzo di Borgo and his gendarmes

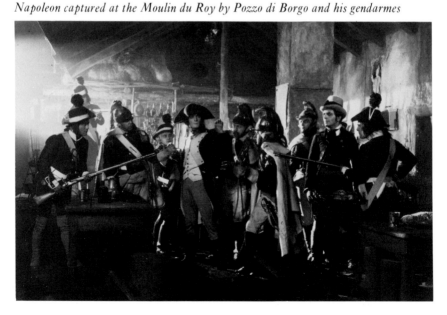

coming at this moment, could be used by France's enemies to her detriment.

Gance replied to Coty that *J'accuse* should have been sufficient indication of his attitude to war to avoid such a slur. 'Do you not remember, sir, that you were one of the first to refuse your agreement—well before our negotiations with foreign financiers? Did you then explain your scruples—or did you put up fallacious industrial reasons?'[9]

So far from exercising political control, Stinnes had neither asked for a scenario nor showed interest in the film's social tendency. He was concerned only with the figures, and the fact that the film would be an impartial historical reconstruction.

Coty did not retract his accusation, and in his angry reply, it became apparent that it was the involvement of 'international finance' that really upset him, and in his choice of words—'Our land ... our race ... our glory'— he revealed his true concerns.

Month after dismal month, all over Europe, Gance and his associates searched for new backers. Assailed with final demands and lawsuits, Gance's personal debts soared to more than five million. 'The rocks of St Helena are further away than ever,' he wrote. 'I am like Don Quixote, tilting at the windmills of finance.'[10]

It was not that financiers balked at a film about Napoleon. Director Henry-Roussell found no difficulty in setting up *Destinée*, a love story involving Bonaparte's rise to power, and the Italian campaign. It differed from Gance's film in that it was of normal length, and relatively normal budget. (It also turned out to be very inferior—a hint of what *Napoleon* might have been like in the hands of a lesser director.)

But the French film industry was in the throes of a crisis. It had reached the point where those who provided the funds were seeing nothing in return. As for export possibilities, Jean Sapène of Pathé Consortium declared, 'Against England I place a zero, against America a double zero.'[11]

Gance, dependent on both, was shackled by his Napoleonic ambitions.

Rescue, when it came, was from a most unlikely source. Once more, Gance would owe a debt to the Russians. A little company called Rodina—which is Russian for fatherland—was formed in Paris in March 1924 to make money out of the automatic developing of motion pictures, a brand-new idea imported from America. At its head was a Georgian named Alexander d'Arbeloff. He was a wealthy man from a wealthy family, and his partner was a close friend, Annie Tinker, an American, daughter of a founder of the National City Bank.

'The American equipment came to France,' said d'Arbeloff, 'and we hired a building on the outskirts of Paris. But we didn't have enough experienced technicians, and the man in charge, of Italian origin, pretended to know the technique and he didn't. We were failing.'[12]

Another Russian, Jacques Grinieff, a cousin of d'Arbeloff and also from Georgia, was interested in film production. Together with the Comte de Béarn and Henri de Cazotte, he had been involved in the financing of a historical epic, *The Miracle of the Wolves* (1924), directed by Raymond Bernard. When money ran low, de Cazotte, president of the Banque Demachy, brought in the young Duc d'Ayen.[13]

Grinieff acted as a catalyst. When he heard of d'Arbeloff's company, he also heard of the sudden death of Annie Tinker. D'Arbeloff was depressed and Grinieff felt he could do something for his morale, while transforming Rodina into a production organisation.[14]

The name Rodina was too Russian, Grinieff decided. It needed to sound thoroughly French, so he changed the name to Société Générale de Films. While d'Arbeloff remained President, de Cazotte was soon heading the organisation, and his name appeared as President long before d'Arbeloff's eventual resignation.

Grinieff knew the importance of appearances. He abandoned the Rodina office in the suburbs and centred the organisation at the *Miracle of the Wolves* headquarters at 36, avenue Hoche, in one of the most exclusive sections of Paris. The first project was to be a film by Raymond Bernard, *The Man Who Laughs*. But when Grinieff heard from Michel Feldman, Simon's brother, that Billancourt studios were available, and Gance in trouble, he undertook to rescue the project. Gance would have to surrender his rights and be placed under contract like any other salaried director. Gance agreed; anything to get his film made. But he was still talking of six films, for which the budget was now twenty million francs.

Grinieff put the idea to the board, and it was turned down as being too ambitious. 'So Grinieff was very clever,' said d'Arbeloff. 'He broke the problem by suggesting that Gance made just the first episode—and then they agreed to finance it, but without specifying just how much. They accepted to finance it by instalments. But it was difficult. D'Ayen was okay, but de Cazotte would not give the money. Jacques had to do some hard fighting before de Cazotte would give him the next instalment.'[15]

Gance's letter of agreement with SGF stated that eight—later reduced to four—million francs would be put at his disposal to complete the first part, that his artistic and technical control would be absolute: 'I will not take on the responsibility except under this express condition.' His 45 per cent participation was reduced to 5 per cent.

Buried among the clauses were the seeds of the film's eventual destruction, a paragraph protecting SGF from the celluloid inflation that had overtaken *La Roue*: 'I undertake to establish a definite version of a total metrage not exceeding 3,000 [9,300 ft]. Should this not be the case, I will allow you to make all the cuts necessary to bring the film down to this length.'[16]

Cuts were also necessary in the scenario, and Gance eliminated an elaborate subplot about a street trader called Cadet Rousselle, 'a man happy under the Terror'.

He agreed that the final cut would be ready to be shown by October 12th, 1926, at the latest and there would be a bonus of 100,000 francs, on top of his salary of 8,000 francs per month (and 7,000 francs per month expenses), if he finished on time. If he failed to do so, he would have to work for nothing.

Once the money started to filter through, the main drawback to progress was Grinieff's commitment to Raymond Bernard and *The Man Who Laughs*. Gance told him that Raymond Bernard was a good friend, and that if he had promised to do the film, then he should do so. 'Afterwards we might arrange something, but I couldn't steal somebody else's work from him — not from a sensitive, charming man like Bernard.'

Raymond Bernard heard about this and came to see Gance. He told him to go on with his film, that it was most important that he finish it and get it shown. 'He was making the sort of generous gesture one never finds in this profession.'

SGF acquired *Napoleon* — and Gance — on advantageous terms, and Grinieff created what he had dreamed of — a prestigious production company capable of financing outstanding French films.[17] He brought Charles Pathé and Léon Gaumont together, and also two prominent members of the aristocratic families of France, the Comte de Breteuil and the Comte de Béarn. Nevertheless, it was an uphill fight to get *Napoleon* completed. The more Gance shot, the more money he needed.

'Without Jacques, *Napoleon* would never have been made,' said d'Arbeloff. 'He financed it piecemeal — an arrangement Gance would never have considered. If they needed a million, and de Cazotte would not give it, Jacques would borrow two hundred here, five hundred there, until he had the money. But it was very difficult. I remember Gance, in our big office, screaming because the money was not coming through. "All right," Jacques would say. "Calm down." And he would play on the patriotic feeling in France to raise more money. It took lots of persuasion. But he always had to change the budget. Gance was not an easy man to deal with. He was artistic; never the businessman. "Money? What's money!" was his attitude until it failed to arrive. Throughout the rest of the picture, he had a very hard time. Very hard. Gance was a real artist, impetuous, impassioned. And lots of people were jealous of him. But he and Jacques Grinieff were like twin brothers. Grinieff understood the mentality of the money people.'[18]

Twenty years later, Gance inscribed on a photograph to Grinieff: 'To the man who sees further than anyone in the Seventh Art of the future — to the father of my *Napoleon*, the only one who understands me.'[19]

11·The Siege of Toulon

Since Gance was paying for the studio and the staff, he managed to shoot certain sequences even at the height of the crisis. One of these was the storm at sea, with Napoleon escaping from Corsica and enduring mountainous seas in his fragile boat. In charge of the sequence was the American, Edward Scholl, who had been set designer for Griffith on *Orphans of the Storm*, and who specialised in the marine aspects of the film. He later filmed the long

Below, *an astonishing photograph revealing how the storm scenes were filmed: the boat floats in the tank; soon it and Dieudonné will be pulverised by thousands of gallons of water from the barrels above the chutes. (In the background, on the left, the Cordeliers set under construction for the Marseillaise sequence.)*
Right, *the resulting scenes.*

shots of the storm with the German special effects cameraman Eugen
Schüfftan. For these, he used a miniature vessel. The close shots were
staged in the studio, and were almost as gruelling for Dieudonné as a real
storm.

The studio swimming pool was opened up and enlarged. Ten 500-litre
barrels were raised on scaffolding and connected to the water supply.
Aeroplane propellers were set up on the sidelines to act as wind machines
and 100mm pipes — part of the fire-extinguishing equipment used in schools
and shops — were fitted in the roof to supply the rain. At a signal — the
customary revolver shot — the wind howled, the rain hissed and the great

drums tilted mechanically, first one and then the next, pouring their contents into chutes which opened suddenly to release vast quantities of water.

Dieudonné said he would have no objection to doing this scene—'But please, make sure the water's *warm*.'

'The first lot was warm,' he said. 'But after that it was extremely cold. I gasped with the shock. Gance kept yelling, "Look frightened!" I didn't have to act.'

The exercise was repeated on three consecutive days, but never lasted more than ten or twelve minutes a day. 'There is no need to explain what courage and stamina are needed when 1,000 lbs of water are falling on you from forty feet up,' wrote Arroy. 'Dieudonné emerged from his boat—almost literally dead—and was rushed to a hot bath, to drink one toddy after another, and to be carefully massaged. Films are full of such unknown bravery.'[1]

The siege of Toulon was the next to be tackled, once normal production had resumed.

In 1793, Napoleon arrived at Toulon as a replacement artillery captain. He was to serve under General Carteaux, a former court painter, whom Napoleon quickly recognised as incompetent. In Toulon were 18,000 foreign troops, mostly English and Spanish, committed to destroying the Revolution. Napoleon's arrival had an immediate effect on French morale, but Carteaux refused to acknowledge the importance of artillery. He was removed from command by the government commissioners and succeeded by General Dugommier, who appreciated Napoleon's ideas. They formulated a plan to seize a vital fortress, and Napoleon began the attack at midnight in appalling conditions of driving wind and rain. The French troops were forced to retreat. Dugommier and the commissioners were anxious to give up, but Bonaparte forced them to try again. He led the troops himself, and at three in the morning the fortress fell. The English set fire to the French fleet and abandoned the town. Next day, the French entered Toulon. The commissioners, under orders from the Committee of Public Safety in Paris, took revenge upon those suspected of collaborating with the English; hundreds of men and women were shot without trial. Bonaparte was powerless to stop the bloodshed. The capture of Toulon saved the Revolution, and brought Napoleon the rank of brigadier-general. He was only twenty-four.

Gance decided to depict every stage of the battle. Bonaparte's decision to attack in the middle of the night *and* in the middle of a storm, however, gave all the technicians enormous difficulties.

In the silent days, the standard film stock (orthochromatic) was not nearly so sensitive to light as modern film stock. Its speed was the equivalent

Antonin Artaud as Marat, in a scene inspired by the David painting. Artaud was an actor and poet who suffered so severely from nervous disorders that he eventually had to be committed to an asylum. He once said he risked insanity the way normal people risked a cold. 'In every madman there is unknown genius,' he wrote, and he set out to lead the surrealists. He managed to make a reasonable living from his acting, but his film roles dissatisfied him. He had a passionate admiration for the German films and identified with Conrad Veidt's Cesar in Caligari. *Unlike that sleepwalker, however, he wanted to be the storm-centre of artistic protest.*

of 25 ASA, the speed of today's slower type of Kodachrome, and one would hardly consider shooting night scenes with that. An emulsion called Pathé Extra-Rapide S gave a little more latitude, but still required an enormous amount of light.

The Americans had long had the habit of shooting in daylight and toning the resulting scenes blue. The French called this *nuit américaine*, even though they did exactly the same. Gance had been obliged to shoot a lot of day-for-night scenes in Corsica. But the battle had to be shot in the dark to reproduce the conditions in which it was fought, at night in driving wind and rain.

Rain was another element everyone avoided in the silent days, since it was damaging, unreliable and seldom registered anyway. After a great deal of discussion, Gance and his team decided that since the battle took place at

The ragged army marches into battle. The dog, at right, is Gance's pet dog, which he adopted as a stray at Briançon and named Brienne. Jean Arroy third from left, by flag.

night *and* in a rainstorm, they might as well shoot the whole thing in the studio, where they would have the necessary control and could light the rain to ensure it showed up. The pipes which had provided rain for the storm at sea would do the same for this. The effect would be augmented by firemen with hoses. How the fire brigade at Chaligny could spare the men and equipment for so long — six men were permanently attached to the production — is hard to determine. Perhaps the fact that Gance's associate, William Delafontaine, had made a documentary tribute called *The Firemen of Paris* had something to do with it.

Rocks were cast out of concrete, pine trees planted and aeroplane engines once more set up in every available corner. The studio was already large, but false perspective and specially designed mirrors gave the impression of miles of territory, with distant cannon capable of spouting flame. The swimming pool where Dieudonné had been bombarded by torrents of water had been converted into a stagnant pond, full of mud and slime and corpses. The battlefield around it was littered with shattered limbs and mutilated bodies, all specially constructed for the film.

Assistant director Tourjansky went to great pains to position these corpses realistically, and makeup man Wladimir Kwanine painted them with theatrical blood. The syrupy taste appealed to Gance's dog, Brienne, who followed behind them furtively licking off the blood as soon as it had been painted on. When they finally straightened up and stood back to examine their handiwork, they were stunned to see no sign of blood anywhere. Brienne's tongue, hanging out hopefully, was bright red ...

During the siege of Toulon, Napoleon was wounded. The restaging of the battle proved equally hazardous for Gance. He had written in parts for Tristan Fleuri and his family. The scullion of Brienne had now become an innkeeper at Toulon, and several important scenes were set in and around his inn. At the height of the battle, Fleuri, Violine and Marcellin reload muskets for French troops, oblivious of the bullets flying through the window. For one scene, English soldiers were shown outside the inn firing at the window.

In charge of explosives on the film was the armourer, M. Lemirt. Because of a marriage in the family, he took a day off and handed the job to a younger and less experienced man, who was not familiar with the safety procedures. A great deal of magnesium was required. It was made up into small packets, so that if one caught fire, there was still a chance to isolate the others. The replacement armourer, who knew nothing of this, was simply anxious to

Scene based on the famous picture by Raffet, 'You can't smoke, but you can sit down.'

keep his powder dry. He decided the best place for a kilo of magnesium would be underneath the tent-like canopy where the cameras were turning.

No one is quite clear what set the explosion off. Gance said that the English soldiers fired blank rounds and a wad of burning paper fell on to the magnesium. Simon Feldman said it was his impression that Gance fired his revolver right into the box.

'There was a tremendous explosion,' said Gance. 'Tremendous! That stuff burns at one thousand degrees. There were nine of us, and we were all set ablaze. I tore off my jacket and protected my face as best I could. We were all blinded. Georges Lampin, right beside me, was seriously burned. There was another young man, a prop man, who was so badly injured that for a month, no one knew whether or not he would lose his sight. Happily, his eyelids had protected him.

'In those days, we had a special ointment for use on burns. We had a bottle with us. I shouted to everybody to use this ointment as quickly as possible. We tore off our clothes and rubbed it all over ourselves. But it wasn't powerful enough. Somebody shouted, "Come on, we'll have to get you all to the hospital as quickly as we can." '

Feldman had grabbed Maryse Damia, the singer, who had been standing behind the cameras, and pulled her out of danger. Now she offered the use of her car. On the drive, a journalist, René Délange of *Excelsior*, did all he could for the victims.

'From the chemist,' said Gance, 'we went to a surgeon, who took one look at us and immediately treated us with *ambrine*. That's a kind of wax. You light it, like a candle, and cover the wounds without bothering to clean them first. We were so badly burned that Délange suddenly became sick. I felt perfectly all right until, after a while, the pain began. And you can never imagine how bad that pain was. I went home with bandages all over me, and there I took a tall glass of cognac—and I don't usually drink—to try to lessen the intense pain. I walked up and down in absolute agony.

'But *l'ambrine* saved me in the end. Without that, I should have been covered in scars. At the end of the month, it had all healed and I was better. Although, while it was healing, I could see through the wax all the black, charred flesh. And I wondered if it would ever heal. Georges Lampin took longer to heal. But less than eight days after the incident I was back on the set.'

Gance said that one could hardly expect to shoot battle sequences without risking real accidents and real wounds. 'I do not consider the cinema to be mere pictures. Films are something great, mysterious and sublime for which one should not spare any effort and for which one should not fail to risk one's life if the need arises.'[2]

Eight days, even on so lengthy a production as *Napoleon*, was too long for

After the explosion: Abel Gance at his apartment, 27 avenue Kléber, with his mother, his wife and the journalist René Délange, in March 1926

the company to hang around with nothing to do. Tourjansky worked on the less important aspects of the Toulon sequences with Gance's old cameraman, Léonce-Henry Burel, who had joined the company as Directeur technique des Films Abel Gance, an all-purpose title which he requested so he would not appear to be taking over anyone's job. Burel promoted Roger Hubert, one of France's great cameramen of the future, to Chief Cameraman with Tourjansky. When Gance returned, with his head and arm bandaged as though he himself were a victim of the battle, they became the second shift, filming at night while Gance filmed during the day.

The explosion was widely reported, attracting the attention of more and more newspapers and magazines. The publicity was encouraging. The eye-witness reports all referred to the remarkable atmosphere, and the dedication of the extras.

In the 1920s, films made in Paris seldom needed large crowds of extras. Small groups could be obtained from a café near Réaumur-Sebastopol, and larger groups from the vegetable market at Les Halles. *Napoleon* drew on both sources, but the film required far greater numbers — hundreds for the battle scenes, a thousand for the Convention. How could Gance find a reliable source, close at hand? Without such a source, the film could not be completed.

By one of those coincidences which so often rescue film-makers at the last moment, the Renault factory at Billancourt went on strike. Suddenly, huge numbers of workers were besieging the studios, anxious for any kind of paid labour.

But such workers were an unknown quantity. How would they react to the make-believe atmosphere of film-making? Could they be made to take it seriously? To win their support, Gance posted a remarkable proclamation on the doors and in the corridors of the studio:

Appeal to the collaborators on NAPOLEON BONAPARTE
by Abel Gance

Artists, technicians, extras

It is imperative — please understand the deep significance I place upon these words — it is imperative that this film should allow us to enter once and for all into the temple of the arts by way of the huge portal of history. An unspeakable anguish grips me at the thought that my will and the gift of my life even are nothing if you do not give me your undivided loyalty and devotion. Thanks to you, we shall bring to life again the Revolution and the Empire. The task is without parallel. You must rediscover within yourselves the flame, the madness, the might of those soldiers of the Year II. Personal initiative is going to be of the utmost importance. I want to feel as I watch you a great surge of force capable of sweeping away with it all critical barriers, so that from a distance I can no longer distinguish between your hearts and your red bonnets. Quick, mad, tumultuous, gigantic, insolent, Homeric, with diminuendoes, and grand orchestral bursts that make the moments of silence even more formidable; this is how the Revolution, that runaway horse, wills you to be. And then comes a man who looks it in the face, who understands it, who wishes to make use of it for the good of France and who, suddenly, leaps on it, seizes it by the reins and little by little calms it, to transform it into the most magnificent instrument of glory. The Revolution and its laugh of agony, the Empire and its giant shadows, the Grand Army and its suns; upon you falls the duty of recreating their immortal figures. My friends, all the screens of the world await you. From everybody, collaborators of every order, lead players, secondary players, cameramen, painters, electricians, stage hands, from everybody, and above all from you, humble extras, who will have the heavy burden of rediscovering the spirit of your ancestors and of giving by your unity of heart the formidable face of

France from 1792 to 1815, I ask, nay, I demand, total forgetfulness of petty personal considerations, and absolute dedication. Only in this way will you truly serve the already illustrious cause of the finest art of the future through the most marvellous of the lessons of history![3]

The Renault management had never talked to their workers quite like that.

Whether it was the proclamation, the atmosphere, or the exhilaration of being free from the production line that inspired them, the extras behaved exactly as Gance had hoped.

André Cerf (later a screenwriter) was among them: 'These fellows from the Renault factory had been split into two camps. They began to hurl insults at one another. Because of the delays, because of impatience and jangled nerves, the insults deteriorated into squabbles. I don't know if it was done on purpose, but then Gance arrived and began to put the two camps under further pressure. This had the effect of making the two sides—one because they had the enemy uniforms, the other because they were French—reach the stage of wanting to smash each other's faces. Really. Towards six o'clock, Gance gave us the signal to attack Toulon and then we started in earnest.

'On the whole, fake weapons were used—wooden muskets, rubber bayonets. But there were some there hadn't been time to fake—real ones. I

W. Percy Day (centre) as Admiral Hood. Day became the leading matte painter in the British film industry; his work for Korda included Rembrandt *and* Things to Come.

was young and full of enthusiasm, and this gave me the strongest impression of combating the enemies of France and taking Toulon under Napoleon.'[4]

Each time a fragment of the battle was staged, the auxiliary equipment went into action.

'In apocalyptic tumult,' wrote Arroy, 'aeroplane propellers began to rumble, blowing a hurricane as firemen's hoses spat out torrential rain and a great electric arc blinded us, flashing like lightning. All around us were fans, pumps, frantic horses, bucking and rearing, the dry crack of guns drowned by the thunderous roar of cannon.'[5]

The sheer physical excitement undoubtedly justified such a description, but Arroy exaggerates; the cannon did not roar. Simon Feldman had developed a special powder for the cannon which was non-explosive, but which provided a lot of smoke. The cannons were built of wood, with steel cylinders from which the powder was discharged. To provide the recoil,

Below and right, *the Wall of Hostages, perhaps the most daring scene in the film, given by Gance to the Cinémathèque in 1958 and never seen again. According to Arroy, 'It is the synthesised expression of collective horror. An incredible crescendo of rapid cutting. The soldiers open fire, an enormous gun fills the screen. A face in the extremes of terror, a jolt, a forehead covered with blood, the eyes turn upward. Then the lens itself becomes a bullet, rushing towards one victim, then another, until it enters their skulls. Finally, a paroxysm of all these visions; an incredible effect of panic. Then a final, static image; the dead lying on the ground.'*

Feldman attached strong rubber as a kind of truss, triggered by a pedal. The gunner lowered his match to the touch-hole; as the smoke appeared, he jammed his foot on the pedal and the cannon recoiled. Gance was so fascinated by this that he had Tourjansky and Burel shoot second-unit inserts with the camera on the cannon.

The lightning emanated from an arc lamp in the middle of the set, shielded from the rain by glass and from the cameras by strategically placed rocks, and operated by remote control. The cameras and cameramen were protected by tent-like canopies, or they were contained in small, portable cabins, rather like the 'iceboxes' of the early sound era, which could be manhandled from one setup to another.

The Danish director Carl Dreyer watched a battle scene covered by as many as twenty-five cameras.[6] 'Gance's preparation is so carefully planned,' he wrote, 'that the battle can be filmed without a rehearsal. Officers on horseback can gallop over the hills, flags fly, a general falls from his horse, cannon from a distant fort fire volleys on to the battlefield, and, in the midst of the fray, one can perceive a soldier wearing a camouflaged camera attached to his chest. The camera is connected by an invisible cable to a motor off the battlefield. The rain falls on the whole scene, the screeching propellers send powder smoke over the undulating mass of struggling men. Lightning flashes. The effect is astounding.'[7]

On following pages '*After the victory*'

Playing Captain Desaix was Robert de Ansorena. The son of the Mexican consul in Paris, he went to Billancourt in the hope of playing Napoleon. Instead, he was thrown into the thick of the battle. Struggling in the mud, he fought back against the onslaught of the English troops until his sabre broke. 'They kept shooting at me and I kept shouting "No, no! You can't kill me now! Desaix was killed at Marengo!"'

De Ansorena had one big scene when Napoleon saw him fighting like a dervish and orders him to be brought over. When the two men meet, Desaix, his magnificent eighteenth-century face glistening beneath his plumed helmet, unexpectedly bursts into laughter. It is an extraordinary moment, one that captures something of the exhilaration of danger.

The brief scene over, de Ansorena turned to go. He leaped from the hillock and, blinded by the lights, headed straight for one of the unprotected aeroplane propellers operating in the darkness. 'Abel Gance saved my life. He grabbed me by the seat of my pants, shouting, "Look out! You'll kill yourself!"'[8]

Perhaps the most memorable effect in the siege of Toulon occurs when the French drummers are killed, one after the other, as Bonaparte orders: 'Drummers of the 6th, sound the charge!' And the charge is sounded, the drummers having been replaced by an unexpected auxiliary ... hail.

Simon Feldman was particularly proud of this effect. 'When they ask me what I do in the cinema, I say I am God. I supply the sun, the moon, the rain, the mud—and even the hail. For the hail, I brought crystallised rock salt from Belgium, and fitted mechanically operated sieves in the ceiling. A man was stationed up there to empty the salt into the sieves.'

It looked superb on film, but it had a devastating effect on the studio. 'For thirty days it had been raining in the studio, and when the rain was mixed with the salt, the floor was eaten away. We had to replace something like five or six hundred metres of wood.'[9]

If the floor was damaged, what about the effect of the artificial weather on the extras? Some of them did not enjoy the experience. Robert Braquehaye, who had been keen on the idea of acting in a super-production, was put in charge of a cannon, in the assault on Petit-Gibraltar. When he saw the horses, he was glad that he had been assigned to the background. But for reverse angles, his cannon was brought to the foreground and, as he remembered it, 'tons of ice cold water poured down my back all day.' One morning he woke up completely hoarse, and since he was an amateur singer, he was thoroughly disgusted with the cinema and never worked for it again.[10]

But this was an isolated case. However much they suffered—and in the cold weather, the relentless 'rain' and 'wind' must have been wretched—the other extras showed a commitment which was nothing short of heroic.

When Gance asked them to work even longer hours, the protests of the few were drowned by the fervour of the majority.

De Ansorena remembered that at the end of the day, Gance would climb on a rostrum and tell the extras, 'It is not just the leading actors who are making this film, it is you, the crowd. You have been splendid. Unfortunately, the budget is not large enough to enable me to take you all back tomorrow. It is very sad.' He would break off for the disappointment to take its effect. And then he would add, 'No, no. It's too bad. Come back tomorrow, all of you.'

'It was charming,' said de Ansorena. 'I'm sure he did it because he was a bit of an actor, but all the same, he did it with his heart. He thought, they're all here, they're all working hard. If I tell them I need only a hundred, that will hurt the others. No I can't do that. So, "Come back tomorrow, all of you," and everyone shouted, "Bravo!"'[11]

Carl Dreyer wrote that he left the studio overwhelmed by what he had seen, and he had to pass the wounded in the corridors. 'The combatants have been so realistically involved in the fighting that they are scratched, they have long cuts and serious wounds. Blood flows. Two nurses are bandaging them up. In an administrative office, a doctor examines those who are more seriously injured. Gance has certainly forgotten all about them.'[12]

If he had forgotten, Gance was reminded by one of the unit nurses, Mme Mélinot. 'Do you realise', she said at a rushes screening, 'that forty-two people were wounded today?'

'Really?' said Gance. 'People seem to be getting wounded every day now. It is a very good sign. These children are really putting their hearts into their work. The momentum of the film will be remarkable.'[13]

12·Cordeliers and Convention

The set represented the chapel of the former convent of the Cordeliers. Seven hundred and seventy-one extras jammed the floor and the galleries. The sense of expectation was as strong as at the first night of a long-awaited play; the scene, the introduction to the revolutionary crowds of La Marseillaise by its composer, Rouget de Lisle.

Behind the scenery was concealed a band, with two bugles, two drums and half a dozen other instruments. An automatic camera glided on a wooden rail beneath the glass roof of the studio. Other cameras were propelled on dollies. Long-focus lenses searched out faces from the crowd without the

Above the set of the Cordeliers, a camera travels on a wooden rail. The pillars are curiously stunted because the top half of the set—the vaulted roof, the stained-glass windows—is to be provided by a device known as the Hall process.

The Hall process, or glass shot, shown out of register, is nothing but a jumble. But look closely: the top half of the set, with light streaming through the windows, is painted on a sheet of glass. When the camera photographs the glass in perfect register with the set beyond, the effect is absolutely convincing. (The painter, W. Percy Day, played Admiral Hood in the Toulon sequences.)

The introduction of the Marseillaise to the revolutionary crowds at the Club des Cordeliers

owners of those faces realising they were to be honoured with closeups. 'You only had to walk on the stage to be seized by the electric atmosphere,' said Harry-Krimer, who played Rouget de Lisle.

Gance climbed into the pulpit, explaining to the extras that he was going to try out a new technique which was a little complicated. 'I must ask you to make a special effort, which will not be beyond you if you enter into it heart and soul. May I ask you to sing La Marseillaise twelve times running in crescendo?'

He emphasised the importance of each and every one of the crowd. 'He spoke to them with sincerity,' said Harry-Krimer. 'He spoke to them as though they were serious people, understanding the artistic nuances, the spirit of history.'[1]

'They were no longer extras, because he *talked* to them,' said Robert Vidalin, who played Camille Desmoulins. '"These pictures", he said, "are going to be shown all over the world. You aren't film extras, you are taking part in the epic of the French Revolution. Don't look above your heads. There are cameras up there and all around to distract you. Pay them no attention. You mustn't break faith with the character that is yours, each one of you individually. I ask you to live the epoch as if you had really been there." After that harangue, he was like Napoleon with his troops.'[2]

The band started up and Alexandre Koubitzky, who played Danton, led the crowd into the song. Koubitzky was a celebrated singer. He transformed the rendering of La Marseillaise by the power of his voice. Since Maryse Damia, also a famous singer, was present (as La Marseillaise), the extras were given an aesthetic experience in which they, too, were participants. It had a profound effect on them. As Émile Vuillermoz wrote, 'These men and women felt transported by an enthusiasm much stronger than their will-power. Gance directed their emotions as a conductor directs an orchestra.'

An assistant director blew a whistle at the end of the scene, but the enthusiastic singing continued. There were tears in many eyes. Gance returned to the pulpit, and he thanked the extras with heartfelt gratitude for their magnificent performance. The extras burst into a spontaneous ovation. From every part of the hall came the cry 'Vive Abel Gance!'

'In the thirty years the cinema has existed,' wrote René Jeanne, 'with its procession of petty hostilities and mean rivalries, in the thirty years there have been directors and extras, this is the first time such a demonstration has taken place in a studio.'[3]

Émile Vuillermoz wrote that it was a moving moment, because it was both magnificent and terrifying. 'If Abel Gance had 10,000 extras under his command, drunk with history and a determination to obey that overcame all reason, he could have invaded the Palais-Bourbon or the Élysée and been proclaimed dictator.'[4]

Napoleon greets Rouget de Lisle (Harry-Krimer). 'I thank you on behalf of France,' he says. 'Your hymn will save many a cannon.'

'The people who worked for me on *Napoleon* had an *esprit* I have never again encountered,' Gance told me. 'I have met goodwill, but never the spirit and enthusiasm of this film.'

The spirit and enthusiasm were inspired partly by the subject, partly by Gance himself. Throughout the making of the film, he seemed possessed by an extraordinary mental electricity. Gance's attitude to the making of epics mirrored his veneration for the art of the cinema. He felt one had to rise to the level of the heroes one wanted to depict.

Curiously enough, when I interviewed the veterans, they often made the same slip of the tongue, saying 'Napoleon' when they meant 'Gance'.

'While one cannot exactly describe Gance as a leader of men, as one would a general,' said Dieudonné, 'he was a most extraordinary leader for his actors.' He considered his direction 'masterly...incomparable'. 'He knew the perfect word to turn the most thick-headed extra into a character from legend. He believed himself within the epoch or the situation of his scenario, and he made others believe it. Those people in the Club des Cordeliers were no longer themselves – they *were* the people of the Revolution.'

Another quality Gance shared with Napoleon was his remarkable equilibrium. 'I never heard Gance raise his voice in all the time I worked on the

Gina Manès as Joséphine. 'During my test,' said Gina Manès (whose real name was Blanche Moulin), 'Gance told me to sing a comic song. I sang, thinking this was just a joke. Then he said, "Sing a sentimental song." I told him I didn't know any. "Doesn't matter: sing 'la-la-la'." So I did. After that, he said, "Right, go and sit there. I shall be behind you. There's the camera. Don't look into it. Listen to what I say but don't move." He started the camera and said, "As I was leaving home this morning, I saw a woman run over by a bus. Don't turn round!" Then he said, "Now you can look round. The prop man's dropped his trousers."

'That was my screen test!'

film,' said Harry-Krimer.[5] 'My memory is of his calmness and self-control.' Gina Manès, who played Joséphine, agreed. 'I never saw that man get angry. He was always calm and kind. If something went wrong, he'd say, "Let's do it again. Sorry, mes enfants, it's my fault."'[6]

He remained relaxed until with a whistle blast or revolver shot he signalled the start of an action scene. Then he seemed to contribute all the vitality in his body for its benefit—his arms flailing the air, his hair flying. Such an expenditure of energy helped nobody, least of all Gance, who would fall back in his chair at the end, exhausted. But it was vivid proof of his commitment, of how much he cared.

The crucial element in Gance's character which mobilised everything else was his contagious enthusiasm. He never became bored, and those who worked with him were never bored, either.

'Without enthusiasm,' he told me, 'there is no cinema, there are no films, there is nothing. There must be enthusiasm, and it must be communicated like a flame—the cinema is a flame in the shadows. If one does not feel it, one cannot transmit it. That is why I believe anyone who doesn't have this enthusiasm is not for me and cannot produce what I consider to be a great film.'

The enthusiasm profoundly affected one extra who, for some reason, was rejected three or four times in succession. 'No, absolutely *no!*' he was told. 'M. Gance has no use for you.' His behaviour indicated that he had mental problems anyway, and this was the last straw. He threw himself into the Seine and had to be rescued.

I confess that when Gance told me this story, I was sceptical. It sounded like a publicity man's fantasy. But a reporter from *Cinéa-Ciné pour tous* was there when it happened. 'The young Turk had no money,' he wrote. 'He loved the cinema and passionately wanted to play a role in *Napoleon*. After he was saved, Gance came to console him. The Turk left the studio radiant, and full of hope. "M. Gance told me such things—ah, such things!"'[7]

Once the set of the Convention was complete, Gance faced a daunting challenge: how to shoot the scene where Robespierre's Jacobins seize power from the moderate Girondins. Victor Hugo came to his aid with a dazzling passage:

'To be a member of the Convention was to be a wave of the ocean. This was true of the greatest there. The force of impulsion came from on high. There was a Will in the Convention which was that of all yet not that of any one person. This Will was an Idea, an idea indomitable and immeasurable, which swept from the summit of Heaven into the darkness below. We call this Revolution. When that idea passed, it beat down one and raised up another; it scattered this man into foam and dashed that one upon the rocks. This idea knew whither it was going, and drove the whirlpool before it. To ascribe the Revolution to men is to ascribe the tide to the waves.'[8]

Gance had translated this vision into his scenario. Opening with the Hugo quote, it continued: 'Souls at the mercy of the wind. The eye takes in the entire hemicycle, from top to bottom. There are three thousand people present. "Nothing in history can be compared to this group as it bends in the wind. But this wind issues from the mouth of the people and is the breath of God. Nothing more chaotic or more sublime. A crowd of heroes, a mob of cowards. Fallow deer on a mountain, reptiles in a marsh. A convocation of Titans."[9]

'This is a brief visual impression, in the same rhythm and movement as that of the storm. Tight correlation between the two storms. The deep significance becomes apparent. The boat seems to sink. The eye plunges from the galleries down to the Girondins gripped with horror before the fury of the Assembly.

'Ten times the boat is on the point of sinking, the sky is lit up with lightning flashes. The tumultuous Assembly rising and falling in a terrifying swell, streaked with flashes of the guillotine blade, a head falling with

The rarest photograph of all: Simon Feldman's pendulum for the Double Storm. Feldman says there were three, but only the footage shot by the largest — this one — was used. The camera is fixed beneath the platform.

each flash. WORDS CAN NO LONGER DESCRIBE THE PARALLELS. Who can try to explain music in words? Indescribable double storm. INNER DYNAMISM. Suggestion rather than evocation.'[10]

Gance sent this page to Simon Feldman with a letter. All the letter said was, 'Read it and let it inspire you.' He had no idea of what Feldman would come up with. Nor, for a long time, had Feldman:

'In the text it spoke of movement — the movement of people, the movement of waves. What could I do? After long reflection, I decided to give the camera the movement of a wave. I ordered from a welder three sets of parallel beams connected to little camera platforms. The devices swung in an arc overhead, like a trapeze, but to enable the cameras to keep the crowd below continuously in view, the platforms were supported by metal arms on ball bearings, and were always parallel to the floor. The device was called "le pendule parallélogrammique".

'These three "pendules" were each shorter than the next one, so that their movements conjugated in a kind of wave. When the pendules were fixed on the runway of the studio, it was a great surprise for everybody. The largest "pendule" was calculated so it just passed over the heads of the crowd. At first, there was a little panic among the extras.'[11]

'The actors were terrified the camera would fall on them,' said Gance. 'Their cringing improved the scene considerably.'

Three 'pendules' were constructed, but only the results produced by the longest one were used in the film.

Feldman also constructed something which Gance had specified in his carnets — a sort of gyroscopic tripod head so that cameras could duplicate the rise and fall of the sea. The ordinary head was removed and the movable head substituted; it operated on the principle of two universal joints — Cardan mounts — which gave a realistic heaving movement, like the ocean's swell, when the cameraman applied his weight.

Thanks to Feldman and his imaginative technical devices, the Double Storm sequence was transformed into that realm of pure cinema for which Gance so earnestly strove.

When the set for the Convention was crammed with extras — not quite the 3,000 specified in the script but somewhere in the region of 1,200 — Abel Gance appeared in the costume of Saint-Just and explained what he was about to do by reading them the passage from Victor Hugo. A few simple instructions were issued and a bugler sounded a single blast. Jacobins clambered out of their seats and fell upon Girondins. The guards rushed up with fixed bayonets but the human rush was too great for them. At the end of the first take, a woman was found to have been trampled, and was rushed in a coma to the infirmary.

An extra, with bleeding face, complained to an assistant, 'I want to change

The Convention, with Robespierre at the tribune

parts — I don't want to be a priest any more. Some fellows started attacking me, shouting, "Down with the clergy!" I never imagined the movies were like this!'

The assistant put his arm round him: 'Please go back to your place. We're starting again in a minute.'

'Thank you, gentlemen,' declared Gance. 'That was very good. But don't worry about your wigs. If you get them knocked off, don't try and pick them up. Let's start again and if you possibly can, do it with a bit more conviction this time, a little more fire.'

The complaining extra went back to his place groaning in misery: 'What's going to happen to me?'[12]

What happened was that the riot was repeated thirteen times that day.

'It ended in incredible tumult,' wrote Arroy. 'The crowd poured down the steps, swelling like the sea. Men jumped three or four rows in one go and fell over in large numbers. Acrobatic hand-to-hand fighting took place. We rolled over chaotically, one on top of another ... We were almost as angry as we would have been fighting for real. Acrobats like Robert Guilbert,

Engeldorff and de Canolle jumped off the assessors' tribunes into groups of fighting men. It was both magnificent and terrifying. A single word from Abel Gance had been enough to release this tumult no other director could have conjured up.'[13]

While the orchestrated violence led to some injuries, an accident occurred when the scaffolding supporting the seats collapsed at the height of the fighting, and more people were taken to the infirmary.

Annabella, who was present as an observer, said she was scared to death from beginning to end.

Abel Gance in the role of Saint-Just. 'I like the character,' he said. 'I find his ideas beautiful. He was far ahead of revolution.'

13 · Sweep of Empire

In the summer of 1926, the company left for Toulon, the last location. Here, they would film the daylight scenes for the siege of Toulon, and what turned out to be the final sequences: Napoleon's proclamation to the troops, their descent into Italy, and the battle of Montenotte.

Vehicle adapted for the filming of Napoleon in the coach, en route to Italy. Kruger at the wheel; Léonce-Henry Burel; Lucas; unknown; makeup man.

The Army of Italy assembled at the quarry of La Garde

The invasion actually began from Albenga, but Gance had found a location at La Garde—in the same part of the world as Albenga, but far more striking visually than anything available there.

He had secured permission to use both troops and sailors. A convoy of trucks left Paris with the equipment, and a train, specially chartered for the picture, carried the personnel.

René Jeanne was on the spot when the first columns arrived at La Garde, a small town eight kilometres from Toulon: 'One morning, the inhabitants were awoken by the tumult of a huge crowd on the march. In the twinkling of an eye, scarcely dressed, they were at their doors. Long columns of soldiers from the colonial infantry, sailors from the depot of crews for the fleet and long lines of mounted colonial artillery filled the street, making their way to the squares.

'There was general stupefaction. "Good grief! All those soldiers!" said the worthies, vaguely alarmed.

'"It is", I said, smiling, to a local café owner, "the departure for the Italian campaign."

'"Are we fighting against Italy now? I always said it would end badly, all this Locarno business![1] Foch's in charge, isn't he? Naturally."

'"No, Bonaparte."

'The café owner looked at me ... then he went back inside, shrugging his shoulders and grumbling, "These Parisians!"

'The assistant directors divided the soldiers into groups, which they led towards the sheds and the courtyards, where each swopped his khaki shirt, trousers and puttees for a blue outfit with red facing, striped linen trousers and a cocked hat. In some cases, this metamorphosis was accompanied by laughs, cries of joy and jokes. The chief wardrobe manager then reassured himself that the effect of the costumes was not being spoiled by some anachronistic detail, no small task when his glance had to encompass 1,700 extras. Armourers replaced the Lebels with the heavy flintlocks of the eighteenth century. Blank cartridges and smoke grenades were also distributed, to make the battle as realistic as possible.

'And the detachments reported to the area where the battle was to take place. General Vincent was there,[2] and the officers who normally command the troops had supplied the director with improvised collaborators—a mixture of uniforms which history could never have guessed at.

'The whole population of La Garde had observed with an amused eye the metamorphosis of the young soldiers, but no one had noticed that Senegalese infantrymen had taken up positions at all the exits of the little town, in order to isolate the battlefield.

'The Senegalese infantrymen only knew their orders, and their orders were to let no one through. So they aimed their bayonets at the chest of anyone who approached.

'The inhabitants of La Garde could not believe their eyes. "So we're no longer masters in our own home?" In the end they crowded together, with no more complaints, behind the barricades of the Senegalese, waiting under the leaden sun for the moment they could slip through to where the film crew was at work.'[3]

The town of La Garde had grown up around an ancient and picturesque village which clung to a steep hill crowned by the ruins of an eleventh-century castle and chapel. The rock upon which these ruins stood had been quarried, and the abandoned workings left dramatic and curious shapes. Here was where Gance made his main location. Everything he needed for the final sequences was within reach. Thanks to the Mediterranean style of building, he could use the old village for the Italian town of Montenotte. Some of the buildings had been deserted, and permission was secured to smash the walls with pick and shovel, as though they had suffered the effects

The village of La Garde doubled as Montenotte for the triptych battle scene. A smoke grenade in the church tower provides most of the effect of 'burning'.

of cannon fire. The church had a stunted tower; once a smoke grenade was placed on its roof, it was transformed into an apparently blazing ruin.

Alexandre Lony was a 21-year-old sailor from the 5th depot, Toulon. 'The battle was a very imposing affair, with wooden cannon, Bengal fire, explosive charges. It was magical. Only a man like Gance could have done it. He came among us and shook hands. "You sailors have been marvellous," he told us, "and so disciplined." From time to time there were clashes with the soldiers, who were rather rough, but that made the film more realistic. Some of the old peasants moaned about their farms and most of all about their henhouses, but they were all compensated.'[4]

The scene was of great historical significance, for it was the first time the triptych camera was used.

Gance had originally thought of using a triptych screen when he was writing the scenario, and he mentioned it in a confidential carnet.

'I felt in certain scenes that I lacked space, that the picture was too small for me. Even a big picture was too small. And it was while I was in the Midi writing the scenes of the Convention that I had the idea of stretching the screen.[5] I didn't know how. I vaguely thought that if I put one camera on the right, one in front and one on the left, I would have an enormous panorama.[6]

'I asked Debrie about it and he said it wasn't possible, that I would have severe parallax problems — when the actors passed from one camera to the next, they would be disjointed. I said if you haven't tried something, you can't be sure. Do it. And so I ordered the equipment.'

It was not quite as simple as that. First, Gance had to convince SGF, who must have been reeling under the floodtide of expenditure, that this was not just a costly and hare-brained scheme, a sort of circus act related to the memorable *Cinéorama* of 1897.[7] The apparatus was eventually paid for personally by the Comte de Béarn.[8]

A simple panoramic vision was not the sole aim of Gance's device. He wanted to extend the emotional and psychological range of montage, and compare and contrast images across the three screens. It was thus not only a technical step forward, but an aesthetic leap as well. Gance had tried to get this across to SGF before, without success. It was probably the knowledge that the film would need a stunning publicity gimmick that finally persuaded them. On February 8th, 1926, the Debrie technicians under chief engineer Maurice Dalotel took their first shots with the new apparatus.[9]

Although their work was secret, rumour spread, and at the end of April 1926 Gance received a deputation from Paramount. Until the merger of Metro-Goldwyn-Mayer in 1924, this had been the leading American production company, and, like M-G-M, it had recently spread its undertaking into Europe. The representatives included Al Kaufman, a member of the board of directors, and Adolphe Osso, head of Paramount in France. They showed an eager interest in the new invention, even though Gance explained that the equipment had not yet been perfected. But when he explained how it would work, they became sceptical. First, they pointed out, it was not commercial, and second, it was technically impossible. Gance, presumably hoping for backing, replied that in the next ten years it would know its highest destiny and change the face of the cinema. The Paramount people asked how much it would cost, and left. There were no further meetings. But by a curious coincidence, the company soon afterwards introduced a new process called Magnascope, by which the screen was greatly enlarged for spectacular sequences. It was not as complicated as the triptych, since it involved only a wide-angle projection lens and a larger screen. But it aroused a great deal of excitement. And when, in 1929, Paramount brought out a wide-gauge film — Magnafilm (56mm) — they ordered the apparatus to be constructed by André Debrie.

The triptych was not the only problem Debrie had to deal with. The company manufactured cameras, printers, perforators and developing ma-

The first triptych camera setup — three Debrie Parvos, one on top of the other, driven by a motor with flexible shafts. Invented by Gance, built by André Debrie.

chines for the entire film-producing world and the output could not be interrupted. But Gance was reaching the end of production. He realised that he could never include the whole of his script for the Campaign in Italy in the first *Napoleon* film. He reluctantly agreed with SGF that it would have to be condensed as a symbol. Since the film had to end in a blaze of glory the symbolic Entry into Italy was the obvious place for the three-screen idea.

'Debrie didn't believe in the idea,' said Gance. In later years, Debrie implied that he had invented it,[10] but confirmation for Gance's statement is contained in a letter from Debrie acknowledging that he had patented it in Gance's name.[11] Marcel David said that Debrie doubted the device would be adopted by enough theatres to make it commercial, and in this he was right. But Debrie was careful enough to take out his own patents.[12]

Gance presented an entirely confident face to Paramount, but how could he possibly be sure of the triptych? He knew that the title of the film would raise expectations of spectacular re-enactments of Austerlitz and Waterloo which he could not fulfil. He desperately needed an effect so remarkable that it would dazzle the audience into forgetting what they *might* have been seeing. So he decided to shoot a roll in an experimental colour process as well, using the Keller-Dorian process.

Even this was not the end of his experimenting. Gance told me that he filmed at La Garde in colour and 3D. This was an astonishing claim. I recently searched for evidence to support it, and found nothing. I assumed he was confusing the 'relief' of the Keller-Dorian embossed film base with the 'relief' of 3D. But I should have known that if anyone knew what he was talking about, it was Gance. Just before this book went to press, a telegram and some letters came to light proving that negotiations had taken place in late 1925 and early 1926 for Gance to use a colour and 3D process developed by A. Carchereux of Marseilles. The cable, dated January 14th, 1926, reports Carchereux's final breakthrough—RESULTS MARVELLOUS—and the letters offer Gance a personal involvement in the society formed to exploit the invention. In the light of this, it is safe to assume that the process was used at La Garde, albeit in an experimental form. (In 1928, Gance suggested

The logistical problems of the film are well suggested in this photograph, as the Army of Italy assembles at La Garde

to Studio 28 that they show the scenes in colour and 'relief', proving that they had been shot.)

The triptych apparatus was completed only just before it was needed. A Debrie technician called Paul Briquet delivered it to La Garde at 5 a.m. on August 11th, 1926—a historic day in the evolution of the cinema. And it happened to be the very day Gance was scheduled to use it. There was no time for tests. He had to take Debrie's workmanship on trust, and so he covered the same scenes with the colour process as insurance.

When the camera was assembled—'a pyramid', Debrie called it, with one camera mounted above the other, linked to a motor by flexible shafts—the technicians regarded it with amazement. Kruger and Roger Hubert took charge of it, helped by Briquet.[13]

Since the review of the army and the proclamation were covered by fifteen to twenty other cameras, it is hardly surprising that the extras were unaware of the new device until Gance explained it to them. In another of his magnetic speeches, he conjured up the pitiful state of the Republican camp—the thinnest soldiers were selected to emphasise its wretchedness—its struggle against the cold and hunger, its stubborn will. As always, he had a strong emotional effect on the extras, an effect offset by his playful sense of humour. He certainly needed that, for shooting was interrupted by an airship from a naval base which passed overhead at a crucial moment, and goods trains steamed through the background at regular intervals.

The company moved to the nearby Plaine de la Crau, where Gance filmed infantry engagements and cavalry charges. Near La Crau was the Château de la Castille. One vital scene of the earlier part of the film remained to be shot, and the Château was chosen as a location for the long-vanished Hôtel Chantereine, where Joséphine lived during Napoleon's courtship. The Château was the holiday home for the pupils of a seminary at Fréjus, and in charge of the place was an old abbé.

Gina Manès (Joséphine), dressed in a pale costume which was almost transparent, stood with Dieudonné on the balcony while Gance and the cameramen appraised the light. There was too much shadow. Gance decided to move the cameras to another set of steps, but here he found all the windows shut. The abbé in charge was most uncooperative. He had already protested that morning about the scantiness of Joséphine's costume. Everybody, even the curé of La Crau, pointed out that it was historically accurate. But the abbé refused to open even the smallest window.

The only thing to do was to break for lunch. A journalist and an artillery officer volunteered to drive off in search of an alternative location, and before long they found one. But when they returned to the Château, they saw to their astonishment that all the windows were open and the scene was

British troops defending the Old Port of Toulon. According to Dieudonné, who was leading a detachment on the quay, soldiers playing the French grew over-excited and pushed soldiers playing the British off the edge into the sea. 'And they couldn't swim,' he said, with fellow feeling. They were fished out, injured only in their pride.

being shot. One of the members of the board of Société Générale de Films had arrived to find the crew at a halt, and immediately demanded to know why. Not long before, he had been made a Papal Knight. He even had the official letter granting this distinction in his wallet. The old abbé's objections crumbled before the Pope's signature; he quickly decided that a man so highly honoured could scarcely be a party to the corruption of public morals … [14]

Next the company moved to the Old Port of Toulon, where the daylight scenes of the siege were staged with the co-operation of the navy, who removed the fleet from the harbour,[15] the police, who stopped the traffic, and the army, who provided the extras and opened up the historic forts. The old port then looked much as it did in the eighteenth century.

Explosive charges were placed on the ramparts, on the quays, in the water, even in the mountains overlooking the town. When everything was ready, a red rocket was fired, and the crowds of onlookers were treated to a historical re-enactment on a grand scale, the troops being deployed according to an account left by Bonaparte himself.[16]

'At last we come to the final great scene of the film,' wrote Arroy. The departure of the Army of Italy; every item of military equipment is included — wagons, cannon, mortars, even Gance's pet dog Brienne. Camera cars run up and down the column. A cart travels with troops. Attached to it is a gigantic cardboard eagle, suspended like a kite to cast a shadow in front of the marching men.

Police and troops have stopped all activity for a radius of seven kilometres. Peasants have put at the company's disposal their horses, their houses, their fields. Schools and tramway depots are requisitioned.

Trucks rumble down the dirt roads ahead of the marching columns, with cameras mounted in the back. Gance drives up in a staff car and gives the troops his last morale-boosting speech:

'You have not eaten for two days, but you are about to enter Italy. You are going to conquer it and you shall be kings! You are about to make this superhuman effort for the headstrong man dragging you on. You will make him glorious throughout the world and he will lead you a long way forward! Your troubles are only just beginning. There will be plenty of others like these on all the battlefields of Europe. But you will follow him everywhere because his star is irresistible, because he pays a higher price himself for all this than you do, because he is noble and disinterested. This is not Napoleon, this is Bonaparte! Look at the eagle leading you on the road to martyrdom and apotheosis. Never lose sight of it! Go on, my boys, you are magnificent. I wish you could all see yourselves. At the moment, you really deserve everything the cinema has to offer you. Carry on! *La victoire en chantant* ...'[17]

The soldiers pick up the refrain of the *Chant du départ*. Out of sight of the cameras, by the side of the road, a crowd of civilians follows the army in parallel formation, and they, too, pick up the song. The Marseillaise follows the *Chant du départ* exactly as it will when the film is brought so triumphantly to the screen a few months later.

'The return. Our eyes were full of dreams, and modern Paris seems dull, lifeless,' wrote Arroy. 'We lack our *raison d'être*. Suddenly we are all projected into the next century. We are no longer of our time and we live in the past. But when we come across Gance, it is as though he drags in his wake all the visions that have just appeared before us. He seems surrounded by a cloud of dust and by flashes of light against steel. Around him, the roar of battle, the clash of weapons, the songs of war and the whole great symphony reawakens.

'If Gance had not taken us back to Paris, we would still be playing at soldiers.'[18]

14 · Flame in the Shadows

The end of shooting on *Napoleon* was marked by a triumph such as the French cinema had never known. On October 9th, 1926, the Société Générale de Films signed a contract with Gaumont-Metro-Goldwyn for the release of the film in France, the United States, England and the Empire, Belgium and Switzerland. The advance was 1,500,000 francs ($43,000).[1]

For a long time, Marcus Loew (known as 'little Napoleon'), head of Loew's, Inc., had been trying to forge links with the Gaumont company in France, and he had succeeded the previous year. In fact he was more interested in expanding his vast theatre chain than in importing French films. However, the French government saw their chance, and awarded him a Legion of Honour (a decoration introduced by Napoleon). Marcus Loew controlled Metro-Goldwyn-Mayer, and that company dutifully purchased Tourjansky's *Michael Strogoff*, Volkoff's *Casanova* and, at a far higher price, *Napoleon*.

M-G-M had already proved itself the leading American production company with films like *The Big Parade* and *Ben-Hur*, and a release through the Loew chain assured *Napoleon* of 'an incomparable fortune; in the United States alone, it will be seen by 100 million people.'[2]

A spectacular banquet was held by SGF at the Ritz to announce the news to the press, in the presence of Arthur Loew, Marcus's son, Charles Pathé and French and American film dignitaries.

Henri de Cazotte praised the sympathetic understanding which Mr Loew and his father cherished for France. Arthur Loew, in reply, said he was happy to have reached this Franco-American rapprochement which had been advocated for so long. 'With *Napoleon*, France has made a film of great value. We await it impatiently in America.'[3]

Abel Gance rose to his feet, amid much applause. 'M. Loew is putting at our disposal the most powerful cinematographic force in the world,' he said.

'I can only be touched, and profoundly grateful, towards this gesture which surpasses by a great deal the range of the usual commercial transaction. It is for this, Messieurs, that I will ask you to raise your glasses in tribute to the Society Loew-Metro and its directors, and also to Messieurs Gaumont and Costil, who have supported its cause in extolling my work. But this friendship, this new point of departure for cinematographic relations between Europe and America, does not close my eyes to the grandeur of the sacrifice, devotion and trust which I have found in France, and I could never forget that it was due to the personal friendship of Charles Pathé that I was not forced to abandon ship several months ago, when the storm was raging around me.'[4]

Marring Gance's euphoria as October passed was the fact that he had failed to meet his deadline. He had therefore lost his 100,000 franc bonus and from now on had to work for nothing. He had spent a great deal more than anyone could have foreseen — the final cost was estimated at 17 million francs.[5] And Gance had budgeted 20 million for all six! In Hollywood terms, however, his expenditure was not excessive. The million dollar feature (35 million francs) was becoming more and more common — and Gance's film was likely to be far longer than two hours.

Gance had also taken so long over his film that he was in danger of being left behind. Raymond Bernard's *Miracle of the Wolves*, which several members of SGF had been involved in and which contained even more spectacular battle scenes than *Napoleon*, had become one of the few French films to be imported into America. It made no money, but its New York première was a critical success and Raymond Bernard had been hailed as the D. W. Griffith of France.[6] This had always been a description reserved for Gance. More dismaying than that was the appearance of a German film which used the camera in the very style for which Gance had been so effective an evangelist. Not that Gance ever expressed his dismay; he had the highest admiration for E. A. Dupont, the director. But *Variety*, released at the end of 1925, was hailed as a masterpiece wherever it was shown, and while it had far fewer innovations than *Napoleon*, it was bound to be used as a comparison. As one critic put it, '*Variety* burnt its way through these United States and came near demoralizing the matter-of-fact technique of Hollywood.'[7] Its staggering success would inevitably make *Napoleon* seem that much less of an event.

Gance's health had suffered from the gruelling period of production, and this added to his anxiety. 'Whatever it costs,' he wrote, 'I must finish my film by January 31st, 1927.'[8]

Editing had been in progress throughout the shooting, in the form known as 'rough-cutting'. Now Gance devoted all his creative concentration to it. No one measured precisely how much film had been shot in the eighteen months of production; the most reliable figure, quoted in the contract with M-G-M, was 400,000 metres.

'Gance was King of Editing,' said Simon Feldman. 'When you came to see the rushes, you said to yourself, "It's chaos. It's impossible. What could you do with it?" When he cut it together, it was *montage* ... Gance was superb. Nobody does it like he did it. Even today, when people have learned from Gance, it is not the same.'[9]

Gance was fortunate in being able to fuse his genius with the talent of a great film editor, Marguerite Beaugé. She began in the industry in 1908 and graduated from her first job of punching sprocket holes, via laboratory work, to editing. The first film she cut for Gance was *La Folie du Dr Tube* (1915). Subsequently she worked on all his silent pictures, including *La Roue*. 'If I am a good editor,' she said, 'it is thanks to Gance. He is the one who taught me. He was a great, great editor.'[10]

Marguerite Beaugé, editor

Marguerite Beaugé's daughter, Yvonne Martin, became a distinguished editor herself; she cut Orson Welles's *The Trial*. (She also cut *Austerlitz* for Gance.) At the time of *Napoleon*, Yvonne was twelve; and as her mother spent most of her time in the cutting room, she did too — when she wasn't at school.

'I was only there to play, but I was right in the middle of things, and it interested me intensely. I watched some of the filming — it was incredible — and I learned how to splice, and what a negative was.'[11]

Gance, she said, was almost never absent from the editing but according to Marguerite Beaugé he had an elastic sense of time: 'He'd say he'd arrive at eight in the morning and he'd come at twelve. And then at night you couldn't go — maybe he wasn't tired! — until 11 p.m.'

Yvonne Martin remembered that the viewing machine they used was an American Moviola — 'they called it a *mitraillette*' ['a sub-machine gun'] because of the way it chattered. Presumably, the *mitraillette* was in constant use by Marguerite Beaugé or one of her twelve assistants, because Gance told me there was no viewing machine at all, and peering at the film was such a strain on the eyes that he had damaged a retina.[12]

The cutting room was in the SGF suite at Avenue Hoche. 'It was an enormous editing room,' said Yvonne Martin. 'I have never seen anything like it in the French cinema. It was very bare, although there were curtains everywhere, and the assistants worked behind the curtains. There was an index system — although my mother had every number in her head, the shots were classified like a library. And there was a projector. When Gance wanted to look at the film — and this happened often because everyone came — he'd pull back the curtains and M. Bonin, the projectionist, would show the film in the cutting room. Gance liked having lots of people to give life to projections.

'The longest time was spent in the selection of scenes. We had so much material. I remember especially the chase across Corsica with the camera on the back of a horse ... there were kilometres of it!

'The choice was incredible, which was why my mother had so many assistants. Each assistant was in charge of so many shot numbers. If Gance asked for a certain shot, the appropriate assistant would locate it. Gance worked to a process of elimination. He would start with all the scenes for a sequence, like the Cordeliers, joined together. He would then look at it carefully, removing scenes and sections he regarded as inferior. Then, and only then, would he begin the creative work.'[13]

His style of editing was extraordinarily fluid and rhythmic. What was his system?

'I wouldn't try to explain. I just felt it,' said Gance. 'For instance — four frames too many, that really hurts me. Take away those four frames — everything works. To have a sense of this sort is luck, pure luck. But I don't rely on this good fortune.

'The whole thing is musical, of course. There were many scenes which were interesting in themselves, but which I had to exclude because they would have broken up the rhythm of the film. The whole film is cut to a rhythm; there isn't a moment without this rhythm. But many shots, particularly closeups made with the portable camera, were too jerky and had to be discarded.'

An example was the intriguing experiment in which he sent Roger Hubert, the camera strapped to his chest, up the steps of the pulpit in the Cordeliers to reproduce all the things Rouget de Lisle would have seen, substituting the camera for the actor. 'After having registered his gestures, it records his perceptions.'[14] But the idea did not work.

'Obviously I took a great many shots which aren't in the film. I was trying to find the best ways of getting the best results. With so many innovations, there were bound to be a few failures.'

Yvonne Martin said that although he changed a lot in the editing, it had all been very well prepared. 'He had a very good memory for shots. You couldn't say a shot didn't exist. He knew it did, he knew what it looked like, and you had to find it. Gance was an intuitive editor; my mother would cut the picture according to what he said, he would look at it and make corrections.'[15]

With the triptychs, Gance was as blind during the editing as he had been during the shooting, for there was no equipment upon which he could view the three images at once. He could look at the three images individually to check that they were technically satisfactory but all he and Marguerite Beaugé could do in the cutting room was to line the shots up on pins and imagine the effect.

The trouble with the triptych shots was that there were so few of them. The proclamation to the Army of Italy was well covered in panoramic shots, and so was the Battle of Montenotte, but thereafter the film resumed, somewhat anti-climactically, on the single screen.

However, Gance had also photographed the triptych scenes in colour and 3D.

'The 3D effects were very good, and very pronounced. I remember one scene where soldiers were waving their pistols in the air with excitement and the pistols seemed to come right out into the audience. I felt, however, that if the audience saw this effect they would be seduced by it, and they would be less interested in the content of the film. And I didn't want that at all. The 3D effect did not encourage the same feeling for rhythm in the audience. I felt that if it fascinated the eye, it would fail to do the same for the mind and the heart.'

He returned to the triptychs, and began to experiment with the vast amount of footage of the army on the move. By placing identical but inverted scenes on the outside screens, with a separate image in the centre, he suddenly became aware of a splendid architectural effect; he realised that by a careful orchestration of single-screen shots — many of which were superimpositions — he could create as powerful an impression as with the panoramas. This was one of the most significant of all the technical innovations of *Napoleon*.

Yet he still had no proof that the triptych process would work. It was essential that the money be found for the proper equipment. He managed to persuade Charles Pathé to arrange with Debrie to synchronise three projectors, which were then installed in his cutting room. 'They were very noisy but very steady. When I switched them on, my heart was beating furiously. But it was perfect. I cannot describe the pleasure it gave me. It was one of the greatest moments of my life.

'At that moment I realised that here was a new alphabet for the cinema. I had only to create the grammar. From then on, the ordinary cinema lost its interest for me.'

So euphoric was he that he recut other sequences to give the triptych effect. The Double Storm had no panoramas, of course, but when the boat was placed on the centre panel and was seen tossing in the same rhythm as the Convention on the outer panels the result was mesmeric.

Gance did the same with the Bal des Victimes but decided, before the première, to remove this section. 'I had done it in a triptych because the dances were lovely in the triptych form, but I decided against it because it reduced the impact of the triptych at the end of the film.'

The immense amount of work demanded by the triptychs meant that he and Marguerite Beaugé had less time to devote to other sections, some of which, like the siege of Toulon, seem never to have progressed much further than the rough-cut.

Gance refused to let anyone see the film, even though the date of the

première at the Opéra was looming closer and closer. Originally arranged for October 1926, delayed to January 1927 and then postponed again, it was now fixed for April 7th, 1927. The film would have to be shown then, whatever its state. The President of the Republic and all the dignitaries had been invited.

But the length was causing concern. Rumour had it that *Napoleon* would be as long as *La Roue*, a fact which dismayed SGF as well as Gaumont-Metro-Goldwyn.

They managed to persuade Gance to restrict the première version to a reasonable length – say three hours. Gance had no alternative; the full version was nowhere near ready. To produce a short version, however, involved a great deal of work all on its own. With so little time left, Arthur Honegger had to abandon the idea of a full original score; he wrote whatever he could for the completed sequences, even though they tended to be changed without warning.

'We worked until twelve at night or two in the morning,' said Marguerite Beaugé. 'Spring had come and the leaves were out and I didn't realise it. I was working with my heart as much as with my mind, and it really didn't bother me. But in the end I fell ill. The last scene, with the triptych, I was up all night. Nobody could take me away – there was too much work. After that, I was in bed for eight days.'[16]

This was something of an understatement – Yvonne Martin said that her mother had a nervous breakdown. It took the form of a profound depression in which she was haunted by the shot numbers of *Napoleon* and by all the scenes still awaiting her. 'The doctor told her to stop work immediately. For eight days she was kept at home in total seclusion.'

At last, Gance showed a rough-cut of the full version to his closest friends, Blaise Cendrars, who had assisted him on *La Roue*, and the writer t'Serstevens.

'Abel put a lot of faith in our judgment of his films,' wrote t'Serstevens, 'Blaise's above all. I shall never forget the day he showed just the two of us, in a studio in the suburbs somewhere, the first cut of his *Napoleon*. For *seven* hours we sat and watched the history of that cumbersome man from Brienne to Austerlitz [*sic*]. All of it without a break, and, what's worse, without a drink, either. Finally, after the last military fanfare, the author came up to us and asked shyly: "Well, what do you think of it?"

'In thorny situations like this, I always let Blaise do the talking. There was a pregnant pause. Finally, in his hoarse voice: "Ma vieille, there are some great bits in it, but I think if you cut three-quarters of it, you might avoid having the audience leave in the middle to catch the last metro."'[17]

Gaumont-Metro-Goldwyn gave Gance the deadline of March 1st, 1927, to produce a print for the première. He failed to do so. A week later he showed the long version, perhaps in the hope that they would change their minds and agree to a première spread over two or three days, as with *La Roue*. The G-M-G people were appalled. 'The film we saw was chaotic, and asked for weeks and weeks of hard work,' they wrote.[18] This first contact seems to have had a permanently damaging effect on G-M-G's attitude to the film.

Another show was arranged for Charles Pathé and Léon Gaumont. Both men were aware of the unfavourable reports and both were extremely upset. They had counted on the film being the contracted length of 3,000 metres, which would give them no distribution problems, and here it was more than three times as long.

'They kept muttering about how long it was,' said Gance. 'As the film progressed, their mood changed and their expressions became lighter. At the end, Pathé said, "It is a great film, but how are we going to show it?"

'Gaumont said, "I thank you profoundly. We are not going to cut a frame. We will show it in four parts."

'They got up to leave. "Wait a minute," I said. "I have something more to show you — something you haven't seen yet."

'"What?" said Gaumont. "More? It's long enough as it is ..." And I showed them the triptychs. Both Pathé and Gaumont were astounded.'

While all this was going on, the negative cutting was under way at the Laboratoires GM at Billancourt. In charge was Henriette Pinson. Today, neg cutting is relatively straightforward; every foot of film is numbered on the edge and can be easily identified. In the 1920s there was no such thing as edge numbering. Identification depended on the picture itself. Since *Napoleon* had more footage shot for it than for any other feature in film history, it was an overwhelming task. In static shots, there was often nothing to differentiate one take from another, and the neg cutter had to peer through a magnifying glass, hoping to identify it from the blink of an eye — or even a speck of dust.

Several negatives had to be assembled — the domestic master negative was made from first takes, to match the cutting copy. Subsidiary negatives, made from second camera material or second takes, were for use by foreign distributors. Not surprisingly, there were wide differences between each negative.

Tinting and toning tests had to be made so that Gance could choose which colour would suit the emotional mood of each scene. The original prints were toned in five separate colours, with some scenes remaining in black and white.

While all the technicians involved in *Napoleon* felt they would explode from the pressure, the publicity campaign was just warming up. Paris cinemagoers, eagerly awaiting the opening, were given a foretaste on April 1st at the Cinéma Madeleine and the Gaumont-Palace, where the Brienne prologue was shown as a special attraction.

At the same time, a small group including Jean Mitry and Jean Arroy was invited by Gance to a preview at the Opéra. Mitry was dumbfounded. 'At this first viewing,' said Arroy, 'I felt the most powerful, the most unexpected and the purest aesthetic emotion that I have ever felt. It was both magnificent and overwhelming. I believed I had caught a glimpse of everything the cinema of the future would be — a fantastic, synthetic form. When the curtains that masked the side screens parted, I received a stunning visual and mental impulse ... In a cascade of bewitching light, these visionary apparitions burst on to a wall four metres high by sixteen in width.'[19]

After the preview, Arroy wrote a letter to Gance which captured his reactions and reservations far more spontaneously than that more studied description, written for publication:

Will you hear my weak voice in that unanimous concert of praise, approval, criticism, advice?

Élie Faure was the only one to tell you the truth. 'Save at all costs the paroxystic passages, the figments of visual symphony. The rest is without importance.' Some will say to you 'the audience', others 'balance' or 'psychology' or 'historical truth'. To all that, merde. The moment has come to make no compromise. You have conquered the fanatical followers whom you needed to support you. What do you fear? The version at the Opéra is not the one the distributor intends for the crowd. And the crowd can stand epic, without compromise.

Is there any need for Violine and Tristan Fleuri? I don't think so. An average member of the audience is the brick wall one hits oneself against. But the crowd is electrified by the crowd. Galvanise it with the Cordeliers, the Convention, Toulon, Albenga.

Here are the remarks I have to make after this first overwhelming contact: — One or two flashes of Robespierre are missing during your speech. You defend him, one does not see him. You may be in the right. One has to see him through you.[20]

The indication in the subtitles of Bonaparte's and Joséphine's accents is, in its spirit, as far away from the cinema as possible. Dangerously shocking.

The mystical marriage of Violine has deeply irritated me. I don't feel it at all. Apart from the embrace with the ghost, which moves one profoundly. But the small statue, the candles, the ecstatic virgin who suffers from inhibition … (No, I would not like to hurt the blonde Suzanne.)

Touch absolutely nothing in:

> The Three Gods
> Cordeliers
> the scene in the Corsican inn: 'our country is France' — eagle
>   head of closeup of NB
> the chase
> the triptych of the storm
> 'order, calm, silence'
> the ghosts in the Convention
> the coach in which NB is writing his commands
> the departure for Italy, with the symmetrical views on the side
>   screens

But cut out completely the final eagle on the road, which does not give the result proportionate to the effort. There is a brutal falling down after such a taking off. This, I assure you, I felt deeply.

One would like to see this rhythmical paroxysm end with a sliding into a vertiginous whirlwind in the clouds. Maelstrom movement; very good! But the eagle does not seem real. It is static and seen only at the men's feet. No dynamism. And the real eagle appeared right afterwards!

You certainly know of better remedies, but here is mine. Show the eagle in the full width of the triptych only at the last moment, link it up with apocalyptic clouds on the three screens, flashes of lightning, and link them to the final maelstrom.

Please don't bear a grudge against me. I don't have the pretension to offer advice. I am suggesting an idea. I assure you the end falls off brutally. I speak to you with my eye, which sees. What one calls seeing, anyway. And with my heart, too, which loves you. And I believe that I am a small part of the cinematographic truth, which you hold so completely.

And, as everybody admires you, let me just love you a little.

Jean Arroy[21]

'*Les Ombres*' — *the ghosts in the Convention. Gance regarded this sequence as the best in the picture. Left to right, Saint-Just (Gance), Robespierre (Van Daële), Danton (Koubitzky), Marat (Artaud) and Couthon (Viguier). Frame enlargement.*

15 · The Music of Light

A special version of 4,500 metres (13,800 ft), lasting about three hours, was announced for the première at the Théâtre National de l'Opéra. The title was now *Napoléon vu par Abel Gance*. Although Gance had agreed to this shortened version, he kept adjusting it until the length had reached 5,600 metres (16,800 ft), lasting three hours forty minutes. With intervals, the première would now be well over four hours long. SGF were upset when they realised Gance had misled them, but it was too late to do anything to remedy the situation.[1]

'No film in the world has been awaited with such feverish impatience,' said *Cinéma*.[2] The Opéra's capacity was usually 2,300 seats, but fewer for a film because of bad sight-lines. For this charity gala all had been sold. A specially built projection box had been installed on the first balcony, containing Debrie's original triptych equipment — which he had constructed for Gance's cutting room — and two ordinary projectors. Four projectionists were on duty.

There was no standard speed for projection in the silent days. Operators were given a suggested running time, but as the speed could alter during a reel it was left to them to work it out with the musical director.[3] The music had been assembled by Honegger to the best of his ability in the absurdly short time allowed him. According to Honegger's collaborator, Arthur Hoerée, Gance had been making alterations to the editing right up to the last minute, and Honegger was growing desperate: 'He told Gance, "It will be impossible to move another piece of music to another section if you keep on making changes in extremis." They had rehearsed the day before, and finalised all the musical parts. Then Gance had changed another little bit, and the poor musicians, who had already been there since nine in the morning, found themselves doing "just another little quarter of an hour". No time for lunch, they started again at two o'clock. By five o'clock, the musicians were exhausted and Gance changed the editing again. Honegger

Arthur Honegger, photographed with Gance and William Delafontaine on the Cordeliers set. (Gance's hand is still bandaged after the explosion.) The composer followed the company on location, and paid great attention to the film, but his work on the score proved next to impossible when Gance kept changing the editing right up to the last moment.

said, "You've done it once, you won't do it again. At least, not to me." He walked out and caught his train.'[4]

Two hours before the great event, Gance had a row with the conductor, M. Szyfer, about the spill of light from the orchestra stands on to the screen. He insisted that some kind of cover be placed over the orchestra, otherwise the picture would be adversely affected. The conductor was furious, but he finally did as Gance wished.

The Garde Républicaine in full dress uniform took their positions outside the Opéra and up the stairway. The arrival of celebrities from the stage, from politics and from high society was watched by an awe-struck crowd. Since the proceeds from the event were to be divided between charities for war wounded, there was a strong military and government presence. Beside the President of the Republic, Gaston Doumergue,[5] and many of his ministers, there were Marshals Foch, Joffre and Fayolle, and two men whose fates would be intertwined in later years, when each would pass sentence of death upon the other — Marshal Pétain and a young captain called Charles de Gaulle.

The Opéra was flowing with rich dresses, dazzling uniforms, flowers and lights. 'It was a real gala occasion,' said Yvonne Martin, 'no pullovers that evening! But although everyone had been told to arrive promptly, the show started late. Because Gance had been making alterations up to the last moment, the lab was still printing the reels on the day of the première. Titles had to be inserted by hand. A man then rushed the completed reel by car from Billancourt to the Opéra. Then there was another problem of the reels being in the wrong cans.'[6]

Marguerite Beaugé had worked all night, and had slept in the cutting room. But now she had managed to change into a new gown for the occasion, and, tense as she was, she could only be optimistic about the reception for the film.

At first, everything went well, despite the occasional badly printed scene. There was a full chorus accompanying the orchestra and Alexandre Koubitzky sang in synchronisation with Rouget de Lisle on the screen. The audience applauded the scenes they admired, and the applause was frequent, especially for the triptychs of the Double Storm.[7]

But one profoundly disappointed spectator was Annabella. She was horrified to discover that practically all her scenes had been cut. She had worked so hard and for so long that to see her part reduced to a handful of brief sequences must have been heartbreaking. As she remembers it now, her first closeup was upside down. But this is merely a symbol of what she mistook for deliberate humiliation. The film had to be reduced, and her scenes with Tristan Fleuri, as the synopsis (pages 264–85) proves, were given footage out of all proportion to their part in the story.

It was something else that was upside down, and that something was sufficient to ruin Marguerite Beaugé's evening: 'I had worked all night and hadn't received the letters Napoleon was writing to Joséphine in the coach. At the last moment they had arrived and an assistant had spliced them in — upside down.'[8]

When the first one appeared on the screen, she and Gance rushed to the projection box and stopped the show.

'Nowadays there would be an outcry if you stopped the projection,' said Yvonne Martin, 'but people were more friendly then and they waited patiently. My mother respliced all the inserts of the letters and the show started off again. The public accepted it.'[9]

Marguerite Beaugé's new dress was ruined. 'I perspired so much, and I was so hurt and angry, I could not return to the auditorium.'

The appearance of the full, panoramic triptych on a screen 40 feet wide had a stunning effect on the audience. Émile Vuillermoz described it: 'The curtains are parted without a sound, displaying side panels where the action unfolds with extraordinary scope and strength. The audience feels miraculously liberated. Reality and dreams no longer appear through a tiny casement; a whole wall grows transparent like crystal and opens up another universe. The spectators suddenly become a crowd watching a crowd. The onrush of this magical world causes an emotional shock of rare intensity. This is one of those inventions which one knows to be absolutely essential immediately one first contemplates them.'[10] Vuillermoz later christened this process Polyvision.

As an added dimension, Gance had asked Harry-Krimer to deliver the proclamation of Bonaparte to the Army of Italy.

'I was hidden in a box on the third balcony,' said Harry-Krimer, 'and I waited with anxiety for the first closeup of Bonaparte: "Soldats!" Dieudonné's voice, good as it was, did not have enough strength to carry across the vast auditorium of the Opéra and we didn't use microphones. I delivered the address following the lip movements. It only lasted a few minutes, but the tension was enormous. At the end I got terrific applause, but my legs were trembling and you could have wrung out my shirt.'[11]

At the end of the film, flanking strips were tinted blue and red and the triptych became a tricolor. Thunderous applause continued for several minutes, together with cries of 'Vive Abel Gance!', until Gance, from his box, shyly rose to thank the audience. They gave him a standing ovation which lasted for fifteen minutes.[12]

'It was unprecedented, unbelievable,' said Gance. 'André Malraux told me de Gaulle was in the audience, as a young captain. He stood up and waved his great long arms in the air and shouted, "Bravo, tremendous, magnificent!" He never forgot the film.'

People surged forward to congratulate Joséphine. 'I was so overwhelmed,' said Gina Manès, 'I could only think of escaping.'[13]

'I met a banker outside,' said Gance, 'who told me a woman had thrown her arms around him and said "It's too beautiful for words! I have to kiss somebody!"'

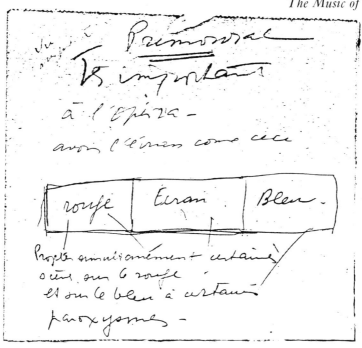

Gance's carnet suggesting that at the Opéra certain paroxysms should be projected on a tricolor triptych. Perhaps the idea of a tricolor—which he has the wrong way round—developed into the triptych?

If the film exceeded hopes, the music did not. Arthur Hoerée said the musicians had been playing for twelve hours that day and they were so tired their arms were dropping off. 'One could no longer hear the bass. It was a musical performance that fell well below the standard and was derisory compared to the quality of the film.'[14]

Gance admitted that although there were some 'magnificent passages' the general standard of the music was defective because it had been chosen so haphazardly.[15]

Some of the critics were savage. 'The musical adaptation is impossible,' wrote J.-K. Raymond-Millet. 'One could not, in all truthfulness, imagine a worse cacophony.'[16]

Poor Honegger! He may have deserved these attacks, but to try to write a score for a picture which changed both length and shape by the hour could hardly have been easy.[17]

Paris-Midi the next day hailed the event as 'sensational', and described how the distinguished audience had again and again burst into applause. But they criticised the projection—blaming the interruptions on the operators—and added that they would have to describe the last third some other time since at twelve-thirty a.m. the film was still going on.[18]

Paris-Soir called it a magnificent visual epic. 'Gance has translated the most beautiful page of our history on to the screen. It is a gigantic work, a truly titanic poem, worthy of the hero who inspired it.'[19]

But not many of the commentators were so uncritical. I have pored over the reviews, trying to find a perceptive critic who expresses unqualified enthusiasm, and I was not able to find one.

When Gance came to select quotes for publicity purposes, he was able to isolate some impressive sentences: '*Napoleon* is the most important work to have been shown to us ... M. Abel Gance is definitely an initiator, practically unique in the cinematographic world' — *Le Petit Journal*.[20]

'It will remain in the history of the cinema as one of the most powerful and the most grandiose. There is, throughout the film, colour, light, movement — a superb production' — Raymond Villette, *Le Gaulois*.[21] J.-L. Croze, in *Comoedia*, was unintentionally ironic: '*Napoleon*, in conquering the world, will do better than its hero, for it will not have a Waterloo or a St Helena.'[22]

The press reactions contained sufficient praise for the film to be called a critical success, and yet the notices were extraordinarilly mixed, passionate raves contrasting with angry denunciation, sometimes in the same review. What is one to make of a notice which hails the film as 'a great work ... it surpasses all productions of a similar type' yet derides it for being 'full of incoherence and puerility' — Jean Prévost, *Les Nouvelles littéraires*.[23] This reviewer was annoyed by the chase, where the dragoons on horseback shoot at Napoleon from a mere fifteen paces behind him; by the storm in the Convention — 'infinitely overdone' — and by the scene of the ghosts in the Convention, which was worse than annoying — 'it disrupts the action.'

Those who knew their history paraded their familiarity with the facts. Jean Mitry retaliated: 'Are the facts precisely right? What does it matter! He has written a cinematographic poem based on a real person, on real facts, which defeats history. I no longer wish to see Bonaparte except through this film.'[24]

Napoleonic expert, art historian and theoretician Élie Faure said, 'If the real Bonaparte came back, I should recognise him only on condition that he resembled Dieudonné's interpretation. If he did not, I should beg him, as an impostor, to please go about his business.

'Dieudonné's expression, his stature, his whole attitude, is all that the real Napoleon must have been. But he does more than resemble Napoleon physically. That alone would not have produced the impression he creates on the screen. He seems to have caught the very spirit of the hero.'[25]

Many critics were antagonistic to the technical innovations. Raymond Villette, who had written in such glowing terms in *Le Gaulois*, wrote in *Mon Ciné* that the snowball fight ended by being tiring 'mainly because of its excessive length, but also because the camera oscillates, shakes, slips—in short bounces around, which has an unpleasant effect on the retina'.[26]

G. M. Coissac, who ran *Cinéopse*, deplored the portable camera, 'which induces headaches in the spectator'. A. P. Richard thought that Gance's knowledge of technique was his weak point; 'it makes him commit unfortunate errors'.[27] He was one of the few critics to find fault with the triptych—he objected to the parallax problems. Virtually everyone else hailed the invention with unqualified enthusiasm.

The triptychs had an immediate effect on one member of the Opéra audience, although it would be years before the full significance of their impact became apparent. Professor Henri Chrétien wanted to bring panoramic pictures to the screen without the use of two additional projectors. To do this, he designed the Hypergonar lens. Years later, he wrote Gance a letter saying that he had been influenced in his design by seeing *Napoleon*, and he dedicated his first Hypergonar to Gance. He formed his own company in 1927 and after working with the French army, fitting the lens to the periscopes of tanks, he offered the Hypergonar to the French film industry.

It failed to arouse much interest, although Marco de Gastyne used it in the battle scenes for *La Merveilleuse Vie de Jeanne d'Arc* (1929) and Claude Autant-Lara experimented with it for *Construire un feu* (1929). In the 1930s, Autant-Lara tried to interest M-G-M, but failed. It was not until 1953 that Twentieth Century-Fox bought the rights from Professor Chrétien and renamed the process CinemaScope. In 1953 Chrétien received an Oscar, as did Fred Waller, inventor of Cinerama.

Gance discovered that *Napoleon* divided his friends. Jean Epstein, for instance, who had written with such enthusiasm of *La Roue*, was very muted on the subject of *Napoleon*. The surrealists had always disliked Gance's work, and most of them loathed this one. Even for those of the avant-garde, less extreme than the surrealists, *Napoleon* was a retrogressive step after *La Roue*.

Gance's chief fault, in their eyes, was to have made a film with nationalistic overtones. Léon Moussinac went so far as to call Gance's Napoleon 'a Bonaparte for apprentice fascists',[28] although, even with fascism on the upsurge in France, the word had not assumed the emotive quality we now impart to it. And no one accused *Napoleon* of being a fascist film. Books, plays and films about charismatic figures who restore order were understandably popular in a period which had just passed through the First World War and revolutions in Russia, Hungary and Germany. But this concept was no more unique to the fascists than it was to the communists.

In the 1920s, extreme right and left found common ground; Trotsky was quoted in 1924 as saying Mussolini was his best pupil.[29] And Napoleon as statesman and soldier united a surprising number who were bitterly opposed politically.

'Socialist authors, like the great socialist historian Tarlé, speak of him with admiration,' Gance told Welsh and Kramer. 'Even Karl Marx and Engels spoke of Napoleon in terms that may astonish you.'[30]

But fascists such as Robert Brasillach were not overly impressed with the film.[31] For fascism required a scapegoat, a focus for hatred. There is no such group, racial or political, nor any sign of hatred in the film. Gance's clear disapproval of the excesses of the Revolution did not please the communists, and his disapproval of the excesses of war did not please the fascists. 'I did not attempt to deal either with morals or with politics,' said Gance. And yet Napoleon waged war, and this figure was not simply romanticised but glorified. It was not enough for Gance to point to his unrealised scenarios, to explain that he left Napoleon in a cloud of glory to make the future tragedy all the stronger. The effect of his film was too powerful.

Émile Vuillermoz wrote that Gance was an artist he admired above all others, but he would never fulfil himself until he had cleared his head of romanticism:

'To adorn the figure of a despot with romantic traits, to decorate with cinematic flowers the statue of a tyrant, is to do a detestable bit of historic and philosophic work. This is what Abel Gance will realise in ten years' time when the evolution of our poor, limping civilisation will have shown him the terrible consequence of war-like cinematography such as is organised by international commerce nowadays ... To ennoble the technique of massacre through romanticism, to make killing respectable or simply joyous, is to take on, my dear Abel Gance, an enormous responsibility with regard to mothers whose children will be machine-gunned tomorrow.'[32]

The same charge could equally be levelled at Griffith's *The Birth of a Nation* and Eisenstein's *October*, two masterpieces which head a battalion of productions far more bellicose than *Napoleon*. In those films, warfare is treated in brilliantly exciting sequences which leave audiences exhilarated. In *Napoleon*, Gance acknowledges the courage involved in warfare, but leaves one in no doubt as to the obscene carnage that results. The violence of the hand-to-hand fighting at Toulon was the most graphic permitted on the screen since *Intolerance* and until the relaxation of censorship in the 1960s.

Nevertheless, for many the paradox remained: that an artist whose pacifist credentials included *J'accuse* could give to a film about France's greatest warrior 'my soul, my heart, my life, my health'.[33]

16·Ten-day Wonder

Napoleon was shown ten times at the Opéra, grossing 562,009 francs, a record for any film shown there. Admittedly, that did not amount to a very extensive list;[1] at the same time, no film had stayed so long. The ten performances had not been scheduled, but the demand had been so great that extra ticket offices had to be opened and the shows sandwiched between operas, the projection box being dismantled each time as a fire precaution. Once all the expenses had been paid, a grand total of 165,240 francs went to charity, another record.[2]

A month later, in May, the *version définitive*[3] was shown to the press and the trade in two episodes, alas without the triptych, at the Apollo. The musical score incorporated the best themes of Honegger, together with Beethoven's 'Eroica', 1st, 2nd, 5th and 7th symphonies and works by Haydn, Mozart, Massenet, Litolff, Franck and Tchaikovsky.

Most critics declared the Apollo version far superior to that shown at the Opéra. 'The proportions are more harmonious, the rhythm better sustained, the events are clearer and they link together more effectively,' said *Echo*.[4] However, everyone regretted the loss of the triptychs, even though Gance had provided an alternative version of the Double Storm and the Entry into Italy edited for the single screen.

Now the two versions of *Napoleon* were clearly established, what happened next? The answer, from the newspapers and documents of the time, becomes all too obvious: nothing. The press preview was not followed by a public showing. Gaumont-Metro-Goldwyn were clearly under pressure from Culver City to hold back *Napoleon*, and to concentrate their resources upon the release of *Ben-Hur*. *Napoleon* had only cost M-G-M $75,000. *Ben-Hur*, the most expensive film ever made, had cost them $4,000,000 (100 million francs). *Napoleon* had been booked into the Cinéma Madeleine, but *Ben-Hur* settled in for a long run and no alternative venue was provided. There were questions in the press, but G-M-G gave no hint of their plans. It was difficult to avoid the conclusion that they had none.

Gance still had high hopes of the film's international success. In Germany, the distribution was handled by UFA.[5] The première at the Ufa-Palast was arranged for October 1927. UFA changed the title to *Napoleon Bonaparte* and planned an elaborate publicity campaign. They were somewhat startled to discover a rival concern, Trianon-Film, embarking on a similar campaign for a film entitled *Napoleon Bonaparte*—'The youth of the great Corsican—the Epic of a Hero in 9 Acts'.

In a flurry of anxiety, it was established that this was Henry-Roussell's *Destinée*. UFA managed to get a provisional court order against Trianon, but they could not persuade them to change the title. In one letter, UFA's representative Herr Meydam said that Roussell had been involved in the early stages of *Napoleon*, and after a disagreement had left and had started a rival film.[6] In his reply Gance neither confirmed nor denied the charge, but enclosed letters from Roussell and producer Jean de Merly. De Merly simply said he had sold the film as *Destinée* and he had taken steps in Berlin to ensure that the title was not changed. 'I am completely of your opinion that this constitutes disloyal rivalry.'[7] Roussell's letter tried to prove that his film was a romance of pure imagination. Even if 'the irresistible silhouette of the little general without a command' should appear, and even if Roussell had dealt with Napoleon's career up to the departure of the Army of Italy, 'we are not working on the same subject. *Destinée* can do no harm to your *Napoleon*—they are two very different films created by two producers who are not in the habit of looking for ideas from neighbours.'[8] In the event, UFA won their case against Trianon, but *Destinée* still appeared in distant parts of the world, such as Argentina, under the title *Napoleon*.

Gance was at work on the scenario for *From Waterloo to St Helena* while the German première was being arranged; even so, he had to deal with a mountain of problems concerning it. Gance hoped to release the second part of *Napoleon* in the winter of 1928/9, so the success of the first part in Germany was of crucial importance. He made some significant suggestions, one being that the 'elite of society' be left out of invitations; 'they are generally sceptical and incapable of appreciating an effort of this sort. I would prefer to see you concentrate on the intellectuals of Berlin, poets, novelists and cineastes, with, obviously, the maximum of officials.'[9]

He coped with problems over the triptych, over the music, over possible cuts and over clashing dates, and with another difficulty which taxed him more than all the rest. As anyone who has worked on a film will understand, friendships are subject to the severest pressure. This applies to the most routine film, let alone one which has taken the best part of eighteen months. Exhaustion can express itself in irrational resentment and jealousy. Thus

Gance found himself at loggerheads with, of all people, Albert Dieudonné over the matter of publicity. Dieudonné felt his contribution swept away by the concentration of the critics on Gance, and he wrote to several German journalists. Gance at first declined to attend the première because of this,[10] but eventually reason prevailed and the friendship resumed.

Napoleon was a critical triumph in Germany, but then German audiences were more accustomed to accepting startling technique with their entertainment. 'Abel Gance', said *Welt am Abend*, 'has destroyed all the traditional forms of film. He carries off complete victory.'[11] The box office returns, however, were disappointing for the whole of UFA's area of distribution.

Still there was no general release in France. In England, the elaborate plans to hold a spectacular première at the Albert Hall were shelved and an ordinary opening substituted at the Tivoli, the flagship theatre of M-G-M's British subsidiary, Jury-Metro-Goldwyn. Yet no firm date was announced.

In Paris, Gaumont-Metro-Goldwyn allowed *Napoleon* to return seven months after the première,[12] when the publicity campaign had been all but forgotten. Was it the *version définitive*? It was not. The version opening at the Marivaux, in November 1927, was an adjusted Opéra version, with only the final triptych.[13] Unspecified 'technical difficulties' prevented the presentation of the other. While the Opéra version was in its own way magnificent, the *version définitive* had been acclaimed as far superior in the press. Cinemagoers in Paris were denied it (although it was shown in various forms in certain provincial cities — see page 286).

However, Gance arranged the Marivaux programme so that Brienne and Toulon could be seen at the matinee and the rest in the evening. Italy was repeated at both. Having been stung by some of the criticisms, which betrayed such lack of understanding for his technical innovations, he wrote a heartfelt message to the spectators. It provides a graphic testament of how he regarded his film, and how he saw Napoleon. And it is a rare example of an artist challenging his audience to keep pace with him, or keep quiet. One can imagine Stravinsky writing something similar in response to the furious hostility aroused in 1913 by his *Rite of Spring*:

Ladies, gentlemen, my friends,

And under the heading of 'my friends' I should like to include you all, for it is only through the secret door of sympathy that one can penetrate deeply into a work like the one you are going to have to judge.

With *Napoleon* I have made what I believe to be a tangible effort towards a somewhat richer and more elevated form of cinema; and this has not been achieved without creating additional hostility and incomprehension towards myself. I should not like you to misjudge this by too swift an opinion.

Let yourselves go completely with the images. Do not react with a preconceived point of view. See in depth; do not persist in confusing that which moves with that which trembles. Discern behind the images the trace of the tears which often imbue them, or the trace of the flames of passion which precipitate them, violent, tumultuous, self-destructive. It is only after this effort that you will know whether or not the journey into history that I have made you take comprises a lesson or a poem.

My aim has been to offer to all weary hearts the most wholesome, the most sustaining and the most pleasant nourishment, that bread of dreams which, to our age of harsh necessities, becomes as indispensable as the other kind, that music of light which, gradually, will transform the great cinemas into cathedrals.

I did not want to serve any political party. I say simply that Napoleon Bonaparte is one of the most outstanding figures of humanity. The angle from which one views him will not affect the psychological and dramatic interest. I say simply that Napoleon was a fervent Republican throughout his entire youth.

It is not my purpose in this film either to judge or prejudge Bonaparte's evolution after the Italian Campaign. It could well be that from 18 Brumaire onwards I might be among his detractors. I do not know, and what is more I do not wish to know in this film. My Bonaparte, up to the point at which I present him, remains in the great line of idealistic republicans, of whom Christ was the first.

From the dramatic point of view, I have made the minimum of concession to the romantic, to anecdote, and consequently I have had to break that elementary law of continuity without which, it seems, the cinema cannot live. I wanted to try to prove with this version that a 'story' was not necessary in History, and I should still like to believe that the thinking public will share my view.

In certain paroxystic sequences, I have created for the first time a new technique, based on the strength of rhythm, dominating the subject and violating our visual habits. I speculated on the simultaneous perception of images, not only of a second's duration but sometimes of an eighth of a second, so that the clash of my images against one another would cause a surge of abstract flashes, touching the soul rather than the eyes. Then an invisible beauty is created which is not impressed upon the film and which is as difficult to explain as the perfume of a rose or the music of a symphony.

You must pardon my audacity in this sphere. It stems from the sincerity and ardour of my researches. And, if you do not understand entirely, do me the favour of believing that maybe your eyes do not yet have the visual education necessary for the reception of this first form of

Gance (left) directs the Army of Italy at La Garde.
Note the triptych 'pyramid' partially dismantled.

the music of light. It is the future of the cinema which is at stake. If our language does not stretch its potential, it will remain no more than a dialect among the arts. It will become a universal language if you make the effort to try to read the new letters which, little by little, it adds to the alphabet of the eyes. Thank you.

In aiding my *Napoleon* you will help our national film to take the place due to it, which should be, and soon will be, first.[14]

Napoleon had a successful ten-week run at the Marivaux. The documentary about the film, *Autour de Napoléon*, was the opening attraction in February 1928 at the Studio 28 in Montmartre. The presentation included the cut triptychs of the Bal des Victimes, under the title *Danses*, and the chase across Corsica, edited for the triple screen, as *Galops*. Also edited for the triple screen was *Marines* in which production footage was contrasted with seascapes shot for the Double Storm and Sanguinaires sequences, and a Dutch scientific film by Ed. Pelster Films of Amsterdam: *Cristillisation*, renamed *Cristaux*. (The main feature was a Soviet film recommended by Gance, *Bed and Sofa*.) Studio 28 was the only cinema with faith enough to install permanent triptych equipment.

In March 1928 a version appeared at the Gaumont-Palace. What a contrast to the rapturous reception at the Opéra! For Gance, it must have been as painful as seeing his film reshot and recut by a hack director. Gaumont-Metro-Goldwyn had not merely removed episodes—they had completely re-edited it, without any consultation with Gance. It was an act of astonishing arrogance. Using a negative consisting of second and third camera material—probably lodged with G-M-G for insurance purposes—the company re-organised the film. Shots from one sequence were put in another, titles were cut out or rewritten, scenes of technical bravura were mutilated or removed, and the picture was transformed from a *chef-d'oeuvre* into a masterpiece of ineptitude. It was indicative of G-M-G's attitude towards the film that they did not bother to tint or tone it, and they used the cheapest style of titles. There were two parts, each heavily reduced, yet each was preceded by prologues with orchestral and organ solos and even a newsreel. In the interval, a jazz band played. Each part ran only a week.

Why did they do it? Throughout film history, distributors have been frustrated in their desire to be involved in the creative process. Having to sell the product, they feel they know the market's requirements. Unfortunately, when they do become involved, they tend to be afflicted with the twin drawbacks of incomprehension and incompetence. G-M-G no doubt thought they had done their duty by showing the *version définitive* to the press. Now they appear to have assumed they were within their rights in reducing it to a length which they could exploit more easily. Episode films were a feature of European production—Henri Fescourt's *Les Misérables* was 32 reels—but they represented a great risk for distributors, who could not export them without cutting them. Gance had already agreed to a cut version being shown at the Opéra. He should not object too strongly to a version being *recut* for the *hoi polloi*. G-M-G anticipated, rightly as it turned out, that most critics would repeat what they had said about the Opéra or Apollo showings without seeing the film again.

Unfortunately G-M-G had breached the contract, which contained a very important clause: 'G-M-G undertakes, inasmuch as commercial necessity will permit, to respect the version of the film which will be given them by SGF and to make no change or cut which would modify the idea or the spirit of the film or betray the historical truth without the prior agreement of SGF.'[16] The same applied to the contract with M-G-M.

Contracts are invariably weighted in favour of those who draw them up, and the phrase 'inasmuch as commercial necessity will permit' probably gave G-M-G the idea that they had licence to do what they liked. The film was so badly mutilated, however, that Gance was able to enrol the support of some of the country's most eminent critics. 'They have so muddled the chronology', said René Jeanne, 'that you see Bonaparte in general's uniform *before* Toulon, when he was still only a lieutenant!'[17] André Antoine, the distinguished theatre and film director and critic, reported, 'What mutilation, what obscurity, what imbalance; one could almost say that care had been taken to disfigure this great French production and prove the superiority of our competitors, with complete contempt for agreements.'[18]

Jean Toulout, president of the Cinematographic Section of the Union des Artistes, the French equivalent of Equity, officially protested against the emasculation of the film, pointing out that many actors had already been hurt by the reduced versions shown at the Opéra and Marivaux. They had not protested because they had confidence that Gance would re-establish their roles in the long version. Now their hard work, and their prospects, were being wiped out.[19]

Gance took Gaumont-Metro-Goldwyn to court. A ruling of July 3rd, 1928, stated, 'No interpretation of the contract gave M-G-M the right to make cuts or mutilations that would distort the work or the author's ideas.'[20] Gance obtained a formal engagement from G-M-G to re-establish the long version.

Gaumont allowed the long version to be seen in some provincial cities, such as Nice. Exhibitors were free to 'adjust' it, and many of them did. But it was not shown again in Paris. And the ruling of the French court did not apply in England where, in June 1928, the film had been treated even more wretchedly than in France. A letter from Gance to Antoine related what happened.

'A version of *Napoleon* called "the English version" is at present being shown in London at the Tivoli cinema under conditions extremely painful to me, as the prestige, both commercial and ethical, which I have built up with difficulty over the years, could be wiped out in a few days.

'I sent a version to London which was exactly like the one shown with such success at the Opéra. (I sent Brienne and the siege of Toulon separately, specifying to M-G-M that they could show the Opéra version or make two films of the whole thing by adding Brienne and Toulon.)[21]

'The company took no notice of my suggestions, nor did they tell us that they had deceitfully prepared another version.'[22]

When Gance heard that the film was to open at the Tivoli on June 28th, 1928, the SGF sent its secretary, M. de la Rozière, to London to ask for information about this version before it was shown. He was refused. De la Rozière attended the opening and had a sworn statement drawn up asserting that the mutilations made to the film in France were as nothing when compared with those made in England.

De la Rozière spoke of enormous gaps made from a total lack of comprehension of Gance's work.

'When the time came to protect the triptych scenes, a green curtain was lowered several metres in front of the ordinary screen. On this was placed a white sheet, half the height of the ordinary screen. This made a disagreeable interruption to the film—about two minutes on June 28th. The screen was not three times the size of an ordinary screen, but was merely a panorama seen on a screen half the height so the effect of visual enlargement was lost.'[23]

Official intervention by the French Foreign Affairs department merely obliged M-G-M's London branch, Jury-Metro-Goldwyn, to hide behind a smokescreen of mendacity. They claimed they had repeatedly tried to secure the participation of the author to make judicious cuts, but in vain.

This attitude was illogical, said Gance, since his one preoccupation was to ensure that the version shown all over the world corresponded with the one shown with such success in Paris, and in Berlin, Prague, Vienna and other places.

The reaction in England was much as he might have expected. One critic said he left the cinema with a migraine and a squint.[24] The all-important trade press was patronisingly dismissive. The *Illustrated London News* said the picture omitted such trifling details as Austerlitz, Jena, Moscow and Waterloo. 'As for the direction, it seemed that the producer had been studying the more complex examples of German technique after an indigestible supper. Restless and meaningless devices were employed throughout the film. The chief impression I retain is a vast, whirling phantasmagoria of the Convention mob, engulfed by waves, tricolour sails, pet eagles, more waves, Napoleon's face, Josephine's face, Danton, Marat, Robespierre and a final seething ocean in full spate.

'It made one wish that technique had never been invented, and that, for once in a way, it might be found possible to direct a straightforward story in a straightforward manner.'[25]

Admittedly, England was self-conscious about the shortcomings of its own industry, which lagged so far behind the others that English critics leaped to the offensive where foreign films were concerned, and were only too happy to pull an expensive epic to pieces. But in this case, Jury-Metro-Goldwyn had given them every excuse.

What would they do in America?

17·Defeat in America

'Tomorrow,' wrote Gance in his letter to Antoine, 'America will show a version with perhaps greater mutilations, rendering the work incomprehensible, even to me, the author.'[1]

Gance was being ironic; he didn't know how right he was. Metro-Goldwyn-Mayer had taken delivery of a negative and a print of the *version définitive*. But the company which had cut von Stroheim's *Greed* from ten hours to two was hardly likely to view *Napoleon* with any more sympathy. Editor Frank Hull, working to orders from producer Harry Rapf, squeezed the sprawling masterpiece into a neat eight reels. When it came to cut the negative, it was discovered that the negative did not match the print. A frantic cable from Louis B. Mayer to the New York office said, 'LOOKS LIKE TWO OR THREE HUNDRED SCENES AND CLOSEUPS WILL BE MISSING STOP AS ALTERNATIVE IF YOU CAN'T GET NEGATIVE WE WILL HAVE TO DUPE FROM OLD SCRATCHED POSITIVE STOP GOD HELP US IF THAT HAS TO BE DONE.'[2]

The tone of the cable suggests Mayer was worried. Had there been a conspiracy to destroy the film, he would not have expressed such concern. Who would have worried about a few thousand feet of poor quality film?

But when the problems were overcome, and the M-G-M version completed, it was clear that most technical innovations had been removed. This adds weight to the theory that M-G-M were anxious to suppress foreign competition. (After all Stinnes, the original financier, had invested in *Napoleon* to help crush American competition.) M-G-M had advanced only $75,000 — a fraction of the sum they spent on their regular releases.

SGF had sent the triptychs, but M-G-M had no intention of using them. It was 1928. *The Jazz Singer*'s success had set theatres converting to Vitaphone, at a cost of between $16,000 and $25,000.[3] Why should these same theatres be expected to install triptych equipment when there was no guarantee the process would ever be used again? Instead, Frank Hull used the elements of the triptych to produce a crazy-paving of the Entry into

Italy. There was no attempt to reproduce the triptych in any form. There was no rapid-cut snowball fight. There was no 'checkerboard effect' in the pillow fight. The Marseillaise was re-edited.

M-G-M considered they had done well by *Napoleon*. (They even named their dog star Bonaparte!) They knew their audiences expected a proper narrative, and would react against an episodic film. Their new story-line made sense. It was, however, dry and dull where it was not absurd. Whenever the film was in danger of taking off, a title and a change of sequence put it firmly back in its place again.

The title-writer, Lotta Woods, had a hard job to cope with some of the vast gaps. 'Then, in the peacefulness of his wooing, the Republic advanced him another step on his road to fame which does not wait for love.' Original titles were inaccurately translated, and additional titles were often sentimental; when little Marcellin appears as a drummer boy at Toulon, he is introduced with the words 'And a little child shall lead them.' In the first romantic encounter between Joséphine and Napoleon, there should only be one title: Joséphine's remark, 'When you are silent you are irresistible.' This was converted to 'I fear I bore you. You find nothing to say to me.' And Napoleon was made to reply, 'My love is too great for speech.' This went against the grain of the original treatment, which was humorous, and which showed Napoleon tongue-tied and gauche in the presence of the woman he loved. The rest of the film was belittled less by its titles than by insensitive editing. A good example of this is the way the film is made to end – not on the road to Italy but in the Convention, among the ghosts of the Revolution, where Napoleon declares he is striving for 'A United States of Man' and we cut to a closeup of George Washington and the American flag.[4]

M-G-M's publicity department produced a detailed pressbook, which suggested they hadn't seen the picture; Napoleon in the boat with the tricolor sail was captioned 'escape from Elba'. Dieudonné's hair was adjusted on press advertisements to make him resemble the Napoleon more familiar to Americans; they even painted his hand inside his coat. As was their usual practice the publicity department provided local papers with ready-made reviews: 'Even the subtitling, with its total absence of wise-cracking, shows the keen delight these French producers have taken in giving their Napoleon to the world.'

When the real reviews appeared, they were guaranteed to put people off seeing the film.

Variety: 'Napoleon doesn't mean anything to the great horde of picture-goers over here. Nap isn't good looking enough and they didn't put in the right scenes for the flaps over here ... Al Gance gets most of the credit. Whoever impersonated Napoleon looks more like Hearst ... Sending it into Loew's New York as its first metropolitan showing place sorta tells what

Poster for the M-G-M version, with characters suggested by adverts for a forthcoming historical picture, Divine Lady

M-G-M thinks of it.'⁵

Zit's: 'Cinematically, it is wet. The sets are dowdy and badly lighted. Most of the exteriors are poorly photographed, and there is one battle sequence in the rain that suggests the efforts of the 16mm amateurs getting ambitious.'⁶

Motion Picture News: 'If you are an exhibitor and you play this one, the chances are that your audiences will send you to St Helena for life. It is a very poor apology for a motion picture. The French company that made it should have been ashamed to send it to America, unless they intended it as an example of how badly they make pictures there.'⁷

New York Post: 'It must be pointed out that M. Gance does not realize the things that can be done with the motion picture. He does not know his camera.'⁸

Wherever *Napoleon* was shown, box office receipts plummeted. Whenever they could, exhibitors who had read the advance notices cancelled the picture. Some theatres went so far as to pay for the picture but not to play it. One small theatre in Florida ran the picture for two days, and made a grand total of $77.35.⁹

Had D. W. Griffith seen it — and there is no evidence one way or the other — he would have been justified in thinking his disciple had wilfully squandered the opportunity of a lifetime.

Could Gance have done more to prevent this debacle? There is no case on record of a foreign director objecting to the re-editing of his film in the United States, and having his cuts restored — not in the silent days, anyway. Every European director knew that his film would be cut for the American market. Gance himself knew it; his first budgets talk of the series of six films being reduced to 3,500 metres (11,482 ft) in America. But he clung to the hope that even a cut version, such as was shown at the Opéra, would be a huge success. The films of his colleagues Tourjansky (*Michael Strogoff*) and Volkoff (*Casanova*) had both been bought by M-G-M, and Tourjansky's film was so successful it had triggered off a whole series of Russian films. Tourjansky had been invited to Hollywood.

Napoleon, in its full version, was almost avant-garde. It really belonged in the specialised theatres that showed such films. However, M-G-M had spent too much money for such a restricted release. There was no reason why, with a little cleaning up, it should not have enjoyed the same popular success as *Strogoff* and *Casanova*.

M-G-M was, on the face of it, the most intelligent of all American production companies, and its head of production was the brilliant Irving Thalberg. It is doubtful, however, that Thalberg had either the time or the inclination to look at the full-length *Napoleon* — a picture lasting several hours would have brought back grim memories of *Greed*. The job was assigned to Harry Rapf.

Rapf was the third member, with Thalberg and Mayer, of the M-G-M triumvirate and the one who is always overlooked. He had been a producer of girl acts in vaudeville. His previous productions were all very modest. He had supervised a series of kid pictures at Warner Brothers. At M-G-M he had a hand in the re-editing of *Greed* (which makes one regret the loss of the original all the more). He was hardly a man likely to respond to *Napoleon*. Simply because he did not understand it, he was likely to be harsher with the material than with a more straightforward film like *Michael Strogoff*.

On top of which, M-G-M was a conservative company. It disliked technical innovations which came from outside. Its own technical experiments were conducted under conditions of secrecy. *Napoleon* was awash with revolutionary ideas, many of which violated the 'picture sense' which M-G-M so prided itself upon.

Variety had rocked the American film industry and whether Rapf understood the picture or not, he could tell that such unconventional technique might lead to further seismic explosions. By removing the threat, he destroyed the impact.

Gance would undoubtedly have fought harder had he not been hamstrung. But in December 1927, SGF had agreed that whatever profit the film should earn from abroad should be given to the Comte de Béarn, in recognition of the large sum he had invested in the production. 'I was away in the navy until 1927,' said de Béarn. 'I just passed through Paris occasionally and signed cheques. They told me, I suppose, whatever they wanted me to hear. I don't know how much it cost — but I think I spent millions, some of which came from England, incidentally.'[10]

The Comte de Béarn now became the proprietor of *Napoleon*, and he was anxious to have no further obstacles to prevent him recovering his money.[11] Gance was reminded that he had undertaken to produce a film of 3,000 metres — not one of 12,800. Legally he was no longer able to protest.

A heartbreaking admission of defeat survives among the Gance papers. Dated August 9th, 1928, before the American release, it was addressed to 'M. l'Administrateur délégué' of SGF (M. Karmann) and it said, 'Following my agreement today with Metro-Goldwyn, it is understood that I am to stop all judicial action against this Society and against ourselves, as to the argument which has separated us on the subject of the cuts made in my film *Napoleon* in America, England and France. I also undertake not to interfere with these versions, to allow you without encumbrance to receive the profits from your contract.'[12]

In return for this surrender, SGF magnanimously agreed to pay him what was already due to him — 5 per cent of the American advance. In the margin of the letter Gance had written in very small handwriting, 'I do not remember receiving this.'

It is perhaps poetic justice that SGF's wholehearted collaboration with M-G-M did them no good at all. The returns were so meagre that the Comte de Béarn sued M-G-M for their failure to derive more revenue from the distribution and he won by default in 1932.[13] G-M-G agreed to new terms, and de Béarn reduced his claim from 5 million to 100,000 francs. G-M-G failed to honour their agreement. SGF went bankrupt. Before long, Gance too was bankrupt. And to complete the picture, Gaumont-Metro-Goldwyn went into liquidation in 1934.

Gance often spoke to me of M-G-M's handling of the film, saying they had 'suppressed' it:

'They bought it for a very great sum, just to lock it away. They said to themselves, "If we put out these triptychs, we'll cause a revolution, and we'll complicate the whole structure of the business. We'll have to use three projectors and three cameras each time we shoot ... No, let's put an end to it before it starts."'

He added bitterly that M-G-M then proceeded to make their own version of *Napoleon*, in Technicolor. No such film was released, and I thought Gance's imagination was affecting his memory. But I recently saw a copy of *Cinémagazine* for December 1927, which reported that Otto Matiesen was to play Napoleon, with Agnes Ayres as Joséphine, in a Technicolor production of the Emperor's life to be directed by Roy William Neill. The project was cancelled (perhaps because of the Gance film?) and the Technicolor film Neill finally made for M-G-M release was *The Viking* (1929).

Gance felt he had written, produced, directed and acted in one of the greatest films ever made. His disappointment was traumatic. In 1926, he had written, 'I neither can nor wish under any circumstances to start again a similar effort where I have to fight the French windmills of incompetence, egoism, pettiness and jealousy.'[14]

His experience is reminiscent of that of Cecil B. DeMille, who, in 1918, staked all his hopes on one brilliant picture, *The Whispering Chorus*. Its success would have meant everything to him. The public was repelled by its grim theme, and its failure, as one writer put it, 'exhausted his capacity for disappointment'. DeMille turned in cynical despair to what he knew the public wanted, and gradually his skill as a film-maker was eroded.

Gance's fate was to be much the same, but without DeMille's commercial success. And he still clung to hopes that some more of *Napoleon* would be made. In 1928, he was struggling to finance the scenario for the second episode. One of his carnets reads, 'Reduce, reduce, *reduce* the second film, otherwise same catastrophe as first.' Yet knowing he would never reach the end and desperate for money, he sold the final scenario to Lupu Pick who made *Napoleon auf St Helena* in Germany, with Werner Krauss as Napoleon.[15] It soon appeared on the boulevards in Paris, with Gance's name as writer on the advertisements, and the critics, able to cope with this much more straightforward film, praised it with far more unanimity than they had praised the original.

In 1929, Gance embarked on an idea he had had fifteen years before, a film about the end of the world. *La Fin du monde* was taken out of his hands and re-edited by the producers. According to Gance, it was ruined, and he disclaimed responsibility for it. In 1931, he went to Berlin to meet representatives of the Soviet film industry to discuss the making of the Russian campaign. He announced he would pioneer an international sound film in which each army would speak its appropriate language.[16] Nothing came of that (nor of a 1947 attempt to film the Egyptian campaign with Jean-Louis Barrault as Napoleon).

In 1934, by arrangement with the Comte de Béarn, Gance reworked *Napoleon* as a sound film, at two and a quarter hours. He and André Debrie invented a process called *perspective sonore*, in which loudspeakers surrounded the audience. It was a forerunner of stereophonic sound. Actors such as Artaud dubbed themselves. Using some of the silent footage and some cheaply shot additional sequences, Gance produced the kind of film he thought people would pay to see, rather than the sort of film he felt committed to make. He had to work his way out of his bankruptcy. But while the film had some popularity, he was regarded as passé by the new generation of critics. They felt he had burned himself out, had failed to adapt to the modern mood. Worse still, although some of his sound films showed a profit, he was branded in the eyes of producers as a man who wasted money. Simone Surdieux said she lost jobs because of his reputation; 'as if I was going to waste money because I had worked for him.'

Gance cut the original negative of *Napoleon* into his sound version. He was supposed to hand the rest of the negative of the *version définitive* back to the Comte de Béarn. De Béarn did not receive it. It was never seen in its entirety again.

But for those who saw the full *Napoleon*, and for those who saw the Opéra version, the experience was a high point of their lives, as it would be for those who saw the reconstructed version half a century later. Georges d'Esparbès, besides being a historian of the past, proved himself a historian of the future when he wrote to Gance in 1927:

'What young student will ask for one of my books at the Bibliothèque Nationale in 1987? While as for you, with your handling of crowds, your sense of lighting and movement, your feeling for life ... rest calmly on your pillow of glory.'

18 · Nothing to Declare

It was quite apparent to me, even from the fragments I owned, that *Napoleon* was a film of exceptional importance. And it had a profound influence on me. Despite Gance's warnings about the harshness of the film industry, I left school as soon as I could, tempted by a job as an office boy with a documentary film company. I lasted four days before I was kicked upstairs into the cutting room, as a trainee film editor. This was my first contact with professional film technicians, and what surprised me was their lack of interest in the cinema. There were a couple of splendid exceptions, but on the whole their attitude was that they had enough of films during the day without seeing more at night. The supervising editor, a woman who had worked with Humphrey Jennings and the Crown Film Unit, scoffed at my enthusiasm for Gance and *Napoleon*. 'The film has never been an art,' she declared, 'and never will be.'

This prehistoric approach dismayed me, and like the young Napoleon at Brienne, I wrote of my unhappiness in a letter. I was going to send it to Gance, but I was too shy. I rewrote it in a more optimistic frame of mind. I knew that Gance had enough problems of his own.

Fortunately I had another outlet. I was asked by the editor of *Amateur Cine World*, Gordon Malthouse, to write an article for the Christmas 1955 issue. I devoted the bulk of it to Gance and *Napoleon*. But even here I had the feeling that no one took me very seriously. The editor introduced the piece with this caption:

'Here is the French film director Abel Gance. His appearance here is made certain by reason of the fact that he is the idol to whom Kevin Brownlow burns incense. Once the god actually talked to his acolyte, and Brownlow can never forget it. In the following pages, compiled by this young enthusiast, Gance's epic *Napoleon* is discussed at length.'

Fortunately, the article had some effect; interest in *Napoleon* was aroused among those who read *ACW*, and I received letters from readers asking for more information. Above all, they asked, when can we see the film? I could supply no answer, but in their enthusiasm lay some hope that the four-hour print belonging to the Cinémathèque Française might eventually be brought over. I longed to see it, and yet I was almost afraid to do so; could any film be anything but boring at such enormous length?

To his undying credit, Henri Langlois, head of the Cinémathèque, pulled off a coup at the 1955 Venice Film Festival by showing the final triptychs from *Napoleon*. The event apparently did nothing to convince the promoters of Cinerama and CinemaScope that they owed a debt to Gance. But it was a splendid gesture.

Almost single-handedly, Langlois kept alive the cultural richness of the French cinema, and made it aware of its traditions. With his devoted assistants Mary Meerson, widow of art director Lazare Meerson, and Marie Epstein, sister of Jean Epstein, Langlois ran the Cinémathèque as a benevolent dictator. During the war, he had protected his collection from the Germans. After the war, he scoured the world not only for films, but for stills, designs, costumes and props. He collected anything, refusing to acknowledge that a film might be worthless. The next generation, he said, might find it of more value than a so-called classic.

Langlois had no money to make copies, so he projected his original prints. He was thus on Ernest Lindgren's list for immediate execution. Lindgren believed films should be preserved, untouched, for posterity. The trouble was, posterity was always twenty years away. For Langlois, posterity was now. He felt films should live and breathe; they should not be buried in vaults, but should frequently be handled and projected.

It was an exhilarating attitude, and Langlois was an early hero of mine, until I realised that his astonishing achievements as a collector were offset by startling deficiencies as an archivist.

Langlois lost, through decomposition, fires and general carelessness, a terrifying number of irreplaceable films. Among them was the second part of Erich von Stroheim's *Wedding March*, *The Honeymoon*. On the other hand, Lindgren, a consummate archivist who would have preserved it, would never have had the initiative to go out and find such a treasure. Langlois was able to keep one and later two theatres supplied with films night after night from his collection. His presentations were spartan in the extreme. Silent films were shown at 16 fps, whether they were shot at that speed or not (with the result that some silents would last over an hour longer than intended). There was no musical accompaniment. He left the titles out.[1] 'A silent film should tell its story without words,' he would say. And of course the consequences to the films were often grave — torn film, reels in the wrong order, vanished sections.

But despite the drawbacks of this extraordinary man, he raised film culture to a higher level in Paris than anywhere else in the world. The New

Wave sprang up as a direct result of these screenings. And a great many films survived his treatment and continued to exert an influence—whereas they might not have done so without him.

There were also a number of specialised cinemas in Paris, of which Studio 28 was the most famous. Under the management of Edgar and Georges Roulleau, it had become a repertory house for classics of the cinema. In 1955, Abel Gance worked with Edgar Roulleau in preparing a new presentation of the 1935 *Napoleon Bonaparte*, adding to it the final triptych of the Entry into Italy. The triptych was synchronised.

The new version was introduced by Gance on a caustic note. 'Ladies and gentlemen,' he said, 'the spectacle which we have the honour of presenting to you was ready thirty years ago. This showing has been delayed due to circumstances beyond our control.'

In the audience was a young man called Claude Lelouch, who would one day support Gance in yet another sound version.

With the reissue of *Napoleon* and the release of *La Tour de Nesle*, the two main French cultural weeklies began a reversal of the opinion about Gance: François Truffaut wrote an article in *Arts* and Georges Sadoul in *Les Lettres françaises*.

Napoleon Bonaparte had a long and successful run at Studio 28; it aroused such interest in Gance that a television programme was devoted to him and René Jeanne and Charles Ford recorded eight interviews for radio.

I would have gone to Paris, except that I could not afford the fare on my salary of £4. 10s. a week. Oddly enough, that did not prove a drawback to my plans of becoming a film director. Professional prospects being dim, I embarked on my own feature film, to be made at weekends—the story of what might have happened had England lost the Second World War and been occupied by the Germans. It was to be called *It Happened Here*.

After a few months floundering around, accumulating sad experiences and equally sad results, I met Andrew Mollo, an art student a couple of years younger than I was. He signed on as art director, since he was an expert on military matters, and later we formed a partnership to produce and direct the picture ourselves.

In 1958, Andrew Mollo's father took us both on a trip to Paris. I imagined finding further rare films, but a fellow collector warned me against over-optimism. 'I was in Paris myself a short time ago,' he said, 'and I found nothing. If you take my advice, you'll forget about films and just see the sights.'

We didn't see the sights, but found a mass of films. We had taken a wrong turning in the Flea Market, trying to find our way out of a maze of alleyways, and discovered a small canvas-covered stall, laden with old 9·5mm cameras and projectors, and attended by two charming but shrewd old ladies. Yes,

The two old ladies in the Flea Market stall pose for my camera with Andrew Mollo

they had plenty of films — was there anything special I wanted? When I mentioned *Napoleon*, there was a flurry of French and hand-waving, and I gathered I had to go to their shop, in another part of Paris. I located it next day — an old-fashioned store whose glass cases might have held secondhand books had they not been full of film. One of the old ladies blew the dust from a cluster of five 60 ft reels called *Napoléon et Joséphine de Beauharnais* and handed them over. They also showed me an ancient Pathé-Baby catalogue, and I was amazed to find that the French version of *Napoleon* differed from the English; it looked as though I had to start collecting all over again.

I went to the Cinémathèque in high hopes of seeing their print of *Napoleon*, but I quickly discovered that in France nothing is accomplished as easily as that. However, Mary Meerson was very kind. She gave me lunch and assured me the Cinémathèque had all Gance's films, and that one day it might be possible to show me *Napoleon*. When I explained how anxious I was to see Gance again, she lifted the phone, dialled a number and handed me the receiver. I found myself talking to Gance. It was a long time since we had met, but my French had not improved. I stumbled through some explanations in franglais; to my relief, he understood. He said yes, he remembered me, and he fixed a meeting for the following day.

With Andrew as my interpreter, I went to Nelly Kaplan's apartment on the rue de Rivoli. The walls were decorated with magnificent stills including

the nine-frame pillow fight montage from *Napoleon*. A large model locomotive, featured in *La Roue*, was perched on a table.

Gance was very friendly—and amused when Andrew tried to interpret
for me. 'You speak French almost as badly as he does,' he teased, which
piqued Andrew and cast a slight cloud over the occasion. Luckily, Nelly
Kaplan spoke English fluently and was able to take over.

He confirmed that he had given all his films to the Cinémathèque, and he
was fascinated to see the extra reels of *Napoleon* I had acquired. In London,
I had recently seen a 9·5mm version of *Maître des Forges* (1933) which had
Gance's name on it and which had greatly disappointed me. I was hoping he
would deny that he had made it, but his answer acknowledged that the film
was a dud.

'I made it with my eyes shut,' he said, closing his eyes and cranking an
imaginary camera handle. 'I made all those sound films like that, except
perhaps *Beethoven* and *J'accuse*.'

But he defended his *Tour de Nesle* which had been heavily criticised in
Europe. 'It is a good film,' he said, simply.

Gance was deeply involved in his new experiments with Polyvision—renamed Magirama—and this was the subject he was most anxious to talk
about: 'The cinema on one screen is a melody played on the piano with one
hand. Polyvision will orchestrate it, will provide the range and power of a
symphony.' The screen, he explained, could be manipulated to any size or
shape to suit the action or the psychology of the scene involved.

'Polyvision', he said, 'is a sort of visual accordion.'

Gance was very interested in the stills we had brought along of our own
feature project, pronouncing it 'an excellent idea'. He persuaded Nelly
Kaplan to part with some of her precious stills, suggesting that I might be
useful in publicising Polyvision in England.

My last recollection of that meeting was of Gance, crouched over a table
lamp, examining the tiny image on the 9·5mm frames of *Napoléon et
Joséphine*. He pulled the film out from its metal cassettes and squinted at
each shot through a magnifying glass.

'You know,' he said, reflectively, 'I burned the triptychs from this film.
Not the final panoramic one—that I couldn't find. But the others—I threw
the negative into the fire. I was profoundly depressed. I felt the industry
had no place for me. How long ago? It feels like a century.'

No film-maker would throw film into a fire, unless he wanted to start a
larger one, so I held out hope that the missing triptychs still existed.

19 · A Gnashing of Teeth

Work on my film, *It Happened Here*, came to a halt when Andrew Mollo's parents decided he should move to Paris to study at the Sorbonne. This may have taken him away from the film, but it brought him closer to the old ladies in the film shop, and he paid many visits on my behalf. Among the rare prints he had them ship to me was a French 9·5mm version of *Napoleon*. It cost a small fortune—all of £30, for the old ladies knew how much I wanted it—and I had to pay another small fortune to the customs authorities. And when it finally arrived, I discovered that this French version was identical in every respect to the English version I already had. Maddening! It was *a* French version, but not *the* French version. And since the old ladies were acting in good faith, I could hardly return the film and demand my money back.

However, one reel—Rouget de Lisle's introduction of the Marseillaise to the revolutionary crowds—turned out to be from the proper French version, and it was full of fresh material. I decided to incorporate all the new scenes into my version, but when I began work I discovered a very curious thing: they would not intercut. The scenes were different—but they were not different enough. Rouget de Lisle, for example, would climb into the pulpit at the Club des Cordeliers and start to sing in close-up in my version; in this new print, he would start to sing in mid-shot. By examining the film closely through a magnifying glass, I realised that they were the same scene—shot by different cameras.

In the silent days, film stock was sharp and clear, but the moment you copied it, the sharpness and clarity vanished. It was therefore essential to make release prints from an original negative. In America, films were shot with two cameras as a standard practice—supplying a domestic and a foreign negative. On *Napoleon*, Gance used at least three cameras, to give himself the widest possible latitude in the cutting room, and to provide several original negatives.

So my new reel was a separate version, with only a few shots more than I already had. I wondered how many versions of *Napoleon* one might have seen in 1927 ... and how difficult it would be to produce one authentic version.

I was particularly interested in Gance's editing because I had become an editor myself, and I was beginning to appreciate what a difficult and complex job it was. Even though the documentaries I worked on hardly demanded Gance's revolutionary style of editing, I looked for every opportunity to introduce rapid cutting or a furious montage. But they looked sadly out of place in films on detergency or on oil exploration in Abu Dhabi.[1]

Eric Mival had worked with me on *The Trans-Antarctic Expedition* when we were both assistants. I now had a small bed-sitter in Hampstead — too small for proper screenings — and Eric managed to rent a larger room in the house next door. It was possible to install twin turntables and twin projectors and to project *Napoleon* with full orchestral accompaniment. I can only assume his landlady was deaf and his neighbours remarkably forbearing, for Eric's room echoed night after night with the clatter of the projector and the thunder of Tchaikovsky, Mendelssohn and Richard Strauss.

I look back upon those shows with great nostalgia. Many film people came, and many film fans. One regular member of the audience was my new assistant Peter Watkins (who later directed *The War Game* and *Privilege*). He was so impressed by *Napoleon* that he wrote a fan letter to Abel Gance, an act which, in turn, greatly impressed me.

Not everyone was so easily converted. I was disheartened to meet several people interested in vintage films who considered the film 'boring'. I thought this might have been a reaction against my incessant advertising, but it turned out that some of them had seen a version I knew nothing about, a version released on 9·5mm and 16mm in France by Film-Office. A *third* French version! When eventually I saw it, I realised that it was, indeed, boring. Subtitles were printed right across the picture — a barbaric habit to begin with — and the footage I was so familiar with had been forced into an unhappy marriage with footage I had never seen before. This was obviously not original material — it seemed to have been shot in the 1930s. Some of it employed back projection. I slowly realised the awful truth, that this was a mute version of the 1935 sound reissue.

The truth was awful because even in my early twenties I was an ingenuous character, who idealised his heroes. It shocked me to think that the man who had created *Napoleon* was capable of mediocre work. It took me years to realise that even the greatest directors can turn out the most terrible films — and even longer to realise that the Griffith of *Intolerance* is in no way diminished by the Griffith of *Dream Street*, nor the Chaplin of *The*

Gold Rush by the Chaplin of *A King in New York*. At the time, I was profoundly depressed to see how the great Gance had so despoiled his own work, and to realise that his critics had, paradoxically, been as right as they were wrong.

I kept my eyes open for the slightest hint of old films appearing on the market. I was fascinated by the whole silent era, and was extending my collection of 9·5mm films into 16mm. I heard about the formation of the Vintage Film Circle, a small society catering for film collectors. It held monthly meetings in a pub in the City, and it was typical, in its eccentric Englishness, of many similar societies across the country. One of its members invited me to St John's Wood to see his huge collection, which, for reasons of space, he kept in a coal cellar. He admitted he never looked at the films, but he liked having them. One of the titles he wafted under my nose was Abel Gance's *Le Droit à la vie* (1917). No, he wouldn't part with it, nor would he sell it. But I could unwind the first few feet if I liked. The film, though much abridged in true 9·5mm style, began with a portrait of its director. And that was all I was ever permitted to see of it.

On the other hand, the Vintage Film Circle brought about a far more rewarding experience. One of its members, Dr C. K. Elliott, pulled off the most extraordinary coup I had heard of in all my years of collecting. He discovered that Royal Sutcliffe Cine Equipment of Bradford had once had a 17·5mm library. All that remained was one silent film and a projector. The silent film was the unimaginable length of 17 reels, and its price, appropriately, was £17. 10s. He bought the film, together with the projector which cost £21, and was then kind enough to offer to show it: for the film was a tinted and toned print, titled in French and English, of the Opéra version of *Napoleon*.

17·5mm was another French invention from Pathé, like 9·5mm, and it was intended for use by mobile cinemas operating in the country — hence its name, Pathé-Rural. The gauge was wide enough to accommodate a picture of excellent quality (and later a sound track). A few silent films were released, including two about Napoleon — Gance's epic and Henry-Roussell's *Destinée*.[2]

Dr Elliott was an Irishman, from Monaghan, with a face that reminded me of eighteenth-century military portraits — strikingly handsome, with a tall forehead and a distinctive, aquiline nose. He had served both in the Irish army, before the war, and in the British army in the Burma campaign. He was thus very intrigued by our depiction of the Germans in England, and now that Andrew Mollo was back and the picture under way again, he suggested we might find some useful locations near his home in Cambridge-shire. Andrew, Eric Mival and I went up for a weekend of location hunting — and Dr Elliott promised to run *Napoleon* as a bonus.

It proved to be a momentous weekend, one of those milestones by which one charts one's life. On the first evening *Citizen Kane* was shown on television, and I had never seen it. I was stunned by it, as were Mollo and Mival, and, convinced I had never seen a greater film, I felt *Napoleon* could never measure up to such grandeur and originality. I fully expected it to be a wretched anti-climax.

It was summer. The sun was blazing. We had scoured possible invasion sites, and Mival and Mollo were relaxing in the swimming pool. It was hardly the ideal moment to drag them inside to watch a four-hour movie. But they came, and Dr Elliott drew the curtains. The room still glowed with light as he warmed up the old 17·5mm projector and he showed the film on the wall. But once the titles faded and the picture began such drawbacks counted for nothing. The first image — the black hat of the young Napoleon rising above the wall of his snow-fortress — told us at once we were seeing something exceptional. We forgot the weather and were lost in the eighteenth century. Far from being anti-climactic, the picture was powerful enough to overwhelm us — even without the triptych. My 9·5mm abridgement was pitiful by comparison. *Napoleon* was the film I had dreamed it might be.

And yet … and yet … There were still scenes missing — scenes I had viewed on 9·5mm which I felt were essential to the narrative, scenes which, if they could only be reintroduced, would greatly enhance the impact. And what else might be missing, that no one had seen since 1927?

In 1963, Andrew and I went to the French Institute in South Kensington to see a special screening of the 1935 sound version — *Napoleon Bonaparte* (vu et entendu par Abel Gance). I had been prepared for it by the mute version on 16mm and I warned Andrew what to expect, but it was even worse than I feared. Gance had taken the silent version and reworked it into a very different film. Each scene had been post-synchronised, so that spoken dialogue replaced subtitles, and the gaps were filled by newly shot cutaways, and newly shot speeches. Actors like Artaud were brought back to deliver their dialogue in sync, and one saw them age ten years in a single cut. Brienne had been removed. There was a lengthy prologue in an inn, a kind of Napoleonic cabaret, and an even lengthier epilogue which made up for the film ending at Italy with a series of lantern slides of the later campaigns. Unwilling to believe that this represented Gance's true intention, I wrote that it had been 'massacred', although the original footage was still 'incredible'. Indeed, it *had* been massacred, but the perpetrator, regrettably, was Gance himself. Had I seen no other version, I would have shrugged Gance off as 'just another DeMille'.

Two months later, my gloom was deepened by even grimmer evidence of a massacre. Tom Milne organised a remarkable season at the National Film Theatre called The Real Avant-Garde, demonstrating just how advanced were the French film-makers of the silent days. He arranged with the

Cinémathèque Française to ship over their complete *Napoleon*. I had waited for this moment for nine years, and with the memory of Dr Elliott's print still glowing, I invited as many friends as I could, including my girlfriend of the time whom I was very anxious to impress.

On to the screen came a lumbering, uncertain sequence of Corsica. The familiar material was there, but none of the shots were as effective. And they had apparently been put together by someone who knew nothing about editing. Closeups from one sequence were inserted haphazardly into another — thus Yvette Dieudonné, playing a sister of Napoleon, appeared in the garden scene in a closeup shot on the boat. When Napoleon tells his family, 'Now the Bonapartes have one country and one country only — France,' a closeup appears from the sequence of the inn in Corsica. Not only was it tedious to sit through, it was embarrassing. Those friends who had seen my 9·5mm version thought that this must have been the way it was released originally — before it was 'improved' by recutting. The audience apparently thought it was highly avant-garde, for they greeted it with merry giggles. My mind flashed back to that *Bioscope* review: ' … judicious and drastic cutting might result in a film of more logical sequence and greatly enhanced interest.'

After a few more reels, I dragged my girlfriend out of the theatre. I was known to be such an evangelist for the film that several people remarked, 'What! Brownlow walking out of *Napoleon*!'

I still remember the desperate disappointment of that NFT show. And the feeling of impotent anger at being able to do nothing about it.

I have discovered recently that this, the Cinémathèque's 'second best' print — called, simply, *Napoléon* (incomplet) — was the Gaumont-Palace version over which Gance brought a lawsuit in 1928. It had become even more truncated since. It would have been damaging enough if the Cinémathèque had withdrawn it at once, but it continued to be circulated, to cure more and more people of any possible interest in the film.

Such NFT screenings used to form the basis of the next batch of articles and books on film history. I hoped writers would ignore this version, for I feared reviews even worse than Paul Rotha's.[3] But Dr Elliott did something far more valuable — he arranged for his 17·5mm print to be shown to the Society for Film History Research at the headquarters of the Royal Society of Arts in the Adelphi, London. The NFT's pianist, Arthur Dulay, accompanied it. The screening was a great success. E. O. Walker, head of the Vintage Film Circle, who helped to organise the event, wrote to Dr Elliott, 'It was infinitely superior to the footage in the Cinémathèque Française version which contained little of the interesting parts, but had reams of dull-as-ditchwater stuff, where everyone looks like everyone else and there seemed neither rhyme nor reason in any of it.'

Dr Elliott wrote to Gance, telling him of his discovery, and proposing that prints should be made for the benefit of film societies. He received a charming reply, apologising for a six-month delay: 'The struggles which artists often wage against the decadent cinema world are so hard one is never allowed to look back idly.' Gance said it was a stroke of the greatest good fortune to find the print because—and this was to have profound consequences—André Malraux, the Minister of Culture in de Gaulle's government, was very keen on a revival of the silent *Napoleon*. As it turned out, Gance did not call upon the 17·5mm print, but Malraux's enthusiasm led to yet another version of the film. And, indirectly, to my own reconstruction.

Abel Gance and Magirama camera — the same Debrie cameras as were used for the triptych, mounted side by side — in 1956

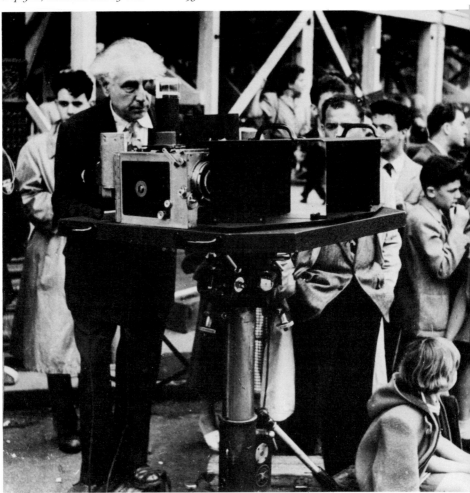

20 · Too Good to Last

If I have given the impression that my entire life revolved around *Napoleon*, nothing could be further from the truth. I only wish it had! I had shown it, publicised it and talked about it—I felt I could do no more. I was deeply involved in *It Happened Here* which, although it had finally been finished in 1964, had run straight into a storm of controversy which did little to aid my professional chances or those of Andrew Mollo. It had its première at the London Film Festival—and, in the same Festival, was the latest, highly praised film by Abel Gance, *Cyrano et d'Artagnan*. What did I think of it? I didn't dare see it. My loyalty to Gance had just undergone the severest possible test; I had seen *Austerlitz*, which Gance had released in 1960, his first feature after *La Tour de Nesle*. Despite this return to the subject of Napoleon, despite the presence of such great stars as Orson Welles and Michel Simon, and despite the co-operation of the Yugoslav army, *Austerlitz* had all the sweep and dash of moving day at Madame Tussaud's. The waxworks were wheeled in, there followed interminable stretches of dialogue about where to go and what to do, and they were wheeled out again. It made me feel terribly sad.

Working at the BFI, and an organiser of the London Film Festival, was a critic called Richard Roud. He staged at the NFT a season devoted to Abel Gance. The BFI invited Gance to attend the opening of the season, and he accepted. To my astonishment, the BFI asked me to meet him at the airport. I thought this might be belated official recognition of my crusade, but it turned out that since Liam O'Leary had left, I was the only person likely to recognise the old man.

My new assistant, Peter Smith (who later directed *Private Enterprise* and the BBC series *Bread and Blood*), was a great asset; he spoke fluent French, and owned a tape recorder. So he came with me, together with Mme Camus of Unifrance Film, in a chauffeur-driven car laid on by the BFI. Gance's plane was delayed, and I stood with Peter on the terminal roof, a long-focus lens fitted to my 16mm camera, taking no chances and filming every aircraft that came in from France, every elderly gentleman that emerged.

We expressed serious doubts about his ability to introduce *J'accuse* at the NFT that evening. 'He'll be far too tired,' we agreed. 'After all, he *is* seventy-five!'

Two hours late, Gance's Trident at last arrived and I filmed the distant figure, with the unmistakable mane of white hair, trudging across the tarmac. When he emerged from the customs hall, he looked fresh and well and he still had that mischievous smile and the endearing glint in his eye. Mme Camus introduced herself, and Peter filmed with my camera as I greeted him. He recognised me from our last meeting — 'when you were *that* high!'

Knowing that he planned to stay in London for only one night, we conducted an interview in the back of the car, and he answered questions all the way to the Savoy Hotel. Fascinating stories ... how he had used strikers from the Renault factory in the Marseillaise sequence ... how one man, thinking he wasn't wanted, threw himself in the Seine ... how he got the idea for the triptychs ... We were enthralled.

At Hammersmith, we discovered the recorder had stopped. Peter jumped out and bought new batteries. When we reached the Savoy, Peter attempted some more shots but the manager said, 'Not in here, sir. Not under any circumstances.' Then he whispered into Mme Camus's ear that the gentleman would not be permitted in the bar without a tie. Gance, who was wearing a polo-necked sweater, grinned. 'Oh well, if they want a rope round my neck.'

At dinner before the show, Gance began talking of his life under the German occupation: 'The Germans thought I was a Jew because someone, whom I will not name, denounced me because he wanted to get rid of me. I felt the shadow of the Gestapo. My name is Abel, and although my family has been Catholic for three hundred years, I myself do not practise. So they insisted on proof; they came to interrogate me and insisted on birth certificates. I had to trace right the way back. I went back sixteen stages and had thirty-two birth certificates. It took three months to go through the archives. When the Germans had this proof, they apologised. Most of the important people, including a collaborator who, like many collaborators, became a minister afterwards, were very apologetic. The Germans asked me if I would come to Berlin to make a film for them — I would be given all facilities. The next day I left for Spain — crossed the Pyrenees on foot. Life there was hard because they were hand in glove with the Germans. I practically starved. Eventually, Manolete [a celebrated matador], who refused to make a film with anyone, accepted to make one with me. I knew nothing about bullfighting, but I wrote the script anyway. I put cameras all the way round the arena, shooting through holes in the barrier. But Manolete was injured … the film was never completed.'

After dinner, we walked across Waterloo Bridge to the NFT. The queue had been held back a few minutes so Gance would be sure to see it. When everyone had been seated, Gance came on the stage and made a charming speech, which Richard Roud translated. A tremendous ovation surprised and delighted him. He had not expected such a reception. Towards the end of *J'accuse*, when Victor Francen makes his great pronouncement about the inevitability of the next war, Gance whispered to me, 'Not bad as a prophecy.'

At the end, after the shattered faces of the war dead — played by Les Gueules Cassées, disfigured war veterans — had marched upon the living, there was a stunned silence, followed by applause. We filed out. Photographs were taken in the foyer, and people flocked around to congratulate Gance. Among them was Bessie Love, Griffith's star.

'Ah, Griffith,' said Gance. 'The only man in the cinema I truly admired. The one great giant.' Almost instinctively, I was about to add another name. But it was Abel Gance talking. For once, there was no need for correction.

The BFI had assured me that for this season the Cinémathèque would be sending their best version of *Napoleon* — an original tinted print. John Huntley, in charge of programming, rang me in alarm a few days before the screening. The print had arrived and was seventeen reels long — a total of about 15,000 ft. 'It will last all night!' he said. It seemed to match the length of Dr Elliott's version — at 16 fps it would last for nearly four hours. At sound speed, 24 fps, it would only take two and a half. John Huntley decided it should be shown at 16 fps.

The audience was warned, and Huntley explained that the print had been put together by Marie Epstein of the Cinémathèque from six other prints. (There was, of course, no triptych.) This version, much of it original footage, tinted and toned, proved the other to have been a cruel joke. The standards I had hoped for were far exceeded. The pictorial beauty was so much greater in this pin-sharp print, enhanced by the emotional use of tints and tones, blues and reds and greens which somehow intensified the grandeur, the excitement and even the tiny details with which the picture was so richly packed.

But on the back of my programme notes, I scribbled details of what I knew was missing. 'Opening shot … no sign of rapid-cut snowball fight … great chunk gone in pillow fight — including the splitting up of the screen into separate shots … titles are in wrong place … the all-important introduction of Napoleon in the Marseillaise sequence is missing.' There was a great deal either missing or in the wrong place after that, including a whole reel from Toulon and vital scenes of the escape from Corsica. And, curiously, this seventeen-reel version was different in many respects to Dr Elliott's seventeen-reel version.

However, it was the best version I had yet seen, and no one could deny its impact. I was so impressed that I went for the second show, and when it was all over, I wrote down my reactions:

'Masterpiece is the word. The only fault I can find with it — and that's only if I'm *very* objective — is a certain tendency to self-indulgence. But that's the easiest thing to forgive when you can't get enough of such breathtaking artistic splendour. I never knew the film was so *funny*! But Napoleon's romance with Joséphine is hilarious, and there are wonderful comic touches throughout the picture. The direction is superhuman — how he kept up his energy after pouring himself into the picture so completely is beyond me. Although I must say, if I saw any of my rushes looking like any part of *Napoleon* I would be stimulated beyond imagination! I've seen the film so often that the characters are old friends to me — I've known them for twelve years. When I see them in new sequences, it's as delightful as meeting people you're very fond of in new surroundings ... Of course, I'm in love with the whole film. It's part of me. It has influenced me. I shoot my action sequences to look like Gance's. I refer to it when I talk about the ultimate in motion picture production. It may be too long — but when you're in love with someone, you can't see too much of them... and it's the same with me and *Napoléon vu par Abel Gance*. As far as I'm concerned, it can last all night.'

The Gance season was presented in chronological order; after a few unimportant thrillers, Gance suddenly flared into a blaze of talent which lasted just ten years, from *Mater Dolorosa* through *J'accuse* and *La Roue* to *Napoleon*. It seemed to end with the coming of sound, perhaps because he found it hard to adjust to sound,[1] perhaps because the producers would no longer give him the freedom he needed. Some of his sound films were effective, but none of them contained more than a hint of the old genius.

I decided to incorporate a lengthy chapter on Gance in my book *The Parade's Gone by* ... There was no justification for it in a book about Hollywood, but I felt that if I didn't sneak it in somehow, the material would never be published. A book by Roger Icart — *Abel Gance* — was of enormous value in providing background. To expand the chapter, I went to see Gance, with Peter Smith, in Paris. In his apartment, packed with books, paintings and photographs, the walls peppered with the quotations he was so fond of — he called them his static explosions — Gance talked in riveting detail about his career. I incorporated a great deal of this into the book, but at this stage the manuscript was turned down by every publisher I sent it to.

Meanwhile, Nelly Kaplan had made a documentary called *Abel Gance — hier et demain*. It dealt with his entire career. It contained some extraordinary material, and in the French version Gance himself spoke the commentary. However, I felt a fascinating documentary could be made on the silent films alone. As usual, this idea was turned down with monotonous regularity by the TV companies. But then I had a stroke of good fortune. I met a BBC producer named Barrie Gavin, who was starting a series called *The Movies*; he arranged that I should produce the film on Gance independently for the series — to run for half an hour, at a budget of £1,000.

I had the inestimable help, as production manager, of Johanna Suschitzky, who had been the continuity girl on *It Happened Here* (and who had married the cameraman). She and I began negotiations with the Cinémathèque, and we learned that what someone said about the Irish — 'they have a word for mañana, but it lacks the same sense of urgency' — could apply just as well to the French. After a great deal of *angoisse*, we were handed over to Marie Epstein, a tiny, bird-like woman, the sister of Jean Epstein, who had made pictures herself in the 1930s with Jean Benoît-Levy. At last things began to happen. When we explained that time and money were running out, she worked very hard to enable us to view the films and mark up the sections we required.

Then, acting on a hint from Gance, we requested some material entitled *Autour de Napoléon*. Marie Epstein carried in a pile of rusty cans. Inside, in separate rolls, were shots of *Napoleon* in production. Johanna and I sat in front of the viewing machine, stunned at our good fortune. All the claims I would otherwise have had to make in commentary were substantiated here before our eyes. Gance had indeed amassed an incredible range of equipment — cameras operated by remote control, cameras mounted on mobile platforms, cameras suspended on overhead cables ... And of course this record of the production was in itself an innovation.

In our excitement, we could not resist calling upon Gance once more. He was overwhelmed with work on his current project, *Christopher Columbus* (which he had last worked on in 1939), but he welcomed us to his new apartment in Boulogne.

'I always had at least two cameras,' he explained, 'and when the extra cameraman had nothing to do, he would shoot the unit at work. Film was cheap in those days, and I knew that one day I'd have someone sitting beside me asking, "How was that done?" I thought of the future.'

His career was so full of interest for film people, I tried to persuade him to write his memoirs.

'An autobiography would be difficult. Such books are usually full of "I" and "Me". It becomes boring to read people talking about themselves. They tend to become "What I have done" rather than "What I was *trying* to do."

Autobiographies contain the qualities one should struggle against — vanity, pride and self-love. Once you get caught up, your narrative revolves around a finished person, instead of what we all are — incomplete, striving.'

I asked him if he ever looked back at his old films.

'No,' he said, 'I just see the faults.'

As far as *Christopher Columbus* was concerned, he was grateful that he had not made it when he completed the first scenario in 1939. 'I didn't have the maturity of outlook,' he said.

Eventually, he pointed to the piles of papers and books. 'If I distract myself, I am like a mariner who has to steer his boat back on course again. It sounds easy, but it is not.'

He also bemoaned his age. 'I could bear one seven, but not two!'

We arranged a date for the filming, and he gave us the address of Albert Dieudonné, ringing him up to explain the project. As we were leaving, he remembered something. From the mass of papers on his desk, he fished out a single sheet which he had prepared for the forthcoming interview. It was his list of preferences among his films, plays and books:

Order of preference:

1 *Prisme* [a book published in 1930, part autobiography, part philosophical sketches]
2 *La Victoire de Samothrace* [a play written in 1912]
3 *La Divine Tragédie* [unrealised film]
4 *Cyrano et d'Artagnan* [his 1964 film]
5 *La Roue*
6 *J'accuse* [he did not distinguish which version]
7 *Napoleon*
8 *Beethoven* [1936 film with Harry Baur]

As for the rest, there is no point in talking of them. They are without value. Perhaps *Christopher Columbus* might be placed between *Cyrano* and *La Roue*.

Abel Gance, September 1967

Two points to discuss which interest me:
   One must think about it [series of great translators of religion]
and an autobiography
   Why have I been only what I am?

21·Vin de l'Empereur

I had been warned that Albert Dieudonné was still obsessed by Napoleon, and I half expected to meet an eccentric from a Raimu comedy. Admittedly, he had a bust of the Emperor on the desk of his elegant Paris apartment. Admittedly, he delivered every year at the Tuileries the speech made by Napoleon on his return from Elba. But Dieudonné, handsome and genial, had too strong a sense of humour to be dismissed as a 'character'.

He gave the impression that playing Napoleon throughout one's life might be unusual, but he had enjoyed it immensely. And he was full of stories of actors who had gone mad after playing the Emperor. One of them was Max Charlier, who, he said, roamed the countryside asking peasants whether he was taxing them too heavily. He wrote a play about Charlier, *Moi, Napoléon*, which won an award and which was performed in every French-speaking country. Dieudonné played the lead in it two hundred times.

After *Napoleon*, Dieudonné might have become one of the great stars of the European cinema, but he turned down parts with which he felt out of sympathy. He was committed to reviving the true image of Bonaparte.

For a while, he hoped to film his novel *Le Tzar Napoléon*,[1] but this remained a dream. He played Napoleon opposite Arletty in *Madame Sans-Gêne*, and he devoted himself to lectures on the Napoleonic era; one was called 'When I Had the Honour of Being Napoleon'.

When we filmed the interview at his apartment, Dieudonné was only too keen to co-operate. He was relaxed and expansive, and gave an excellent performance — he even delivered the speech to the Army of Italy, which he knew by heart, in his splendidly resonant and commanding voice.

Next we filmed Gance, who greatly alarmed me at the beginning by directing the interview. He asked us to film him reading from *Prisme*. I could imagine nothing less compelling than someone reading from a book, but there was no point in arguing. We filmed it, and when he had finished, he allowed me to take over. He gave us a superb interview, full of stark tragedy — the war, the death of Ida — but brightened by shafts of humour. Johanna asked the questions and cameraman Chris Menges twisted himself into contorted positions to capture the best setups. He also took a series of remarkable stills.

The Cinémathèque, meanwhile, had erected a Maginot line to prevent our getting a foot of the film. Money, copyright ... Langlois mobilised every possible obstacle to stop our project. This proved to be characteristic of the unlovable side of Langlois, and is a trait often inbred in great collectors. We sent money, clearances, agreements, *anything* to secure the film without which we would have no programme.

At the time I thought this behaviour was outrageous, but having dealt with many archives since, I have discovered that most of them treat their customers like this. It is an exaggerated form of self-protection, but it is a grave flaw of the archive movement and one which has undoubtedly sup-pressed many worthwhile projects.

Before we returned to England, we went to the Cinémathèque to try to sort out our problems. We managed to see Marie Epstein. She could not reverse an executive decision, but she had assembled *Autour de Napoléon* and we were able to see the amazing footage again. But would we ever be able to use it? The suspense was heightened when I started peering into some more rusty cans Mlle Epstein had left on a table. She shooed me away, saying there was nothing much in them. As soon as she was out of the room, I opened a can and pulled out a roll. There were some shots of Gance with army officers at Toulon. A few sections of tests for the burning of the fleet. These odd pieces fell away revealing a longer roll.

I pulled out a few feet and held the film up to the light. With a shock, I saw blurred shots of small boys fighting in the snow. I realised this could only be the long-lost climax to the snowball fight. Referred to by Bardèche and Brasillach as 'a masterpiece of rapid cutting', the snowball fight had always seemed very tame to me. I suspected the heart of the sequence had been removed, but could never find any proof. As soon as she returned, Mlle Epstein realised what I'd been doing, and protested indignantly. But she had a soft heart, despite her adherence to Langlois's rules, and she relented and obligingly coaxed the fragile sequence through the machine.

I would count the few minutes it took to watch the roll as among the most exciting I have ever spent. For me, it was the equivalent of the famous discovery of a Leonardo da Vinci sketchbook in a Spanish museum. The sequence went beyond any other experiment in the film. It represented the most sophisticated editing I had ever seen. The snowball fight having been established in straightforward long shots and closeups, Gance now orches-trated furious, hand-held tracking shots of the fighting with closeups of the young Napoleon issuing orders. The sequence was impressionistic and avant-garde. The cuts set up a definite rhythm, and rhythm built to a frenzy as the closeups of Napoleon came faster and faster. Gradually, his face was suffused with the smile of victory, and Gance increased the pace until he was literally intercutting single frames to produce the effect of a visual machinegun.

When the sequence was over, Johanna and I had been so exhilarated we were exhausted. We thanked Mlle Epstein profusely. But we could not help wondering why that sequence should have been wrapped up with trims and outtakes, and forgotten.[2]

Back in London, we viewed our rushes and were appalled to find that the equipment, rented in Paris, had been defective; the Dieudonné interview was almost entirely unusable. I considered threatening the company with legal action, but they knew my financial situation, and it would do nothing to restore the lost footage. We were very cast down.

To add insult to injury, the negotiations with the Cinémathèque and the French laboratories had led to so many months of delay that *The Movies* had come to the end of its run. For a while, it seemed as though we would have no showing on television at all, but I reckoned without our producer, Barrie Gavin. He simply switched the film from one series to another — from *The Movies* to *Omnibus* — doubled the budget (to £2,000) and extended the programme from half an hour to fifty minutes, which enabled me to devote more screen time to *Napoleon*. I sent some of the increased budget to Gance, and made sure he would continue to receive money from the film as long it continued to be shown.

When I heard that the Cinémathèque's tinted print of *Napoleon* was to be presented at the New York Film Festival by Richard Roud, I wrote him a long letter detailing the missing or muddled sections. It was a futile gesture — he could hardly have read it out to the audience while Henri Langlois stood next to him. Fortunately, however mutilated, the film had a strong impact. 'Probably no film of the era', wrote Stuart Byron in *Variety*, 'achieved such a quantitative grandeur.'[3] Nine other Gance films were shown at the same festival, including *Marie Tudor* (1965), which had been made for television.

'One of the most useful jobs accomplished by the younger critics of *Les Cahiers du cinéma*,' wrote Roud in the programme, 'was the rehabilitation of Abel Gance. Of course, he was a name in the history books, but that was all. Truffaut, Rivette and Godard actually decided to see all of Gance's films and discovered — as is usually the case — that the books were all wrong. That Gance had not stopped with *Napoleon*. That even if Gance had not invented Polyvision, he would have been one of the world's most important directors.'

Roud's season was another crucial stage in the campaign.

22 · Somebody Has to Do It

February 1968 – a bombshell from Bernard Eisenschitz, calling from Paris: 'Henri Langlois is out of the Cinémathèque!' Apparently, the Board had voted against Langlois on a financial issue. He had taken it as a negative vote and resigned. An enormous row broke out and a press campaign was mounted to restore Langlois to his position. The younger members of the film community, who had benefited from the showings at the Cinémathèque, took to the streets, in a rehearsal for the uprising of May 1968. One of the first to be injured was Jean-Luc Godard, when he jumped on a policeman from the roof of a taxi. Steel-helmeted riot police were posted outside the Cinémathèque. A new administration conducted the press around the film storage areas to show them the cans of rotting film. Nevertheless, petitions of protest contained the names of virtually everyone concerned with films, including that of Abel Gance, who also wrote a crusading article in support of Langlois.[1]

Langlois was eventually reinstated by the Board. The Minister of Culture, André Malraux, then withdrew the representatives of the State from the Board and withdrew some of its financial support, starting an official state archive at Bois d'Arcy.

Despite all the trouble in Paris, Richard Arnell, who was organising a festival of multiscreen films in London, persuaded the Cinémathèque to send over the triptychs of *Napoleon*. His collaborator was the Canadian animator George Dunning, who made *The Yellow Submarine*. The print arrived in poor condition and I offered to repair it. Dunning handed over the three cans. Once I settled down to work I wished I hadn't been so free with my offer. Many sprocket holes were torn and in order that they should pass easily through the projector, they had to be repaired individually. With eight to a frame, that was tedious work. The tape refused to stick because the reels were soaked in oil. It took several days to clean and repair all three reels. They were also out of synchronisation. A few more adjustments, some black spacing, and they were ready for the public show at the Odeon, Leicester Square.

I had never seen the triptychs projected. They were scheduled to be the last item on the programme – following the most sophisticated examples of multiscreen, shown as they were meant to be shown, in colour, on a vast screen with full stereophonic sound. *Napoleon* came on silent, in black and white, on a diminished screen, when the audience's eyes and ears were numbed from the rest of the programme. It being a weekday morning, the house was full of advertising and media people.

The opening shot was a sweeping panorama of the ragged Army of Italy. A subtitle appeared: 'Garde à vous!' And the audience tittered. When Bonaparte called out, via a subtitle, 'Soldats!' the audience shrieked with merriment. It was silent, like the old comedies; one was expected to laugh. At a closeup of Joséphine they hooted. And they sniggered infuriatingly to the very end.

There was loud and enthusiastic applause, but nothing could erase the memory of that maddening, mindless laughter. Those who found it arduous to make a 15-second commercial relaxed at the Odeon, Leicester Square, and mocked one of the great achievements of cinema history.

In spite of the audience, I was extremely impressed by the triptychs; it seemed that Gance had thought of virtually everything it was possible to do with the process. And some of the other films would have benefited from a viewing of Gance's work. Once again I thought, 'This film gets better and better, the more I see of it. Somehow, it *must* be reconstructed ...'

Being a collector, it crossed my mind that someone should copy the triptychs before sending them back to the dangerous muddle of the Cinémathèque. But I myself had neither the money nor the nerve.

One afternoon, George Dunning asked me to come to his office in Dean Street, Soho, a few minutes from my own cutting room. He was a quiet, charming and laconic man, suggesting a university professor more than a film producer. 'Look,' he said, 'Dick Arnell and I have returned the triptychs to Paris.' He saw my face fall. 'But I had them copied before they went.' I tried to look shocked that he would commit such piracy. He added, 'I think you ought to look after them.' I could not conceal my delight. It had obviously cost him a great deal of money, yet he was *giving* me the three cans of dupe negative. It was hard to express my gratitude, and yet I felt a new sense of responsibility. For the gift was a symbol of trust. The reconstruction had involuntarily started.

Not long afterwards, I was saddened to learn of George Dunning's death. He was a man after my own heart, and I was determined not to let him down. I took great care of his triptychs, looking forward to the moment they might be augmented.

Three weeks later, my documentary *Abel Gance — the Charm of Dynamite* went out on BBC-2. One BBC executive, who had previously never heard of Gance, now informed me that he was 'the cinema's original revolutionary and its greatest orator'.

The Times called it 'a stunningly good profile ... It showed Gance to be a superb editor, a remarkable technical innovator ... What was notable was his lack of bitterness about the way his innovations have been exploited by others. "I feel like Aesop," he said, without a hint of malice. "He may have written the fables, but La Fontaine got the money out of them."'[2]

My first book, *The Parade's Gone By ...*, was at last published in October 1968 and I was able to send a copy to Gance, together with some of the reviews of *The Charm of Dynamite*. This was being shown at the ICA cinema in London, thanks to Derek Hill who had become the film's distributor.

In reply, Gance wrote on the notepaper printed for *Napoleon* in 1925:

October 30th, 1968

Thanks, dear Kevin, for your letter and for the tremendous newspaper articles. M. Ledoux — director of the Brussels Cinémathèque — has just phoned to say that *The Charm of Dynamite* is a 'chef d'oeuvre' and has just been shown with *enormous* success. He tells me the audience were completely stupefied to find me because they thought I had disappeared!! Ledoux is astounded that the film has not yet been shown in France. Tell me when you can send it to me, or better, come to show it to me, because I should love to embrace you to thank you. A thousand thanks for the elixir of rejuvenation which you pour into my heart.

Your friend, Abel Gance.

He added on another sheet:

'Strange coincidences! I was just about to write to you to thank you for the articles when I received the phone call from Brussels. I went back to writing my letter to you, and I was just putting it into an envelope when the postman delivered a parcel; it was your beautiful book. That dedication and the many pages devoted to me — there is no longer any such thing as chance. You are my destiny!

'So I am taking the opportunity to ask you to help me. I have been working for a year on my most beautiful work, *Christopher Columbus*. This and *The Divine Tragedy* are the two best works of my life.'

And he spelled out the kind of financial backing he needed, expecting me to find it. I warned him that I had been notably unsuccessful in raising money for my own projects. I was an appalling businessman and he could not have asked anyone less suited. However, I did what I could. I wrote to various organisations; only the BBC replied, saying the *Columbus* project was far too expensive. It was a miserable duty having to communicate nothing but bad news.

Eventually, I arranged to show the documentary to Gance and his family in Paris. Bernard Eisenschitz acted as interpreter; he translated the narration, and at the end there was a chorus of 'très bien'. Gance said he was amazed to see the rapid-cut snowball fight, which he had not seen for forty years. 'Where did you get it from?' he asked.

'From a rusty can at the Cinémathèque,' I said, tactlessly, and Bernard translated. At this, a small figure leaped from the shadows and I recognised Marie Epstein. I could have died. She had been kind and helpful, and I would not have offended her for the world. She indignantly defended the Cinémathèque; they had no rusty cans! Gance said he wanted to get hold of it because he had been asked by André Malraux to reissue *Napoleon* for the bicentennial of Bonaparte's birth in 1969.

'I want to re-edit Brienne,' he said, 'and I feel as if I have a finger missing.'

As an unexpected encore, he screened sections of Brienne and the Bal des Victimes which Mlle Epstein had printed for him from the original negative. The quality was superb, and they contained shots I had never seen before (and, sadly, was never to see again). But the negative was showing tell-tale signs of decomposition.

Afterwards, Gance took Bernard and me to lunch, and expanded on his achievements.

'When you look at the technique I used then, you can see I thought of using everything,' he said, without a trace of modesty. 'What do they do today when they make a film? They place a camera in front of the actors, and they film. There's no life in it. It's true, isn't it? I'm not saying I invented everything in the cinema, but I did give it a good start. If people had followed me, the cinema would have made rapid progress. There is one man who did follow me, actually two. First, Eisenstein, who came twice to see me and who told me it was from *La Roue* that he learned his art. Then Kurosawa, who was also very enthusiastic. Then Dovzhenko ... also Pudovkin and Ekk. But it was mainly Eisenstein, Kurosawa and Dovzhenko who really took aesthetic lessons from me.

'I have a fixation about Polyvision. One should be able to make a film entirely in Polyvision—but I never had the means. I would prove that Polyvision is really the language of the cinema, because now the eye is so rapid that one can see three screens simultaneously. Perhaps not all the time, but let's say about half the time during a long film. With three screens you have a new visual grammar, and you have a synthesis of images—that is, when the multiple images meet the eye, there is a kind of visual explosion, a lightning spark in the brain.'

I put to him the possibility of my coming back to France to sort out the Cinémathèque's print of *Napoleon*—that snowball fight could be restored, the muddled titles corrected and sequences put in the right order. Gance said, 'Yes, so long as Langlois says yes.'

Langlois, of course, did not say yes. Instead, he wrote a letter: 'I think you will be happy to know that there will soon be an extraordinary gala at the Opéra—the projection of the definitive version of *Napoleon*, established by Gance thanks to a grant from the French government. Thus your wishes and those of all the faithful supporters of Abel Gance are fulfilled.'[3]

I wrote back explaining that this so-called definitive version would in fact be the 1935 sound version, whereas my interest lay in the original 1927 silent film. The BFI had arranged a special lecture for Gance, to be followed by the film. It was vital that the film be reconstituted. The National Film Archive had blown Dr Elliott's 17·5mm print up to 35mm; this could provide some of the missing footage. 'I would be happy to pay my fare over, and the hotel bill, to do this important work. But I must have the full co-operation of the Cinémathèque.'[4]

Langlois did not answer. And the BFI got no answer when they made their requests for the print. Nor did Gance; he had to cancel a trip to Holland and Belgium because Langlois would not release the print. Something very strange was going on. The Film Co-ordinator at the BFI, Pam Balfry, telephoned repeatedly, and received only evasive replies. We began to suspect they had lost it, and this was confirmed when Pam Balfry called Richard Roud. He had inside knowledge, and explained that the Cinémathèque could not locate the film. He thought it must still be in the United States.

We contacted Lincoln Center, where the film had been shown during the New York Film Festival, and tracked one of the Festival people to her home.

'What a pity you didn't call earlier,' she said. 'It's been at the airport for months.'

'Is it still there?'

'Yes, now—this very minute it's being freighted to Montreal.'

'Is there a show there?'

'No.'

'Why is it going?'

'I don't know. I tried to persuade Langlois to take them all back.'

'*Them?*'

'Yes, all of Gance's films. But he wouldn't pay the freight.'

When we called the Cinémathèque with this news, they offered to send their 'second-best' print, which we refused. Somehow *Napoleon* was extricated from a customs warehouse at Kennedy airport and it arrived at the

National Film Theatre with strict instructions from Langlois that Kevin Brownlow was not to touch it. ('Who is he?' he had apparently demanded. 'How old? How can he know how *Napoleon* should go?')

It transpired that Langlois, desperate to keep his films from being seized by the government, had squirrelled them away in hideouts of which only he and Mary Meerson knew the location. The nine features and two shorts of Abel Gance were abandoned in America to rot quietly away in the vault of some distant freight agent.

Unfortunately for Langlois, Kevin Brownlow was officially requested by the BFI to handle the print. The NFT projectionists announced that there was no way it could go through their machines, so appalling was its condition. I had repaired the triptychs; would I take a look at this? I raced over to the NFT where projectionists were hauling yards of shredded film out of the reels. I repaired as much as I could and cut out sections which were irreparably damaged.

I was angry at the state of the print, which had been projected so often and so carelessly that on some reels sprocket holes were hanging from the oil-soaked film like miniature hammocks. Before the big show I went on stage and told the audience they were in at the death of a film. I produced from a cardboard box yards of torn film, which I referred to as 'Langlois confetti'. And I read them an apology from Gance, whose doctor had advised him not to make the trip.

On March 23rd, 1969, the packed house — with many people standing — received the film with great enthusiasm. And fortunately, the print went through without further damage. I had the best of the reactions translated and sent them to Gance.

There were two shows. Before the next, the most essential task was to attempt a rescue operation on the torn sections I had removed from the reels. Some were too far gone, and I have their grim evidence to this day. But to do the job properly, I had to take the film over to my cutting room. Upon examining it closely, I noticed a curious thing: the print was on *safety* stock. Film was normally printed on the highly inflammable nitrate stock. The French, however, had never forgotten the 1897 Charity Bazaar fire when hundred of deaths were attributed to nitrate film catching light. The French authorities insisted on safety stock as soon as it became available, although the nitrate stock continued to circulate because safety stock was so expensive. However, the contract between SGF and G-M-G specified safety stock.

Some reels were in such an advanced state of disintegration that I doubted they would ever be projected again. I spent an entire morning on one reel, endeavouring to restore the jagged sprocket holes with Mylar tape. Deep into the task, I asked myself why was I doing this? The print would go back

The worst of the damage

and be damaged all over again. I decided to do something about it, once and for all.

I telephoned Alf Dossett at Studio Film Labs and explained the situation. He said he could do nothing to help. I pressed him with the urgency of the task. The print *had* to go back. The film *had* to be saved. Dossett finally agreed to put some men on to overtime to copy it. Those men managed to do the entire job over the weekend. The work took all the money I had — £800 — but there seemed no alternative. I was usually broke at this period, but I had been supervising editor on *Charge of the Light Brigade* (Tony Richardson) for some months, and I had directed a handful of commercials. So Woodfall, Sparklet soda syphons and Wolsey socks paid for *Napoleon*.

I ferried the print back to the NFT for the second show, which was another success, and it was subsequently returned to the Cinémathèque in considerably better condition than it was received. An act such as mine was extremely reprehensible, but I have never regretted it. For that print, so beautifully tinted and toned, eventually disappeared — presumed to have been destroyed in the last big Cinémathèque fire.

23 · On the Firing Line

1969 was a momentous year for me. In August, I married Virginia Keane (an Irish girl, unconnected with films) and soon afterwards began serious work on the reconstruction of *Napoleon*.

At the same time, Gance was struggling with his own reconstruction and suffering from producer trouble. While I was lengthening my version, he was reducing his. It must have made him despair to be told how to assemble a film he had already made twice. His producer insisted the Double Storm be shortened and Brienne removed. Gance asked me to write an antedated letter, as if from the NFT show, saying how admired these scenes had been and how essential they were to the film. I did so, intrigued that the reaction of a new generation meant so much to him. It transpired that the reason he was embarking on this project at all was because of the adulatory comments from the shows in London and New York.

I thought it a paradox that enthusiasm for the silent film should make him turn it into a sound film. But the future had always concerned him more than the past. I felt obliged to help him in any way I could. He told me he needed the snowball fight; the Cinémathèque were being 'very difficult' and Mlle Epstein was denying all knowledge of its existence. I went to see her on his behalf, and explained that by some means or other, Gance would get the sequence — even if I had to blow up the 16mm print she had supplied to me. That made up her mind for her. She agreed to make a fine grain positive provided I ordered it, I received it and I paid for it. Nothing could have suited me better ... It took ages but eventually an excellent fine grain arrived. I made two negatives; one went to Gance. The other became the first new sequence to be inserted into what I was starting to call my reconstruction.

It was curious that both Gance and I should have been working on a reconstruction at the same time, and also incredibly lucky. I doubt if I could ever have achieved my version, had I not had Gance to fight some of my battles by proxy. For when I asked if I could have access to his negatives, he agreed, but explained that so far he had still not managed to prise all his material from the Cinémathèque. 'You need two revolvers,' he said, 'one for Langlois, one for Marie Epstein.'

Rather belatedly, Langlois had turned protective. Recalling that Gance had cut his original negative into the 1935 version, he was trying to stop him doing so again. I couldn't think why. He didn't have any original negative.[1] Since Gance now wanted only dupe negatives from the prints he held, I assumed that Langlois had been stalling because, until we retrieved the original print from Kennedy airport, he was lacking his most substantial version.

Besides working on his new version, Gance was trying to set up *Christopher Columbus* and *La Divine Tragédie*. Despite my earlier failure, he asked me to help him find backing. I soon realised what he had gone through trying to set up *Napoleon*. The humiliating arrogance of the very rich towards those looking for money has to be experienced to be believed. On one occasion, Gance had the idea of casting Richard Burton and Elizabeth Taylor in *Columbus*, and asked me to check their availability. I spoke to their agent, Hugh French, and when I mentioned that Abel Gance would be producing and directing he lost his temper and demanded to know why I was wasting his time. It turned out he had never heard of him.

I managed to secure small sums for Gance by other methods, and thanks to the energetic distribution of Derek Hill, *The Charm of Dynamite* earned regular sums for us both. And it helped to introduce his name to those who had never heard it before. I took a print to America, where it was shown by George Stevens jr, director of the American Film Institute, at the AFI's Beverly Hills headquarters. There were two screenings, one for Fellows of the AFI and one for professional directors, cameramen and screenwriters. There was a remarkable turnout: historian and screenwriter DeWitt Bodeen, art director Ben Carré, directors Tay Garnett, Rouben Mamoulian, John Rich, George Stevens sr, Jacques Tourneur, William Wellman and William Wyler; cameramen Hal Mohr and Charles van Enger and producer Daniel Selznick.

The reaction could not have been better. They applauded during the film — especially at the multiscreen pillow fight. (Hollywood had just begun to use the device again.) I wrote down the comments and sent them to Gance. George Stevens sr: 'There has never been such vitality, such passion on the screen before or since Gance. I had read about his work; I never for a moment thought it would be so shattering.' William Wyler: 'I thought his work was fantastic. What an incredible man.' Charles van Enger (cameraman for Vidor, Seastrom, Lubitsch): 'That guy was doing things in 1925 we haven't thought of yet.'

The students said they had read Gance's name, but had never dreamed how revolutionary he was. 'We have to start all over,' said one.

Gance wrote to say that the letter was 'the most magnificent of gifts' and he had been extremely touched by the tributes. However, he had reached a crisis. André Malraux had given him all that remained in his small cultural budget before he left. The money was spent; what could he do? The work would be ten times more interesting than the silent film, but editing would have to stop at the end of the week unless he found more money. He also alerted Daniel Selznick. He and I were involved in the AFI Oral History Project and we discussed the matter. He said, 'If I could achieve this, it would be the greatest thing that anyone at this studio [Universal] could ever do.' As for myself, I was even further out of the financial swing in the USA than I was in England.

Selznick had no success, and nor did I. In April 1970, Gance wrote to say that after a great many tribulations, his situation was improving. And he told me a heartening story. 'François Truffaut came to see me and a couple of days after his visit a cheque and a letter arrived. The letter said, "If I had had to pay for all the tickets to the cinema where I learned my business, it would add up to about this much. It's not a gift, just the price of the tickets." I was extremely moved.'

Truffaut did more.

He telephoned Claude Lelouch, knowing he had made a lot of money from his film *A Man and a Woman*, and explained that Gance was looking for a producer to make his *Napoleon* with sound. Would that interest him?

'I said yes straight away,' said Lelouch, 'because Abel Gance for me was a sort of god of the cinema. His kind of film-making corresponded with what I would like to do. So Gance came to my office and we discussed it and he said it was the fulfilment of his work—the end of his *Napoleon*, because it had been a film he was never able to finish.'

Gance managed to obtain backing from the Centre National de la Cinématographie which, together with further finance from Lelouch, enabled the project to begin again.[2]

Lelouch said that he did not act as a producer in the usual sense.

'Gance had a hatred of producers, because they would not let him do what he wanted. At that time, he had a great desire that people should start talking about him again. He wanted people to be reminded of his *Napoleon*. I let Gance do exactly what he wanted. I was sometimes shocked, but when I respect something, I respect it totally. When I make a film, I cannot bear anyone telling *me* what to do. Not for a moment did I interfere with the creation or make any suggestions. I gave him my crew, my stock and he filmed in my building.'[3]

But the situation was a repeat of 1925. To rescue his film, he had to surrender his rights. Lelouch explained that he had to acquire them so there would not be 'parallel exploitations'.

Gance said that the new film would be called *Bonaparte — the unknown*, and it would involve a great deal of additional shooting. He was due to attend the Cannes Festival, and he would speak about it on television; could he have a copy of *The Charm of Dynamite* so that French TV could help to publicise the new work? Derek Hill sent one over.

Meanwhile, I went to Paris to see Gance, with my friend Bernard Eisenschitz as interpreter, to try to get my hands on the *Napoleon* negatives he had at last secured from the material in the Cinémathèque. The *Sunday Times* was arranging to celebrate the cinema's seventy-fifth anniversary with an exhibition called Cinema City. The organisers, George Perry and Colin Ford, were anxious to screen the reconstructed *Napoleon*.

But Gance was already having more producer trouble — Lelouch was being 'difficult'. 'The battle at the moment is between my lawyers and his to better my personal situation. I shall come out of it triumphantly defeated.'

Gance said that Albert Dieudonné was going to dub his own part. 'He is magnificent. He has the same enthusiasm, and, incredibly, the same voice. He is eighty. He rings me up two or three times a day. Formidable! There is a beautiful future for you two.' He glanced at me and Bernard. 'You see what you can do at this age. I shall be eighty-one in October.'

In a few days, he said, they would have finished dubbing some new characters. But there was a problem with Saint-Just, a character who had fascinated Gance so much he had played the role himself. Saint-Just, young and brilliant, was one of the most powerful, and certainly the most ruthless, of the Revolutionary leaders.

'I am making a parallel', said Gance, 'between Saint-Just's thoughts and Bonaparte's — the things Saint-Just said just before his death at twenty-six no statesman could have said. I am worried whether I could do it. I have to split myself to find the character.'

And Gance asked me point blank whether he could do it. 'Give me an intuitive answer.' I assumed something had been muddled in the translation, and that Gance was asking if his voice would be right for the part after all these years. I said tests would have to be done to filter his voice.

'From the emotional point of view,' said Gance.

'Of course,' I said, bewildered, gradually realising what he meant. *He* would act the part in front of the camera! It was one thing to play a 26-year-old at the age of thirty-six, but it was extremely worrying to think he intended to play the role at eighty-one! I stumbled awkwardly over a cowardly answer, intended as a placebo, hoping that he would never go through with it.

Gance thought the script, which was now 95 per cent authentic, could be translated into English and would be very successful. It could be used as a 'scholarly document'.

'I don't want to sacrifice anything, as what people say is important, but if I have to then it would be worth making the script longer than the final film.'

I asked him about his original script. 'If you put explosive between each page,' he said, 'you'd get an idea of the new film.' He insisted that almost everything in the original script had been shot, but that six or seven reels had been lost, probably during the war. 'The scenes with Mlle Lenormant, with Salicetti, the execution of hostages at Toulon and why the shooting happened[4] — all these have been lost. I didn't replace them with new scenes. They were too weak for the new version.'

Gance thought it would be better to do one book with both the original script and the script for his new film. Again he lightened the discussion by becoming skittish. I had handed him some money from Lorrimer Press, who planned to publish the original scenario (they didn't), and he took the envelope and let his hand drop to the floor, pretending it was too heavy to be carried.

Suddenly, he got up. 'You already took my glasses,' he said, looking for them among the books and papers spread across his desk. Then he began talking about my obsession with his work. 'It is strange that such clarity of vision should come from abroad. But there is such jealousy here in France. You have the feeling of pigmies who, when they look up, complain that their eyes hurt.

'I have suffered through this subject, Bonaparte,' he said. 'I will leave it to posterity. I am now doing my St Helena, but there will be no Arc de Triomphe.'

Gance had been very indulgent about the idea of my restoring *Napoleon*, but it took him a long time to do anything about the negative. It was a case of father saying to an importunate child 'of course you can play in the garden' but being too preoccupied to unlock the door.

I had to have the key, and now, at last, he gave it to me in the form of a letter to his laboratories. He even let me go to the labs myself, giving me carte-blanche to help myself to anything I wanted. It was a tremendous moment, and as I entered the laboratory building on the outskirts of Paris, I was only nervous that I would miss something.

Laboratory workers led me to a woman in a white coat who was apparently in charge. She had read the letter. Now she gave me instructions concerning the hours they stopped for lunch and directions to a convenient café round the corner. She showed me a bench and a rewind, pointed to the piles of cans and left me to it. It was like turning an alcoholic loose in a brewery. It was against the rules for the negative to be run through any sort of viewing machine, so I had to stare at the reversed image and try to recognise fresh sequences. After a while, I acquired intermittent eyesight. The familiar scenes were fairly easy to recognise, but it was extremely exciting to catch sight of a totally unfamiliar shot, and, sometimes, to see those shots becoming shorter and shorter in new sequences of frenetic cutting. I was over-generous in ordering the footage, and I broke out in a cold sweat at the thought of all it was costing me. But I realised I would never again have such an incredible stroke of luck. And I realised, too, that my project could never have been achieved had Gance not been doing his new version, for Langlois would rather have died than surrender his material to me. Gance himself had already had to fight hard enough to get hold of it as it was.

I had long left my old cutting room, and as soon as the material I had ordered began arriving in England, I urgently required editing facilities. I talked the matter over with Colin Ford, one of the Cinema City organisers and the new deputy curator of the NFA. He realised that while Ernest Lindgren remained as Curator, the work would never receive official approval. Such individual initiative did not fit in with his views of how an organisation should conduct itself. So Colin Ford made arrangements for me to come to work at the BFI as soon as Lindgren had left the building. I must admit that the clandestine atmosphere added to the fun.

One of the employees at the BFI, David Meeker, was often in touch with the head of the Royal Belgian Film Archive, Jacques Ledoux, who had a magnificent collection of films stored in a former tram depot in Brussels. Jacques Ledoux was an admirer of Gance, and when he heard what I was up to he took it upon himself to contact every archive in the world which had preserved even a reel of *Napoleon*. Had he not done so, I would have missed many vital scenes which I never knew existed.

The enormous air freight charges—£70 per print, on average—were absorbed by Cinema City, and soon my viewing cubicle at the BFI was swamped with cans.

The archives in Eastern Europe responded first, and fragments came in from elsewhere. One print was nitrate, ripped and torn, repaired with a pre-war version of Sellotape. It was a glutinous mess, the cans apparently full of toast crumbs and treacle. But glinting amongst the dross was a scene missing from all other versions, so I spent long evenings cleaning it and making new sprocket holes with Mylar tape and a razor blade. Alf Dossett at Studio Film Labs worked hard to achieve the very best possible duplicate negative, even bringing an original silent-era printer out of retirement to coax through the most difficult sections.

I put every frame of every print through the Arnoe viewer, and was struck by the variation not only between the episodes, and in the way they were cut together, but between treatments of the same scene. When

Bonaparte is visited in his prison cell at Fort Carré by Salicetti (Philippe Hériat), most versions covered it in a long shot and a couple of closeups. But one print began with a closeup of the grille on the cell door, as Salicetti peered through, then tracked back as he entered, and continued moving until he had reached Bonaparte. Following the interchange of titles, the camera followed Salicetti back towards the door, and ended on the shadow cast by the grille.

As far as I could gather from Gance, once the main version was edited by him and Marguerite Beaugé, and the negative cut by Henriette Pinson, assistants were employed to make up additional negatives for foreign versions, following the master plan. Their selection was not always ideal; they included scenes Gance would never have permitted—scenes marred by poor focus, bad camera operating and, in one case, the sun on a diffusion net reflecting the movement of a cameraman's arm.

As far as choosing which section I should use, I simply went for the best. There was usually no argument. Only occasionally did I exercise my editorial prerogative. For example, in the Corsican sequence, Gance was so proud of having as a location Napoleon's birthplace in Ajaccio that he showed a closeup of the plaque, then dissolved foliage over the plaque to obscure it. I always thought that this shattered the atmosphere, and I was delighted at the chance of censoring it. (I have since put it back.) When we remade the titles I cut out the constant repetition of 'Historique' for a more prosaic reason—every word cost money.

I had the scenario to work from—although I was surprised at the number of scenes which did not appear in it—and I had Dr Elliott's print as a kind of master plan—although there were many scenes which did not appear in that either.

The kind of problems peculiar to film restoration soon became familiar—vital sequences, building to a climax, which were suddenly cut short ... important titles missing, their absence indicated by a jump in the action, with no clue to the wording ... sequences which made no sense at all, and appeared to belong to another film. One of these showed a dimly lit room, a corpse laid out on a palliasse, a woman mourning. It was so out of character with the rest of the film that until I saw it in a sound version I put it to one side and forgot it. It was apparently intended to be used as a symbol for starving France, but I have yet to discover how Gance wove it into the original version.

There were tantalising fragments, sometimes single frames, showing scenes which have long since disappeared—Violine being carried unconscious into Joséphine's room ... Napoleon pawning his watch to buy a pair of boots. And there were excellent episodes, such as Paoli's mobs rallying by torchlight in the centre of Ajaccio, which required shots to start and end the sequence before they could be used.[5]

I discovered what I had always suspected was true: that *Napoleon* contained practically every one of the cinema's visual advances. As more and more sections of the film arrived, I was able to catalogue them — from the extravagant use of the portable camera to the kind of editing which most fascinated me, rapid cutting. Ever since I had first seen it in a Russian silent, I had felt it to be the most powerful use of cinema. But since everyone referred to it as 'Russian cutting', I had assumed Gance was merely copying the style. Not until much later did I realise that he was its true inventor, with *La Roue*.

The experimental 'time cutting' of Alain Resnais — a series of flashes of a character's thoughts — was one thing the picture could hardly have anticipated, or so I thought. This style is associated with *Last Year at Marienbad* (1961). I was therefore very surprised when I found an additional fragment for a scene where Bonaparte meets Joséphine at the Bal des Victimes and saw that Gance had rapid-cut shots of their previous encounters.

I feared that this experiment might act like an alcoholic's cure and finish my enthusiasm forever. Far from it. The surprises were frequent and the opportunity I had to examine the editing increased my admiration. When working on other early films, I have often been tempted to adjust a cut to make it more effective. There was no way to improve the editing of *Napoleon*.

Not that creative cutting was unnecessary. When integrating several sections into one sequence, I occasionally discovered that different takes had been used. The action did not always match, and the only way to make them work was to cut them as one would cut rushes in a feature. Once or twice, I came across signs of incorrect negative cutting in a foreign version which had to be adjusted. And sometimes a scene had been partially destroyed, and the only way to save it was to re-edit it. But always, I followed the editing style of the rest of the film and made the transitions as close to the way Gance and Marguerite Beaugé would have made them as I could.

Gance knew that the triptych would not be seen everywhere, and he edited an alternative ending for the ordinary screen. It was not as long, yet it contained an additional scene. At the review, Tristan Fleuri tells his comrades that he knew the general. As Bonaparte rides up, he steps forward, out of the ranks: 'Tristan Fleuri, general. I was at Brienne.'

Bonaparte looks down at him, then barks an order. 'One pace forward!'

The soldiers step forward and Fleuri is absorbed into the ranks again. He almost faints with disappointment.[6]

I considered adding this to the triptych, but on close examination realised it could not be done. The first striking effect of the triptych is the long shot of the review; Bonaparte and his staff ride through the ranks in the far distance. They vanish out of the frame for a moment, then gallop past the whole panorama, close to camera. The horses seem to ride out of the screen. Fracturing that effect with the Fleuri scene would have been madness. And so it exists only in the alternative version.

The Cinema City organisers who had fixed the big show for October, told me that there was no hope of showing the triptych. The projection box at the National Film Theatre could not accommodate three extra machines. I suggested setting them up in a special booth in the theatre itself, but fire regulations squashed that idea. So we had to settle for the single-screen ending.

At the end of this part of the reconstruction, which had taken twelve weeks of evenings and weekends, my cramped viewing room at the BFI was inundated with film cans. I began to return the various versions to their various owners, via the BFI's despatch department. And as I gathered together in one pile all the reels of the reconstruction, I began to have serious misgivings. The seventeen-reel version had seemed long enough. How would the audience take an even longer version? Few of them would ever have seen a film of more than three hours. I felt that the film improved as the flesh was restored to the skeleton, but the public might find it a colossal bore.

Because of my lack of confidence, I held back a handful of sequences which I thought would hold up the narrative. (They later went back in!) And I made sure that *Napoleon* would be projected at the right speed: not the so-called silent speed of 16 fps, which added a spurious hour or so to the length, but the average speed at which it was shot, 20 fps. The proper speed would make it flow more smoothly, and cut down the overall running time.

Even so, it would last the best part of five hours.

24 · A Whiff of Grapeshot

The reaction to the reconstructed version at the NFT in October 1970 was far more intense than at any other show I had attended. As I wrote to Gance afterwards: 'I cannot do justice to the occasion. I wish you had been there to hear the reaction. The audience sat there for nearly five hours. Many had seen the battered, incomplete print from the Cinémathèque. No one had ever seen such a full copy. There was applause at the end of Part One, there was a deafening ovation at the end. People came up and told me how overwhelmed they were. "I am so moved, I just can't speak" ... "the greatest film I have ever seen."'

Gance replied: 'Once more, you warm my old heart. I answer you in a hurry, as I have to complete this version, which will have a new title, *Bonaparte and the Revolution*. I am deeply moved by what you wrote me about the success of this 45-year-old version. I feel the English public has a sounder view of things, that it is not so sceptical as ours. A thousand thanks to Cinema City for their fine co-operation.'

Cinema City had booked the Cinémathèque print, at my suggestion, not to run it but because there were some short sections where I felt the definition in the reconstructed version could be improved. When the reprinted material was delivered, I checked it and then returned the print to Eddie Fairbrother at BFI Despatch. But I committed an act of gross stupidity – I failed to count the number of cans.

A few weeks later, the Cinémathèque complained to the BFI that three reels were missing. Knowing how disorganised they were, I took no notice beyond checking to ensure they were not in the viewing room. The anguished cries from the Cinémathèque became stronger. By this time I was in California, with the American Film Institute; I suggested the reels might have been sent back with another print by mistake. But when I returned, the prints had been checked and nothing found. And I heard, to my dismay, that the Cinémathèque were screening their print – without the missing reels. They explained that these had been 'stolen by Kevin Brownlow'. This alarmed me because it suggested that the reels had really been lost. And the effect on the film would be devastating.

Shortly afterwards I had the shock of my life. I walked into Studio Film Labs and spotted two reels of the Cinémathèque's *Napoleon* on their shelves. They had failed to return them, and because, like an idiot, I hadn't counted the reels, I had never missed them. There was one reel of Corsica, and one of the Bal des Victimes. I was horrified, and wondered anxiously about the third reel. But over that, the Cinémathèque had erred. There were just two reels missing. Eddie Fairbrother sportingly telephoned Marie Epstein and said the reels had come into their possession 'very mysteriously'. They were rushed over by air freight. I was overcome with embarrassment and shame.

In the midst of that drama occurred another: the première of *Bonaparte and the Revolution* on September 9th, 1971. Gance sent me an invitation, and I flew to Paris with a sense of dread. I was afraid the new film would compound the worst errors of the 1935 version. My fears were amply justified. I have resisted writing or even talking about this until now, for fear of hurting Gance's feelings. But while I count *Napoleon* among my greatest cinematic experiences, *Bonaparte and the Revolution* was among my worst.

Had the film been re-edited and reissued by someone other than Gance, my anger would have been explosive, and I would have fought tooth and nail to have it suppressed. Since it was entirely Gance's responsibility, I could only swallow my desolation and keep quiet.

Gance used a great deal of his original film, but he treated it like a TV documentary producer treats stock footage. Whenever he wanted to make a historical point he cut into the original footage extracts from *Austerlitz*, extracts from his television work such as *Valmy*, scenes from the 1935 *Napoleon Bonaparte*, engravings, letters, pamphlets and new re-enactments. Gance had wrested his romantic, symbolic symphony and tried to turn it into an educational film. The rhythm of the Double Storm was fractured by sync dialogue speeches, some shot in 1934, some in 1969 — static talking heads inserted into that wild movement with all the subtlety of a poleaxe. The silent material had all been post-synched, so that the actors now had voices. Dieudonné provided his own voice, even though he was eighty years old, even though the increase in the speed of the film meant that he had to talk extremely fast. The timbre of his voice conflicted with the youthfulness of the figure on the screen. But more extraordinary, and in the most curiously wilful act I have ever known a film-maker to perpetrate on his own work, Abel Gance once again played Saint-Just.

For the majority of Saint-Just's pronouncements about the achievements of the Revolution, Gance used the original shots with his voice, as recorded in 1934. But the new scene began with Saint-Just, silhouetted in an alcove, delivering the speech. The figure was obviously that of an old man, as was the voice. The cameraman had done all he could to cast a shadow over this perverse performance, but the difference was embarrassingly obvious.

The film lasted four hours forty-five minutes even without Brienne (the snowball fight was inexplicably included at the end), and even without the Tristan Fleuri and Violine episodes, the Pozzo di Borgo–Salicetti subplot and the triptychs. I suffered through every frame. The knack of selecting faces and ensuring that the players are costumed properly had completely left Gance. So had his photographic eye. The new material had that flatly lit look of Merton Park quickies of the 1950s.

The speed problem was not as serious as I had expected, although there were some clumsy attempts at stretch-printing. Live action was occasionally combined with engravings. Stills and frozen frames were used as cutaways.

Was it for this that my reconstruction was to be relegated to the vaults? I saw Gance the next day. With his charming inconsistency, he listened sympathetically when I told him that the Los Angeles Film Festival wanted to present the reconstruction, and that they would finance the shooting of English titles. He agreed that they could do this. What he didn't tell me was that he had sold his rights to Claude Lelouch of Films 13 and he was therefore no longer in control of the film's destiny.

Abel Gance and me, photographed by Chris Menges during the filming of The Charm of Dynamite, *Paris, 1967*

25·A Meeting of Eagles

The reaction to *Bonaparte and the Revolution* divided the critics. Gene Moskowitz, sympathetic to Gance, wrote in *Variety*: 'This is still mainly a fine work of reconstruction and a boon for film students and shows what can be done to save film patrimony, with a definite bow to Lelouch who put up most of the coin and is handling the distribution.'[1] The *Hollywood Reporter* said: 'It is so pompous, it is a better joke than the Marx Brothers.'[2]

The review with the most original viewpoint came from Vincent Canby, in the *New York Times* after the film was shown at the 9th New York Film Festival: 'The emotional effect is both immensely moving and more than a little spooky ... Watching it is like looking through an enchanted telescope that allows us to observe, simultaneously, several different ages of one man, which is actually what we are doing in the case of Gance. We see not only the shifting interests and sensibilities of the director, but also Gance himself, who, at the age of thirty-six, played the revolutionary immoralist Saint-Just. He speaks, however, with the voice of Gance in his forties, and then, quite late in the film, we see the silhouette of Saint-Just — Gance, in a scene shot last year, as Saint-Just stands in a shadowy alcove listening to charges being brought against him on the Convention floor. There's no mistaking the silhouette as that of anyone but an indomitable old man. Yet the scene works beautifully within the context of the drama. Saint-Just is the one leader of the Terror who is firmly convinced that history will acknowledge his brilliance, if not justify his actions, and seeing the almost ghostly silhouette of an old Saint-Just, who was actually guillotined at the age of twenty-six, amounts to another one of Gance's more nervy, poetic projections, with which the film is positively dense.'[3]

In 1972, the Institut Français in London arranged to show *Bonaparte and the Revolution* in the presence of Abel Gance. But Gance had been ill, and wrote asking me to deputise for him. I had no sooner finished reading his letter, however, than the telephone rang — the French Institute said that not only was Gance coming after all, but also Albert Dieudonné!

With the Institute's Anne Berthoud, I met Gance, Dieudonné and Mme Dieudonné at Heathrow airport. Gance looked pale and tired from his illness. 'I have come from St Helena,' he said, wistfully.

Dieudonné, who was in considerably better shape, said, 'I've come from Elba!' As we climbed into the car, he said, 'Don't take me to Waterloo Station or Trafalgar Square.'

En route to the hotel, Gance told me about Lelouch and how he had categorically rejected the possibility of the silent version being shown anywhere, in case it jeopardised the chances of *Bonaparte*. I said I understood, but since my version would be shown perhaps once a year for film students only, would he sign a letter of permission? Gance thought for a moment, then said he felt I ought to have the permission; I deserved it. I handed him a letter I had typed out, and he signed it — to my intense relief. Only much later did I realise that Gance was in no position to do this, as Lelouch now controlled the rights in the silent version as well.

Dieudonné told us that he had not been to England since 1910, when he toured the universities in the British Isles playing the classics. We talked of Bondarchuk's *Waterloo*. Dieudonné did not think much of it. Gance said Bondarchuk was a fine director, but his presentation of Napoleon was bad. He was a much more subtle character. Dieudonné, to my surprise, thought the battles of *Cromwell* were better; 'the cavalry charged into the ranks of the infantry, something you do not see in *Waterloo*.'

That evening, a small exhibition organised in the foyer of the Institute by historian Jacques Deslandes was attracting attention. He had the *Marche Consulaire* playing on a tape machine, and a huge slide of Dieudonné dominated the stairway. Dieudonné kept asking if there would be a lot of people, and I assured him the place would be packed. But when we went in, the theatre was only two-thirds full.

The film had been cut by forty-five minutes (as it was for general release a week after the opening), but it was still an agonising experience for anyone who loved the original. The audience was restless and impatient. They tittered ceaselessly and clapped derisively at several points. The sound that I remember most vividly, however, was the clattering of seats as people made their escape. If I hadn't been obliged to remain, I'd have escaped too.

When the vandalised masterpiece had reached its unhappy conclusion Gance stood up and thanked the audience for their sensitivity and tact. No whiff of irony seemed intended. He talked about how old the material was, and said it should be excused because of its age. The combined ages of himself and Dieudonné, he said, was 166. He went on to talk about Bonaparte's dream of a new Europe and the new Europe that was now emerging. The speech appeared to be the start of a marathon, but finally I heard him use the word 'fatigué' and there was laughter and applause and that was that. The survivors went off feeling pleased with themselves.

At the reception afterwards, Virginia suggested we have a lunch party. 'Monsieur Dieudonné,' I said. 'What are your plans for tomorrow?'

'Well, around 10.30 I shall telephone one or two young girls...'

At 1.30 next day, Gance, Dieudonné and his wife, and Anne Berthoud arrived. Gance carried a brown envelope and said, 'This is for you.' It was my rent demand which he had picked up from the table in the hall.

The atmosphere was completely relaxed and neither Gance nor Dieudonné seemed affected by the previous night's ordeal. There was a great deal of joking and banter. Gance was full of flattering phrases: 'How much to move in here?...How much do you charge him for the cooking?...This is the best meal I have had in England.' He held up his hand. 'One moment, I am going to speak in English.' And he began to utter, in the strangest accent, the words of a poem by Robert Browning. He had learned it parrot fashion when he was at school, but he had never understood it. To hear the familiar words pronounced so strangely, not so much like a Frenchman as a visitor from another planet, was uncanny.

Gance said that if he was living now, it was because of Jean Dréville. About a year ago, he said, he had nearly died. He had nothing to eat. Truffaut gave him 10,000 francs...and Dréville, secretary of the Society of Authors, arranged a pension for him. Gance was apt to exaggerate his

Albert Dieudonné (left) and Abel Gance come to our flat for lunch, 1972

poverty, for he lived in an expensive apartment. But I remember once glancing at a paper on his desk — his bank statement. He had 300 francs ...[4]

After lunch, Dieudonné asked to see *The Charm of Dynamite*. It was a fascinating show, because Gance kept throwing out little comments — when Ivy Close falls down the mountainside in *La Roue*: 'That was an accident, and she was nearly killed, but was rescued at the last moment by a cameraman.' They were both delighted with the film, and even more delighted when the phone rang: it was a call from Cinema V of New York, negotiating for *Bonaparte and the Revolution* and *The Charm of Dynamite*.

Anne drove Gance to the airport — the Dieudonnés having already left — and Virginia and I went with him. As Anne started the car, she said she felt a great sense of responsibility. 'You are carrying Caesar and his destiny,' said Gance. (An allusion to a title in *Napoleon* referring to the boat that carried the Bonaparte family to France.)

I asked if he had seen *Woodstock*, the 1970 film about a pop festival, which used three images in a manner reminiscent of Polyvision. He said when it was successful it was only by chance, otherwise it was maladroit.

What directors *do* you admire nowadays?

Gance listed Losey, Bergman, Fellini, Truffaut, Rohmer, Albicocco, Reichenbach ('a witness for posterity'), Bardem, and Buñuel ('he has a bad character and it shows itself in his work'). But most films seemed the same — 'the same stories about crooks and policemen, the same wife ... the only suspense is whether the wife will go to bed with the crook or the policeman.'

He still talked of *Columbus*. 'Will you do it?' asked Anne.

'Like a horse at the bottom of a hill — if he is asked if he can get up it, he will say he doesn't know.'

Virginia blew her nose, and Gance said something which Anne translated: 'Don't cry. He'll come back.'

Due to traffic jams, there was panic at the airport; we arrived too late to check in. We had to rush poor Gance straight to the departure gate. In the confusion, he lost his briefcase. We promised we would hunt for it and send it on. We said many affectionate farewells and Gance kissed us all goodbye.

Gance's briefcase was delivered to Anne Berthoud while I was in her office. She opened it, in a matter of fact way, to make sure it was the right one, and revealed a whole file of material on *Napoleon*. I am not normally given to peering into other people's briefcases, but this material was of enormous historical importance. We began to take a closer, if guiltier look. Gance had equipped himself with everything he might need to provide an

I took this picture of Albert Dieudonné when he arrived at the French Institute, London, for a screening of Bonaparte and the Revolution *in 1972. A slide from the original* Napoleon *was projected on the wall behind him.*

article on his work, and no one had so much as asked him. The file opened at a letter from Eugénie Buffet, who played the mother in *Napoleon*, written right after the première: 'It was so beautiful! I cried! I shouted! I have no words to express my emotions.' There was a letter from Richard Roud with his article in the *Guardian*; one from Truffaut, saying how glad he was to see the new version; surprisingly, one from me, translated into French; 'the most beautiful letter on *Bonaparte and the Revolution*' from Dominique de Roux, editor of *Cahiers de l'Herne*. There was also the astonishing letter written in 1927 by Jean Arroy, trying to make Gance aware of the importance of the bravura sequences — and to make him cut the Violine episodes.

Gance was obviously aware that one day someone would go through all this, and he had annotated the letters — who the person was, and sometimes what he thought of the letter. 'Beautiful letter with the spontaneity of youth,' he had said of Arroy. I realised what a monumental task there would be for the person assigned to it, for Gance's output was prodigious. A letter to the French Institute was laid out in two or three drafts in Gance's minuscule handwriting, using several coloured inks. Everything he attempted, even a straightforward letter, seemed to take on an epic quality. We sent the brief-case back to Gance, but he was less concerned with the loss of his papers than with the lack of publicity. After his success at the New York Film Festival, he somehow imagined a single screening at the French Institute would lead to the same results. 'I am astonished,' he wrote, 'to have received absolutely no news of the soirée on 23 March! Not a single article. Not a single letter. While in Paris there were 15 articles the next morning, and in New York three *extraordinary* columns in the *New York Times*. A flash in the pan in London? It all seems extinguished. Send me a word of explanation of the silence of the press.'[5]

Fortunately, the dependable David Robinson wrote a three-column article in the *Financial Times*. Acknowledging that purists hated the film, he wrote, 'Regarded as a new and independent conception, it is exceptional. Never in its $4\frac{1}{2}$ hours does the vitality or interest lag.'[6] Robinson's article gratified Gance immensely, and he wrote him a letter of thanks in which he called it 'one of the best and most pertinent' he had read.

Robinson was associated with the Chicago Film Festival, and one evening he brought to my flat the festival's director, Michael Kutza. I showed him *The Charm of Dynamite* and Kutza arranged a tribute at the 8th Chicago International Film Festival. Gance was unable to attend, but the Feature Film Jury, of which David Robinson was chairman, awarded him the Gold Hugo. It was an award which made a great impression on Gance, and he often referred to it. It stood in a place of honour in his apartment. I only regretted that an honorary Oscar — one of which was given to Henri Langlois — could not have been set beside it.

26 · Fortune Favours the Brave

In December 1972, David Shepard wrote that the AFI would be willing to help complete my project by providing English titles for all those cards which remained in French. Shepard was a young film enthusiast who had revitalised the AFI's archive project, finding extraordinary films in extraordinary places. In April he had been appointed Theater Programs Manager for the AFI's new theatre in the John F. Kennedy Center in Washington, charged with producing ideas to reduce the previous theatre's deficit. He wanted to programme some of the multiscreen exposition films, including Francis Thompson's *To Be Alive* and *We Are Young*, which required three projectors with interlock. The new theatre's projection booth was equipped with this machinery, and, since it had to be capable of showing silent films, speed controls were also fitted. Thus the AFI ended up with the unique ability to show *Napoleon*.

The AFI's opening programme included an impressive range of new films including *State of Siege*, produced by Jacques Perrin and directed by Costa-Gavras, about the CIA's involvement in torture and repression in South America. The head of the AFI, George Stevens jr, largely dependent on government finance, realised the effect this film might have on the Nixon regime, and rejected it.

'This precipitated an attack by Perrin and Costa-Gavras,' said David Shepard, 'who persuaded fifteen directors to withdraw their works from AFI's theatre, and also precipitated my departure from the AFI staff. In any case, we had a large number of programme holes to plug, and I chose to fill about three of them with *Napoleon*.'

Shepard sent a letter to Gance, explaining what was going to happen and asking for his permission. 'Ours will be the only archive theater in the world in which it would be possible to present the original silent *Napoleon* as it was intended to be shown. Our showings will not be frequent enough to damage the commercial potentialities of *Bonaparte*. Rather, I would hope they would promote enthusiasm for it.'[1]

Gance did not sign the letter of permission, even though Shepard had persuaded the AFI to send $1,000 to ease his financial predicament. He followed this with an offer of a trip to the US, plus an honorarium of $4,000 for introducing the film in four cities. Gance finally replied, saying he wanted a few days to think it over. But no word had been received from him by early March, and the date of the big show had been fixed for April 14th–15th, 1973. Letter or no letter, Shepard decided to take a chance.

The reaction to the screening of the reconstructed version at the AFI Theatre exceeded all our expectations. David Shepard rang me in a state of great excitement. 'They came from four hundred miles away,' he said. 'Standing room only! They went absolutely wild when the three screens came up and the whole audience rose to its feet and cheered, just like the première. They gave it a standing ovation of five minutes!'

Robert Dellett, of Alexandria, Virginia, wrote to Shepard saying he had seen what he called the Cinémathèque's patchwork version two years before, and almost hadn't attended this showing. 'The difference was astonishing. This is a new film. And what a stirring experience! It's hard to believe that this monumental film almost slipped through our fingers.'[2]

The *Washington Post* said, 'It seems only fitting that Napoleon, who dominated a continent for a whole generation, should have inspired three towering works of art: Tolstoy's *War and Peace*, Beethoven's 'Eroica' and Abel Gance's visionary *Napoleon* … it is an exploration of camera art decades ahead of its time … '[3]

By arrangement with the AFI, Tom Luddy of the Pacific Film Archives in Berkeley organised a West Coast première. He, too, had gone to the trouble of installing triptych projection, and this show, too, had a pulverising effect on the audience. One director, Francis Ford Coppola, was so impressed that he declared: 'What a terrific experience. Wouldn't it be wonderful to do it again with three big screens and a live orchestra — conducted by my father?'

But then I received a fateful letter from Gance:

I have obtained from Les Films 13 [Lelouch's firm] something remarkable. Claude Lelouch is willing to renounce in my favour all his rights on *Napoleon* and *Bonaparte* for the USA in return for the sum of $13,000. Obviously that's nothing! And no more problems with Lelouch or with Langlois. Free to restore Brienne and the triptychs! This is how I envisage the operation.

1. You take care of this American operation, with a good percentage for you, which we will agree on together.

2. You make two versions of *Bonaparte* — let's forget the silent film for

the moment. The first version of *Bonaparte* to last 3 hours, with triptych for the big cities. Second version 3 hours for all the cinemas in America, without triptychs.

You are an excellent editor and you know the American public and I give you carte-blanche while indicating to you the sequences I would like to keep intact. Come to Paris to study the details of the operation, and I will let you have all the freedom you want.

Affectionately to you and Virginia
A.G.[4]

I went over the next month and when Gance and I talked, I realised there was no resisting the old man. I would first have to take on the job of selling the film to the United States, and then of re-editing it. Gance smiled when I reluctantly agreed. 'You will be the murderer of the film; you know how English and American audiences react. Find a distributor – or find $13,000.'

A few days after my return, he wrote again.

After your visit, I wrote to Les Films 13 and asked them to abandon the proposition with Don Rugoff of Cinema V. It is not only ridiculous as to the price, but is full of constraints and servitudes which would get you and me involved in lawsuits.

How, indeed, can I give Films 13 the guarantee they demand that not a single frame of the silent *Napoleon* will ever again be shown in America – in universities, academies of cinema or in schools? That is impossible. Apart from you, there will always be in the wings cineastes possessing known and unknown elements of the silent version, who won't hesitate to use them.

How can I make Films 13 understand your disinterested efforts with my silent film, not only without any financial interest, but you have also spent a lot of money on prints, dupes and titles, solely in the cause of awakening the interests of the English and Americans in my work of 1926?

I therefore proposed to Films 13 a solution which I am not certain they will accept. It concerns an option I have asked of them – valid until December 1973, to abandon the Cinema V contract, and making clear that from now on I will make all efforts to pay them $13,000 against their giving up the whole of the American market to my sole profit. It is vital, therefore, that you help me in obtaining a minimum guarantee of $13,000 from an English or American company. It is only after this payment that I will be able to push back the storm that is threatening us. If not, we will have to await a lawsuit, you and me. This dilemma is serious. I am very discouraged that you and I are prisoners for a sum that I consider so small, compared to the intrinsic grandeur of the silent film and the sound.

    If you obtain $13,000 ... I will give you 30 per cent of my profits. Courage — it's the last tribulation of the great work — and act for the best.

Abel Gance

    If you say it's impossible, I shall reply in Napoleon's celebrated words: 'Impossible — n'est pas français!'[5]

And so began months of the most frustrating and time-consuming negotiations I have ever been involved with.

Abel Gance on the set of Cyrano et d'Artagnan

27·Strings Attached

I won't go into the infinitely wearying details of how, over a year, the deal was *almost* taken up by Cinema V—the company also distributed *State of Siege*, which certainly complicated matters—and how they vacillated so long that Gance lost his chance of recovering the rights.

The situation abruptly changed in April 1975 when, out of nowhere, a young man called Bob Harris stepped forward and acquired the US rights to *Bonaparte and the Revolution* for his company, Images Film Archive, for $20,000. I was delighted that someone had gazumped Cinema V after all their delays. But at the back of my mind was the fear that Images might reach too many people with *Bonaparte and the Revolution*—and put them off ever wanting to see *Napoleon*.

Bob Harris was very new to the game. His anxiety to obtain *Bonaparte* was due to the fact that he felt, philosophically, that there was no other way to distribute *Napoleon* in the US. 'From the agreement between Gance and Lelouch,' he wrote, 'the original version cannot be shown.'[1]

This, of course, was saddening news. For in the meantime, David Francis had been appointed Curator of the National Film Archive in succession to the late Ernest Lindgren. He had agreed to purchase the reconstruction for the Archive for exactly what I had paid for it, and he was willing to invest more money in completing it. He insisted on standardising the titles—they were all in English now, but the style was wildly inconsistent. And he said that the Archive would pay the huge cost of cutting the negative and making the answer print. His support came in the nick of time, for I could never have found the money to see the project through.

Bob Harris soon realised that the importance of the silent version far outweighed that of *Bonaparte and the Revolution*. He might have been told that there was no legal way to resurrect it, but he went right out to find one. In the meantime, he achieved a miracle. With financial help from the Museum of Modern Art, he purchased the negative of the 1928 M-G-M version.

This, the least satisfactory of all the versions, had nothing to commend it aesthetically. The miracle lay in the fact that it contained several sections I had never seen before.

Harris made these available, together with some brief scenes from *Bonaparte* (surprisingly, I had missed the nude dancing of the Bal des Victimes when I was winding through the negative at the Paris laboratory!). Once I had cut these sequences into the reconstruction, and had the extra titles made up (by Frameline Productions of London) I felt the film was as complete as it could be. I guessed that six or seven reels were still missing, but Gance had intimated that these had been destroyed during the war. I measured the film, and it came to 22,187 ft—some 7,000 ft, almost the length of an entire feature film, had been added to the Cinémathèque's print, the longest extant version.[2]

The next vital stage had to be handled by the laboratory. The BFI had acquired Henderson's Laboratories in Norwood, South London—the last to specialise in black and white. The neg cutting had been carried out piecemeal by Mike Fraser Associates. Henderson's monumental task was to grade—or, as they say in America, time—the negative. Their chief, an experienced sight grader called John Ling, did the work himself. Although he had 250 light changes in one reel alone, he produced an excellent print first time, and has turned out consistently fine work ever since.

Thanks to the shows in Washington and Berkeley, Bob Harris was besieged by requests for *Napoleon*, all of which he had to turn down because of *Bonaparte*. He stepped up his efforts to recover the rights to the original film, and asked me for information. I told him that if I had any flair for tracking down copyright, I should have done so long ago and would now be in control of world rights. 'The only way for this problem to be solved,' I wrote, 'is for you to do it, for you have the ability, the interest and the incentive.'

Images' agent in France had a meeting in 1976 with Henri Langlois, who refused even to discuss *Napoleon*. He may have been feeling a trifle guilty, for in 1973, when Gance was so desperately trying to secure American distribution for *Bonaparte*, Langlois visited America and offered twelve films to distributors—including the silent *Napoleon*. He quoted the assignment from Gance which predated anything signed by Lelouch. There were no takers.

Bob Harris eventually satisfied himself that despite Films 13 he could safely proceed with the release of *Napoleon* in the United States. He arranged for the BFI to have the British rights, and he ensured that a large percentage of the gross would go direct to Abel Gance.

And for the first presentation, he made an unusual choice—not Radio City Music Hall, nor even Lincoln Center. He chose Telluride, Colorado.

28·Gala Dernière

Telluride is a remote mining town in the Rocky Mountains which has been brought back to life by its young inhabitants, all comparatively new arrivals. The film festival, organised by Bill and Stella Pence, Bill Everson and Tom Luddy, is one of its most invigorating events. They always present tributes to the great survivors, and they asked me if I thought Gance would come.

'Impossible,' I said. 'He's been ill for years. He never travels. His wife has died. He has turned down several invitations to the USA. He has moved out of his Paris apartment and now lives with friends in Nice. What's more, he's almost ninety. Nevertheless,' I added, 'there's no harm in asking. He might appreciate the invitation.'

They asked Gance, and to my astonishment he said yes. 'I have been wondering what to do with the rest of my life,' he explained. 'This will give me the chance to publicise *Christopher Columbus*.'

I thought of a slogan I had seen in his apartment: 'For those with a mission to accomplish, bodily existence will last as long as necessary.'

They asked me to come, too. Since it was my favourite film festival, I was sorely tempted. But I was working with David Gill on the *Hollywood* series for Thames Television and we were racing towards a transmission date. So I was the one who said no.

While regretting my decision, I was confident Gance would cry off at the last minute. He always did. On top of which, the £500 air fare was a strong deterrent. Then work at Thames ground to a halt as Independent Television went on strike. And when Bill Everson's daughter decided not to go, and Bill offered me her ticket, there was no further argument.

August 30th, 1979: Arriving at the opening night party, my attention was drawn to a figure in a bright red shirt and Stetson hat, who was holding forth to a group. It was Abel Gance. I had not seen him for some time. He had changed very little, although he had lost a few teeth. But I thought he would be in a wheelchair, and here he was, at eighty-nine, *standing*!

I went up to him, and it was some moments before he recognised me. Then, in true French style, we embraced.

'A very dear friend,' Gance explained.

'I have known him since I was so high,' said I.

'He had the very good taste to pick me out,' smiled Gance.

The party was enjoyable, but I weakened long before Gance. Yet he had made an even more arduous journey than I had. 'He's having the time of his life,' said someone.

Next day, Gance looked very tired. He had not slept, and had asked for his hotel room to be changed. When his *Beethoven* was screened, he declared that it had been 'massacred'. This puzzled us, for the print was an original from the Royal Belgian Film Archive. Gance saw only ten minutes and refused to watch the rest. The screening of *Beethoven* to the public was cancelled. No one wanted to upset the old man.

This event increased everyone's nervousness for the evening's tribute to Gance. He kept saying he was not concerned with the past, that 'discoveries of the future' were what interested him. Gance's words were translated by Annette Insdorf, a small, intensely energetic girl with an indelible smile and inexhaustible patience. She was a Professor of Film at Yale, and had written a book on Truffaut. Gance teased her about this book, and demanded to know why she chose Truffaut before him. She protested that she had seen none of his films, which was why this festival was so important.

Gance had come to Telluride with the friends with whom he now lived in Nice, M. and Mme de Castro. They took their places that evening in the Sheridan Opera House, a small but charming theatre which Bill Pence had rescued from destruction. Gance and his party wanted to sit in the centre of the stalls, to get the best view of the screen, but Pence said absolutely not. 'They must sit at the side, in the reserved box.' Rather unwillingly, they moved from the plush seats to the hard chairs of the box, with its impossible view of the screen.

I was becoming increasingly nervous, and as I paced up and down I asked Gance if he felt the same. 'I take things tragically,' he said, 'but never seriously.'

The Opera House quickly filled to capacity. I was told that the print of *Charm of Dynamite* which I had brought all the way from London, and which was to be the only film shown at the Gance Tribute, would not go through the projector.

'But that's absurd,' I protested. 'The print is in perfect condition and it's been shown on every kind of projector for years.'

'There's something wrong with the projector,' was the reply. 'But we have another print ...'

Abel Gance at Telluride, aged eighty-nine

I introduced the tribute from the stage, and I gave as warm a welcome to Gance as I could manage, and on came *The Charm of Dynamite*. The audience responded well, and a ripple of applause broke out during the multiscreen section of the pillow fight. After the Marseillaise sequence, something else broke out — the sound of raised voices … speaking French. My eyes darted to Gance's party. I could see Gance standing, and Annette trying to make him sit down again.

Bill Pence came over. 'Gance is objecting to your film, and wants to leave.' The voices became louder, and sibilant French 's's hissed like bullets across the auditorium. I ran over to the box and stage-whispered to Annette, 'Tell him he's seen it twice before,' which was all I could think of.

'I have,' said Annette, helplessly.

I noticed that Bill Pence had the expression of a man going to the guillo-tine. He knew the next event of the evening was to be the presentation of the Telluride Award — and I was to present that Award. With admirable sang-froid, he bundled me into an alcove backstage, and thrust a box into my hands. 'The medallion is in that,' he said. 'Come on stage as soon as the end credits appear. I'll try and get Gance to do the same.'

I wondered what on earth I was doing, standing in that alcove — which was no more than a broom cupboard — listening to Gance's calm and measured tones on the sound track, and his very agitated tones from the auditorium. What could he be objecting to? Bill Pence, Annette and the de Castros all seemed to be talking at once, and the combined *bavardage* threatened to drown the film. 'This cannot be happening,' I told myself.

The film came to an end, and with it the dreadful French chatter. The audience burst into applause. As I walked on stage, the lights came up and to my relief Gance appeared from the opposite side. I held out my hand, and the audience gave him a standing ovation.

So far so good. Maybe this will make him change his mind, I thought. After all, he can't bite the hand that is about to present him with an award … can he? He could. He waited for the applause to die down and said:

'I thank you for your strong reaction to my work … but do not judge me by the mish-mash you have just seen.'

He spoke in French and Annette translated — beautifully — whenever he paused for breath. His language was forceful and poetic, and he elicited many laughs from the audience. I stood there, clutching the box with the award in it, with a smile which was becoming more and more fixed. Gance grew more and more heated as he attacked those people who cut up films and put them in an order their makers never intended. 'Massacre' and 'crime' were French words for which I needed no translation. I had, as the Americans say, egg on my face.

As soon as Gance had finished, I had to try and respond as though he had praised the film to the skies. I shook him by the hand, and said 'Merci' to his somewhat blank face, and presented him with the award. As the flashbulbs went off, and the cameras zoomed in, I remembered that all this was being taped for television.

In the corridor outside, I said to Gance, 'Vous êtes très méchant! Vous avez vu cette film deux fois …' And Annette translated my pidgin French into proper French. Gance looked bemused. 'Am I mad?' he asked Annette.

'You are cruel,' I said with a smile. 'Magnificent, but cruel.'

Gance tried to explain. 'You have the Mona Lisa. You cannot take one little piece of the Mona Lisa and stick it next to another piece and give an impression of the whole thing.'

I had enough detachment to see the irony of the situation. It struck me that academics who write on Joyce and Fitzgerald are well advised to stick to their posthumous studies; their subjects cannot then turn round and abuse them.

Now we had to face the marathon screening of *Napoleon*. There was no building in Telluride large enough to accommodate the vast screen so the show had to take place in the open. Four projectors fixed to run at 20 fps had been installed on the perimeter of Elks Park, three of them operating with synchronised motors.

After the experience I'd just had, I didn't know how I was going to sit through five hours of *Napoleon*—particularly since I'd seen it more than a hundred times before. In any case, I hardly expected Gance to attend. He was exhausted after his sleepless night, and the Tribute could hardly have invigorated him. I thought he might watch a few scenes, but remembered that after *Bonaparte and the Revolution*, his interest in the original had faded.

The print looked beautiful. The BFI's laboratory had done a superb job. The technicians in charge of the projection had already handled the 1973 Berkeley showing; the chief, Chris Reyna, told me that this would be his third time with the picture, and it was one of his all-time favourites. (He had even visited Gance in Paris.) The music came from an electronic piano—the organ had fused—but soon the player had to stop, his hands frozen.

About an hour into the film, a man returned to a seat in front of me, clutching some blankets. 'I hate to tell you,' he said to his girlfriend, 'but I've just seen Abel Gance walking out!'

Just what I expected! I supposed he was feeling the cold, which was becoming more and more intense as the evening wore on. A few moments later, Bob Harris drew my attention to Gance, watching from his hotel window. The New Sheridan Hotel was situated behind the Elks Park field, and Gance had an excellent view.

The audience huddled in sleeping bags and blankets as the temperature sank below zero. Hot soup acted as a lifesaver in the interval. Nevertheless it was an adventure to see the whole of this extraordinary film in one sitting, under such conditions. Somehow, the cold made the experience all the more vivid.

'I can't believe I'm seeing this,' said the man next to me, shivering under several layers of garments.

It was after three a.m. when the whirr of a single projector gave way to the roar of three projectors running simultaneously. The very ground seemed to shake. The picture fused into an immense, panoramic scene. The audience gasped. 'Jesus Christ!' said someone. 'Look at *that*!'

I had taken regular checks to see if Gance was still at his window—now I could see that he was on his feet. The projectors were maintaining perfect synchronisation and the editing of the panoramas with contrasting triple-screen images was magnificent. By the time the revolutionary army had been reviewed by Bonaparte, and had marched into Italy, and the triptych had been tinted blue, white and red like the French tricolor, the audience was stunned.

The emotion of the evening, the sight of the reconstructed print looking so good, the knowledge that Gance was watching the whole thing from his window was all too much for me, and tears stung my eyes. The overriding feeling was of being a part of returning an astonishing work of art to the man who made it, in the midst of an extremely appreciative audience.

The cold had dispelled some of them, but still a large number remained. People were shouting 'Bravo' and applauding Gance, who acknowledged them from his window, like the Emperor.

I went up to his room to find him surrounded by admirers. He was thoroughly delighted. He had misunderstood the documentary, he hadn't realised the entire film was also going to be shown. He said it was as good as the première at the Paris Opéra. He embraced me and did his best to make up for the grim experience earlier in the evening. A television crew scrambled to capture his every word.

The next day, Gance was able to make a public appeal on behalf of his cherished project, *Christopher Columbus*. And he made a public apology to me. His impish sense of humour returned, and he insisted on kissing every girl who came to congratulate him. Telluride lionised him and the other visiting film-makers—Robert Wise, Werner Herzog, Alain Tanner, Jacques Demy—all paid their respects.

A young man said to me, 'I hadn't seen anything by Gance before last night. Now I'm a hundred per cent convert.'

Gance must have enjoyed Telluride, because six months later he paid another visit to America, to appear with *Napoleon* at the Walker Art Center, Minneapolis. This time, I didn't go, and I'm glad I didn't. A physical and mental deterioration was now apparent; Gance tired quickly and became short-tempered with importunate journalists. As he was hurried from one date to another, he said, 'I am used to command. I cannot accept being ordered about.' Shades of St Helena! Nevertheless, both the film and its creator made a profound impression. And Gance was introduced to Francis Ford Coppola and his father, Carmine. Coppola had at last made the fateful decision: *Napoleon* would be shown at the 6,000-seat Radio City Music Hall, New York City. And his father would write the score and conduct the orchestra. Carmine Coppola had worked with Toscanini, and had written music for *The Godfather*.

It was a reckless and flamboyant gesture. Francis Coppola fully expected to lose money, although he hoped to break even. But he was willing to do it at a loss because he thought it was a very important piece of work. 'At least I thought *I'd* get to see it!' he said later.

As his partner Bob Harris put it: 'I expect to be sitting in an empty theatre surrounded by forty of my closest friends.'

29 · Fortissimo

It had always been an ambition of mine to see a silent film presented with full symphony orchestra. It had been tried — Filmex in Los Angeles regularly presented silent films with orchestra, and in Paris *Miracle of the Wolves* had been shown with its Henri Rabaud score. I had only seen one attempt in London, when the Philomusica played Hugo Riesenfeld's score for *Beau Geste* (1926). On that occasion, the 16mm print was of such lamentable quality they might as well have dispensed with the picture and held a concert.

Working on Thames Television's *Hollywood*, a thirteen-part series devoted to the American silent film, made me much more aware of the power of music and film. I had been startled when King Vidor told us, in an interview, 'Probably 50 per cent of the emotion came from the music.' After listening to Carl Davis's music and watching its effect with the films, I realised what he meant. Davis had been a prolific composer for films and television; his best-known work was probably the music for *The World at War*.

Hollywood had absorbed four years of my life, from 1976 to 1980, during which time I had worked in the closest and most rewarding partnership with David Gill, an unsung hero of this story. Gill was extremely musical, and he and Carl Davis were determined that when the series opened there should be a gala screening of a silent film — perhaps Griffith's *Broken Blossoms* — accompanied not by the inevitable piano, but by an orchestra. No one in command at Thames shared their conviction that this would be an exciting and instructional event, so the event did not take place.

Carl Davis's music for the *Hollywood* series was superb; he seemed to understand instinctively the kind of music that would enhance the films. David and I talked of his doing for *Napoleon* in London what Coppola was doing in New York, but only as a dream.

Carmine Coppola came to London early in 1980; he had been nominated for a BAFTA award for his music for *The Godfather*. I met him at the Savoy and asked Carl Davis to come too, to cope with the more difficult musical questions. Coppola was well under way with his score, and Carl was able to help him by supplying French revolutionary songs. Talking about it made us wish there was someone in England with the daring of the Coppolas, Tom Luddy and Images.

Meanwhile, in spite of the success of the Telluride showing, no one in England expressed any interest in running the film. The BFI had had my reconstruction since 1973. Now, five years later, only David Francis talked of showing it.

In a further attempt to get the film shown, I wrote an article for the London *Observer*, announcing (hopefully) that it would be presented at the NFT that summer. It wasn't. Even David Francis had had to abandon hope of a full-scale show when he found the NFT could not be fitted with extra projectors to cope with the triptych.

Bob Harris telephoned, asking me to suggest cuts for the American version. 'We are going to have to cut it down to $3\frac{1}{2}$ hours,' he said, 'or the theatres won't accept it.' It was particularly important to shorten it for Radio City, he said, otherwise they would run past midnight, and they would have to pay Golden Time to all the stagehands and musicians—a mere $15,000. Realising that the full version would still be available, I agreed to produce a version which more or less matched that shown at the première at the Opéra. David Francis was shocked that having put the picture together, I was now being asked to dismantle it again, but when he spoke to Bob Harris he, too, realised that it would have to be done. In the end, Harris balked at so fierce a reduction, and settled for a version of four hours. He said he would run it at 24 fps and thus save a great deal of time. The Violine sequences were the first to go—Gance professed to dislike those scenes anyway—together with eight minutes from Toulon. (This had the odd effect of making a long sequence seem longer.) Brief moments like Napoleon brooding in the grotto at Casone, and mingling with his family at Ajaccio, were also dropped. It was a pity, but rather a shorter and swifter *Napoleon* shown to the public than risk the full version sitting on the shelf, as in London.

During the summer of 1980, the BFI had so many enquiries about *Napoleon*, thanks to the *Observer* piece, that they decided to put it on during the 24th London Film Festival. With a piano.

One evening, a party for the *Hollywood* team was held by the BFI. The series had been a success in England, so Thames were pleased. The BFI were getting all the stills, documents and even some of the film used in the series, so they were pleased. In this atmosphere of goodwill, David Gill heard of the decision to show *Napoleon* with a piano. He asked the new head of the BFI, Anthony Smith, how he could contemplate such a decision, especially since the Zoetrope presentation at Radio City Music Hall had been announced. Anthony Smith agreed the film should have an orchestra, but who would finance such an expensive operation? A possible source of funds, said David, was Thames TV. The managing director, Bryan Cowgill, was present, so Anthony Smith put the problem directly to him. 'Of course,' said Bryan Cowgill, in an inspired and historic moment, 'it's a very good idea. We'll do it.'

Thus began Thames Television's association with silent films and live music. It was agreed that Carl Davis would arrange the score—the longest ever written for a film. The Wren Orchestra would perform it. And David Gill would supervise the operation. He had the assistance of another *Hollywood* veteran, Liz Sutherland. David Gill's first decision was to show the film at the correct speed, whatever problems that might create. The film was transferred at 20 fps on to videotape and in September 1980, Carl Davis began work with feverish haste.

His first decision was whether or not to use Beethoven.

'I reread his letters,' said Carl Davis, 'and a volume of impressions of Beethoven by his contemporaries, and it seemed clear that up to the point when Napoleon declared himself Emperor, Beethoven's view of him was of a liberator. The "Eroica" Symphony, initially, was dedicated to Napoleon. It was only after that moment that Beethoven crossed out the dedication.'

Since Gance's film ended with Napoleon leading an army of liberation, Carl thought he had sufficient licence to use Beethoven. 'Aside from the historical factor, there is also a good match in Beethoven and Napoleon. Throughout the film, one is impressed by the dynamism of the man, the intensity of his feelings and the directness of his actions. This could be a description of certain qualities in Beethoven's music. I researched all the sources of the "Eroica" theme—the Symphony itself, the piano variations and its first appearance in the ballet *Prometheus*. All these found their way into the score.'

Carl decided to use the film as a research project. 'I took great pride in looking for compositions by other composers working in France: Gluck, Cherubini, Méhul, Monsigny, Grétry, Dittersdorf, Gossec. Napoleon was known to have said that he could listen to an aria from Paisiello's opera *Nina* every day of his life—that melody accompanies the picnic scene in Corsica. I also looked at the first printed settings of the songs of the French Revolution and preserved these in their original forms, as well as researching the folk music of Corsica.

'I also decided that when I found the view of the director became subjective and not strictly historical, that would be the moment I would compose original themes. The most important was to describe the Eagle, which starts as a living bird held in a cage, is freed to return to his master, and then recurs thematically throughout the film as a symbol of the spirit of Napoleon. I could not find any music of the period which had a melody to describe his idealised feelings towards Joséphine de Beauharnais, and so I also composed a theme to represent that idea. Otherwise, I gave myself the date 1810 as a boundary beyond which I would not draw on any music.'

When Carl Davis began the score, he had none of the Honegger music. Only after several weeks' work, when he was halfway through, did seven of the Honegger pieces reach him. 'I reviewed this material in the light of my own concept and decided not to use it, except for one piece which was a superb treatment of the *Chant du départ* by Méhul, in counterpoint to the Marseillaise, and which fits perfectly with the march and battle scenes in the triptychs.'

As Carl completed each section, he would call David, me and Liz Sutherland to his house in Streatham to hear it on the piano. Those summer afternoons in Carl's studio, with the sun pouring through the window, and Mozart, Haydn and Beethoven enriching our souls, were idyllic, but I harboured serious qualms about the Big Show. How could he keep in perfect synchronisation with the picture for five hours? It would be chaos.

I said nothing, but Carl seemed to agree. At the end of one of the orchestra rehearsals, he exclaimed, 'We're mad! It can't be done.' I noticed that whenever the orchestra overran at these rehearsals, Carl simply rewound the videotape and started again. He could not do that on the night. Yet there was no time to rehearse the orchestra with the film from beginning to end.

Admittedly, the score, which Carl had written in six weeks, was remarkable. But if he went out of sync, there was no way he could cut the music from the scores of forty-five musicians. He would just have to grind on, getting further and further behind the picture, until the whole thing was laughed off the screen. It was a terrifying thought. The only person who remained calm and confident was David Gill. 'When it fits, it's terrific,' he said. 'Let's count our victories, not our losses.'

The problems of projection were entrusted to Charles Beddow, who had been with the NFT for many years. He was given full co-operation from the staff of the Empire, Leicester Square, which was selected for the Big Show. He and his colleague Billy Bell solved all the problems of projecting at the right speed, and the switch from single screen to triptych.

There was still a lack of confidence in high places. A five-hour silent film at the Empire? 'I doubt if there'll be more than two hundred people in the place,' said one BFI official. The seats were sold out an hour after booking opened.

I arrived at the Empire two hours before the start to find a policeman on duty outside the cinema, and a substantial number of people queuing. The queue was headed by young men with sleeping bags. The manager of the Empire, not accustomed to such dedication, shrugged his shoulders when I asked about these people and said, 'They're probably dossers.'

The first man was a young Yugoslav, Zdravkovic Sinisa, who had already seen *Bonaparte and the Revolution*, and had been outside since 1 a.m.

The administrator of the Wren Orchestra, John Burrows, told me he had been offered £100 for a ticket. The black marketeers were asking £50. A card had been pinned up at the NFT: 'NAPOLEON — ANY PRICE PAID for 2 tickets.' The theatre held 1,400 seats. Out of that number only nine tickets had been returned by people who couldn't make it for one reason or another. The sense of expectation was so high that I was anxious in case the mood of the audience turned against the film. Anxious? I was terrified! I was convinced that the picture would be strongly disliked for its fervent nationalism, and laughed at for its antique qualities.

I introduced it by saying that Abel Gance was not well enough to travel, and I read a message from him. Actually, the poor man was too ill even to think of a message, so I used one he had sent me a few years before, when he thought he wouldn't be able to get to the French Institute in 1972.

'The final creative contributor to the process of making a film is you — the audience,' I added. 'Only you can create the atmosphere which will make this an extraordinary event. So I do beg of you not to break that atmosphere by giggling at the serious bits. There is plenty of comedy in the film. But remember it was made before most of us were born — and be generous towards it.'

Once the film began, and Brienne was on the screen, and the orchestra swelled to the peak of a Mozart symphony, the audience was absolutely gripped. Carl Davis's synchronisation was heroic — almost uncanny. Again and again, as the film faded out, so did the music. The sparks flew from the anvil in the Danton sequence — he had incorporated an anvil into the orchestra. Cannons fired — the percussion was often simultaneous. But quite beyond my powers of description was what he had done with the music to raise the picture to an emotional peak I had never experienced at any of the other screenings.

I looked at the picture as though I'd never seen it before. I recalled Lillian Gish, in the first *Hollywood* programme, talking about the première of *The Birth of a Nation*: 'I sat at the end of a row with men, and during some parts the whole row shook with their sobs, it was so moving.' Well, I shook my row, and I'm not ashamed to admit it. I was overcome with relief

On following pages *Presentation of* Napoleon *at the Empire, Leicester Square, November 30th, 1980, with the orchestra conducted by Carl Davis (Photo: Laurie Lewis)*

and suffused with joy that the film was at last being seen as it was meant to be seen. By the time the film ended I was drained.

I wrote to Gance to try to recapture the spirit of the occasion: 'By the end of the triptychs, the audience, which had applauded each section with intensity, now rose to their feet and gave it a standing ovation. That was the moment for which we should have dragged you across the Channel. That — and the comments afterwards. I could never remember them all.'[1]

Of course, the audience was saluting the heroic endeavours of the orchestra, as well as the film. But had Gance been able to step from the wings at the end of that show, he would have heard an ovation that would have astounded him.

There were film-makers from all over the world, and the place was full of television people. One was Jeremy Isaacs, originator of *Hollywood* when he was programme controller of Thames. Now he was head of the new Channel 4.

'If this film isn't on Channel 4,' he declared, 'there won't be a Channel 4.'

Shirley Williams, about to form the Social Democratic Party, asked me for the speech given by Napoleon to the shades of the Convention; she wanted to use it in one of her speeches. 'I have never seen a *film* before,' she said. Rachel Ford, business manager for Charles Chaplin, admitted that she was usually bored in the cinema, but in this case 'it went like an hour. I was transfixed. I never blinked, except to shed a tear.'

I was delighted to see that Jacques Ledoux had come over — I told him once again that without his initiative in contacting all the other archives there would have been no reconstruction.

The reviews were unanimously enthusiastic. 'Masterpiece of cinema triumphantly reincarnated' was the headline for a six-column review by David Robinson in *The Times*. 'Everyone knew that *Napoleon* would be an occasion,' he wrote. 'No one — not even (or perhaps above all) the people most closely concerned with the presentation anticipated just how completely Abel Gance's legendary epic ... would work the same magic on an audience in 1980 as it did at its historic première at the Paris Opéra in April 1927. The film is still full of lessons for film-makers today, and the Empire was full of directors ready to learn, from Satyajit Ray to Wim Wenders and Nicholas Roeg. Throughout all the five hours, Gance's prodigious invention never flags ... The audience is bombarded with visual experiences ... Gance's use of the triptych is light years in advance of anything three-projector Cinerama ever achieved, whether creatively or technically ... London this week was inevitably full of people asking, "How can you look at any other film after *Napoleon*?" How indeed?'[2]

'"After Sunday,"' wrote Patrick Ensor in the *Guardian* quoting the BFI Director Anthony Smith, '"the world will be divided into those who have seen *Napoleon* and those who haven't." Anthony Smith is undoubtedly right. This screening was an unqualified triumph ... What makes *Napoleon* so extraordinary is not the story, moving though each episode is, but the techniques Gance invented to tell it ... Here is an artist who not only dared to do the impossible ... but knew how to assemble his material with rapid cuts and multi-superimpositions to create cinematic poetry.'[3]

Alexander Walker in the *New Standard* said, 'It was a never-to-be-forgotten occasion. It was a time-travel excursion back into the era when Cinema was spelled with a capital C.' Quoting Anthony Smith's remark, he concluded, 'I missed the Battle of Agincourt, at which similar sentiments were expressed, so I'd just like to commemorate a good deed and a great event which showed that the cinema's past can still hold its present in thrall and say, with modesty as well as gratitude, "I was there." '[4]

'One had seen botched versions and fragments before,' wrote John Coleman in the *New Statesman*, 'but nothing had suggested the sustained bravura scale and invention of the enterprise ... It is my pleasure to report that I came out into the evening streets delighted, admiring and incredulous.'[5]

Eric Shorter in the *Daily Telegraph* referred to 'the amazing, engrossing, enchanting, dazzling, delightful event' and declared that the element which contributed most forcibly to his pleasure was the music from the 43-piece symphony orchestra conducted by Carl Davis: 'No wonder the house rose with a roar of gratitude at every pause in the day's proceedings. For it may not be a marvel to accompany a five-hour silent film on the piano. But how often has an orchestra of this scale and quality done so with such exhilarating charm, precision and discreet sympathy?'[6]

Liam O'Leary, who had spotted Gance in the BFI all those years ago, wrote a review in the *Irish Times* in which he called the event 'the film show of the century'.[7]

I was particularly touched by the letters which members of the audience took the trouble to send to me—for those same people had already sent letters to Gance. Here are some of their comments:

'Briefly, it was the experience of a lifetime.' Stephen Pike, Totnes.

'When you took us through a roughcut at the NFT with Yugoslavian subtitles and all, you hoped one day to give it a Leicester Square showing and I have looked forward to it ever since—but never—NEVER—could I have expected anything like that which you gave us on Sunday.' J. F. Folger, London SW8.

'I don't think I've ever had such a feeling of "having been to the cinema" before. The immaculate images, and the emotions they created, coupled with the beauty and sheer warmth of the music, led to an amazing audience response that was almost tangible.' Mike Ellis (film editor), London NW3.

'It is difficult for me to find the words, let alone the right words, to describe what I felt during the film, and now, after it. Suffice to say that its power, its beauty, its humour, its great vision, but above all its poetry, have fired the imagination and touched the heart.' Richard Turp, London EC4.

Perhaps Mamoun Hassan best expressed the reason for the astonishing audience reaction: 'It was not only that the film was unique — a masterpiece like no other — but also that the occasion itself revived the basic experience of cinema which has almost been lost; a *community* of experience. At the end we were clapping and cheering the film, Gance, you, the composer and the orchestra, but also ourselves. We had seen so much, felt so much and given so much.'

'That was an experience of a lifetime,' said a relieved BFI official. 'I think we should leave it at that.' David Gill had to shout down the telephone to make them put it on again. 'But the number of tickets over don't justify another show.' Each of the next four shows, in March, was packed.

I went to Paris to see Gance, and my old friend Bernard Eisenschitz went with me. I was dreading the encounter — I had been told how acutely distressed he was, and how seriously he had deteriorated.

We were greeted by Gance's neighbour, Mme Salacroup. (She deserves an award for the way she took care of the old man.) She led us first into her apartment, and brought out some of the letters Gance had received — raves from the French Embassy, London, from the French Minister of Culture, hoping for a show in France, a splendid one headed HOMAGE A ABEL GANCE from Veronica Bamfield, and a pile of letters from members of the audience. They had all been carefully written in French and most contained the phrase 'expérience de ma vie'. Gance was to receive an award (by proxy) that very evening from the Young Film Makers.

'It is all too late,' said Mme Salacroup. 'I don't mean this as a criticism of you, but had this happened only one year ago ...'

We went next door, and found Gance in bed. The scene reminded me at once of a photograph I had seen of von Stroheim on his death bed. The apartment looked oddly different from when I had last seen it — the same volumes of Molière, the same pictures, but all looking desolate, drained of life. The huge desk was swept clear of papers, although a letter addressed to Annette Insdorf lay on it. On another table, a pathetic and somehow symbolic sight — a plant, in stale water, its stem trailing out of the glass and lying defunct on the table.

Gance's eyesight had all but gone, and Mme Salacroup had to explain carefully who we were. He shook us gravely by the hand, and I could see how much he had changed since Telluride. And yet ... he was still handsome, and the humour sparkled through the misery. Mme Salacroup told him about the show in London, and Gance began to hum the Marseillaise. I had brought a cheque with me, from Thames Television, and when I handed it to him he grabbed it with delight. 'This will enable me to live! We will celebrate with champagne!' And there was a flash of the old Gance. He insisted on staggering out of bed, and he grasped my hand and did a little dance. Then he settled into a chair and Bernard translated some of the reviews.

'That is written?' asked Gance, in amazement. Bernard confirmed that he was reading from English newspapers. Gance looked absolutely delighted. Meanwhile, I struggled to open the champagne which Mme Salacroup had brought in. Gance could just see what I was doing. 'Are you trying to kill us?' he asked.

We showed him David Robinson's spread in *The Times*, with its picture of the young Napoleon. He held it very close to his eyes. 'Roudenko!' he said, and burst into tears. 'He used to pass the cage with the eagle very often and I noticed that he would speak to it. His intuition, which he did not seem aware of, made me feel he was a true friend at the time. And I can no longer look at the photograph of him without crying.'

He struggled against the tears, and I was touched by the way he concentrated on the answer to a question, pushing himself until he had completed it. Every so often, his hand reached out and felt carefully for his glass, and he toasted us with the customary 'à votre santé' — which, since it means 'your health', seemed a touch ironic.

By the time he had heard a few more stunning quotes, Gance turned to me, grasped my hand and expressed his thanks in the most moving manner. I said that it was I who should be thanking *him*.

When I told him I had been asked to write a book about *Napoleon*, he simply said two words: 'Faites-le!' — 'Do it!'

After a few more toasts, a few more reminiscences, he suddenly said, 'I am so tired.' And we took our leave.

30 · Cresting the Wave

I didn't want to go to Radio City in January 1981 because I thought it would be an anti-climax. The London show had been so amazing I didn't think it would ever be possible to top it. And for me, Carl Davis's music was now the music for *Napoleon*. So when Bob Harris telephoned me, I asked, 'Do I have to go?'

'We would appreciate it,' he said.

Since *Hollywood* was getting the D. W. Griffith Award from the National Board of Review around the same time, both David Gill and I flew over.

Radio City Music Hall did not look very imposing from the outside. A rather pinched marquee anticipated the return of the prisoners from Iran: 'WELCOME EX-HOSTAGES! FRANCIS FORD COPPOLA PRESENTS ABEL GANCE'S NAPOLEON LIVE ORCHESTRA CONDUCTED BY CARMINE COPPOLA WELCOME EX-HOSTAGES!'

Inside, the theatre's foyer soared to the stars, and seemed larger on its own than any cinema in Britain. I was unprepared for the auditorium. You could store six Zeppelins in it, and still have room for the audience. Designed in 1930s style — High Kitsch — it seated 6,000, but the ticket sales were so encouraging that Coppola's company, Zoetrope, were considering extra shows.

Tom Luddy, responsible with Bernard Gersten for staging the event, assured me Gance was coming. I said the poor man could hardly cross the room, let alone the Atlantic, but apparently Gance had told him, 'I would rather die on the stage in New York than sit in my bed.' Mme Salacroup had bought tickets on Concorde, and planned to look after him herself.

However, as a result of the London screening, the French had decided to present Gance with their equivalent of the Oscar, the gold *César*, and the ceremony was to be held in Paris shortly after the New York show. I was not surprised when it suddenly became impossible to contact Gance, and we eventually heard he had been forbidden to travel.

David and I sought our seats. I wondered whether the show was sold out, and was dismayed when the lights went down with many seats remaining empty. A spotlight picked out a man at the microphone. 'It's Mayor Koch,' someone said. There was applause, and there were boos. Koch proclaimed *Napoleon* 'a spectacular film for a spectacular city' and then introduced Gene Kelly. There was a gasp of surprise and tremendous applause, followed by a near-riot from the vast number of people who had been held back from the auditorium by the ushers. They yelled, 'Seat us!' The ushers stood firm.

I was told later that these people were yelling out of sheer desperation and fury. They had arrived at the theatre to find such a crush that they had been told to line up outside. It was extremely cold. Soon the line straggled four abreast round the block. There was pandemonium as some people tried to insinuate their way to the front. Now all these people had reached the auditorium to find their way blocked, and the show beginning. But Zoetrope were determined to start on time — 7.40 — with the threat of Golden Time looming over the whole event.

By 7.35, the safety margin was perilously thin. Gene Kelly read a message from Gance — using phrases Gance had used to Annette when she finally reached him on the telephone, including his remark, 'Je n'ai pas le "pep" pour le voyage': 'When I came to New York two years ago, I fell in love with its excitement and grandeur. I wanted very much to return to New York this weekend, but I don't have the pep for the journey. At the age of ninety-one, I don't have enough confidence in my body. My spirit is with you, and I am deeply moved that my *Napoleon* is being shown to such a large and enthusiastic audience. I hope that its images, although silent, will still have something to say to you.'

The spotlight went off. Carmine Coppola raised his baton with an electric light at its tip. The captives in the foyer were now freed and the thunder of feet was drowned by the opening blast of the sixty-piece orchestra.

Coppola had already conducted a dress rehearsal that day. For a man in his seventies, he displayed an enviable energy and stamina. His score was so unlike Carl Davis's that it took David and me some time to adjust to it. Much of it he had composed himself, with only occasional additions from Beethoven, Smetana and Mendelssohn. It was therefore more of a traditional motion picture score — 'wall-to-wall music' as he himself described it — and, as such, it represented nine months of hard work. It was a titanic effort by any standards.

'It's harder even than conducting an opera,' he told the L.A. *Evening Outlook*, 'because in an opera, the performers are at least looking at you. They take their direction from you. But this just goes on. There are over a hundred cues to catch. What I see, I do.'[1]

In the early stages, there was the inevitable element who expected to find the film old-fashioned and expected to titter at it. A man behind me was forcing the sniggers, as though he felt he ought to. On top of this, people were still streaming in, taking no notice of the seat numbers on their tickets and grabbing a seat wherever they could find one. The place was soon packed, and when the last stragglers had settled down, the picture began to assert itself. Gradually, the appreciative element outweighed the mockers. As if to emphasise this, applause broke out at the end of the pillow fight. After that, bravura sequences were greeted with applause. Sometimes you heard solitary clapping for a moment someone liked. It was, to put it mildly, an exhibitionistic audience—but how Gance would have liked it!

The applause became more frequent and finally annihilated the titterers. Now the laughter was *with* the picture—the audience seemed to grasp every one of the throwaway jokes which, in true Gance style, litter the picture.

An organ took over from the orchestra after a while, to give the players a rest. There was the inevitable loss of temperature, but the film continued to mesmerise the 6,000. *Napoleon* had never been seen by so many at one show, and the enthusiasm was almost tangible. People tended to have lost contact with shared enjoyment on a large scale; they now watched TV in small family units, or alone, and if they went to the movies it was to find the old picture palaces divided into cubicles not much larger than the rooms they had left. A sizeable proportion of the spectators that night had probably never seen a film with several thousand people before, had never experienced the electricity that passes between people and unites them.

If the atmosphere was highly charged, it soon grew positively explosive. When the single screen burst its boundaries into the stunning panoramas of the triptych, the audience was overwhelmed—and one could hear the gasps and 'oh, wow!' as the horses thundered past in the review. When the triptych was transformed into a tricolor, the audience erupted in wild applause. And as the orchestra rose into view on its elevator platform, the audience rose, too, and gave Coppola and Gance a deafening ovation. I had never heard 6,000 people react with such fervour to a film before.[2]

'That was no big deal,' said someone, as we all filed out. 'That was a miracle.'

It was seeing someone using a phone backstage that gave me the idea to place a call to Gance just before the finale of the second show so he could hear for himself that incredible ovation. Since the time difference meant that we would have to wake him early in the morning, Annette Insdorf checked with him: Gance said he would love to be wakened for applause at six a.m.!

Gance was extremely sleepy when the allotted time came round. 'C'est

Annette, à New York! ANNETTE! A NEW YORK!' At last she got through to him. 'Who is this? Annette?' he asked.

'Yes. You will soon be hearing the applause — all for you.'

'It is too late,' he said, bluntly. To soften the blow, he added: 'It is never too late to do good.'

'Here is the music now,' said Annette, holding the receiver out. The orchestra broke into La Marseillaise; the audience into applause. Annette held the phone out to the wings. More applause, then the film ended and the audience rose to its feet in another thunderous ovation. 'They are on their feet now,' said Annette. She put her hand over the mouthpiece, and said that Gance was weeping. The orchestra played a reprise of the Joséphine theme. Gance said, 'I thank you all who did this beautiful thing — I don't have to be there to see it with my eyes. Be sure to thank all the people who have brought the film to New York.' The applause subsided as the audience listened to the music, so David Gill took the receiver and went right out on stage — stretching the cable until I feared it would be torn from its socket. He signalled for more applause, and the audience knew at once what was expected of them. They responded with everything they had. The publicist, Renee Furst, was crying. Annette, too. 'I don't believe I'm hearing this,' said Bob Harris. It was like telephoning heaven and waking Beethoven to hear what we mortals thought of his work. David made the audience cheer again. Annette told Gance who the people were who were standing round the phone, and that we each sent him our fondest wishes, and the conversation came to an end.

Francis Ford Coppola came backstage and we were introduced: 'Don't you wish you could make a picture that would get a reaction like that?' he said.

31 · 'The Measure for All Other Films, Forever'

Napoleon took New York by storm. Coppola's magnificent gamble paid off so handsomely that the film had to be held over for the following weekend — and the one after that. When New York takes up a cause, it does so wholeheartedly.

The rest of that trip is a delightful blur in my memory, a sort of rapid-cut Polyvision storm of praise and approval from some of the greatest names in the industry — including Lillian Gish who had been at *J'accuse* sixty years before — and some of New York's least-known citizens — hotel porters and cab drivers, who had seen the film and had been as stunned by it as the great directors.

It proved to be the top box office picture in New York, and on the strength of that single weekend, number eleven in *Variety*'s top grossing pictures in the whole country. The press coverage was phenomenal. The *New York Times* devoted an editorial to it, an honour they had apparently never accorded a film before. Vincent Canby, Richard Schickel and Jack Kroll gave it raves. CBS nationwide news devoted eleven minutes to the event.

The film has had the same extraordinary effect wherever it has been shown. Zoetrope took it on a tour of American cities, where the enthusiasm echoed New York's. In July 1981 it reached Los Angeles, where the motion picture community filled the Shrine Auditorium and cheered, if possible, even more loudly than anywhere else, and Charles Champlin headlined his review in the *Los Angeles Times* 'The measure for all other films, forever.'

'It is so compelling,' wrote Barry Brennan in the L.A. *Evening Outlook*, 'so sweeping, so totally overpowering emotionally and intellectually, you are practically forced to love it. It doesn't leave you any other choice.'[1]

'It is a uniquely vivid, transporting spectacle,' wrote Gary Arnold in the *Washington Post*. 'It not only strives to recreate the dramatic events of a tumultuous period, but also to reawaken the explosive emotional climate that triggered them. This phenomenal movie derives its enduring power and fascination from Gance's impassioned vision of a heroic national past. It sustains an almost mystic quality of illusion by seeming to bear witness to the very moments in which history and legend merge.'[2]

Impressed by the show at Radio City, director Andrea Andermann staged the film in Rome, outside the Colosseum, with a screen 120 ft wide and a ninety-piece orchestra, in front of 8,000 people, thus fulfilling Gance's dream of films being shown in huge arenas to vast audiences.

The French Minister for Cultural Affairs, Jack Lang, announced that the film would be shown in Paris on Bastille Day, July 14th, 1982. *Napoleon* had established itself as a great work of art *and* a hot commercial property—a rare combination. Now it was all set to return home in triumph.

If all stories of endeavour could have such an ideal conclusion, the world would be a splendid place. But while the film industry purveys happy endings, it seldom encourages them in real life.

Had *Napoleon* flopped at the box office, all would have been well. The trouble was that it was fantastically successful. News of the picture became a regular feature in *Variety*, whose Paris correspondent, Lenny Borger, bravely tried to make sense of everything with a chronology. The *Hollywood Reporter* even announced 'an Abel Gance biopic with John Phillip Law'!

Thanks to the rights he had acquired from Gance, Claude Lelouch was now all-powerful. Even so, he claimed, no one had informed him about Radio City. According to Bob Harris, Lelouch had given permission for the show, 'even though he thought we were mad.' In any case, Zoetrope flew him to New York to attend the second weekend. He admired the presentation, but professed to see no difference between *Bonaparte et la Révolution* and *Napoleon*— 'the images are exactly the same.' However, he appreciated the difference between their respective earning powers, and he left with a new financial agreement, under which he would receive 50 per cent.

He did not want the reconstructed version to be shown in France. The publicity for the Coppola shows aroused new interest in *Bonaparte*, which was exploited as though it was the original *Napoleon*—with sound.

Thames TV planned to record the Carl Davis score and prepare the film to open the new Channel 4, but nothing could be done until the UK rights were sorted out. The BFI, who had been given the rights by Images in exchange for their material, were dismayed to learn that Images had reassigned all rights in the UK version to Lelouch. 'Lelouch will honour the agreement,' they were assured.

We were further dismayed to hear that Lelouch had thrown open the world distribution of *Napoleon* to the highest bidder. According to *Variety*, from which we received most of our news from the front, he was offering three versions: Coppola's, 'when an agreement was finalised'; *Bonaparte et la*

Révolution; and what was airily described as 'an English version with music by Beethoven'.

More than twenty distribution companies scrambled for the rights. And what usually happens in such situations happened in this one.

'A quarrel has developed over who has ... Lelouch's authorisation to pursue distribution rights in territories outside of France and the U.S.,' reported *Variety*.[3] Independent distributors Alex Massis and Red Silverstein declared that they were the exclusive representatives worldwide, and threatened legal action against anyone who challenged their status.

David Gill and I went to the Telluride Film Festival in September 1981, and had several long and difficult meetings with Bob Harris and Tom Luddy. Now that so much money had been invested in what the press had hailed as *the* reconstructed version, the existence of another, longer version was an embarrassment. The fact that it had another score angered Tom Luddy, who declared that I had betrayed him by not informing him. 'I wouldn't have involved Carmine if I'd known,' he said. David Gill pointed out that a silent seldom had an exclusive score — the music could differ every time you saw the film. There was absolutely no reason why the two versions could not co-exist as alternatives, the commercial version and the archive version.

But, on behalf of Zoetrope, Luddy resisted the idea of the Carl Davis version being shown outside the UK. We said this was tantamount to suppressing the most complete print. 'Not at all,' he said. 'We'll show it — and have Carmine write more music.'

He and Harris acknowledged the BFI's rights, but were worried about Thames's involvement. Without that involvement, we explained, none of the English shows could have happened. Luddy and Harris were concerned about competition; in reality, there was little question of it. By the end of the Festival we had established an atmosphere of agreement, if not the agreement itself. The full version could exist, but we should avoid head-on competition.

When we got back, we found the BFI disturbed by the way its contribution had been ignored in America, and by the continuing lack of evidence of its rights. Thames was refusing to proceed with the television version without an indemnity from the BFI, and despite all the reassurances the BFI still had nothing. We invited Harris and Luddy to come over. They agreed initially, but one thing led to another and the trip never took place. Having concluded a deal with Lelouch for world rights, Images were finalising a deal with Universal Pictures to distribute their version with sound track. Zoetrope, sadly, was in trouble.

In the midst of all this, Abel Gance died, aged ninety-two. I flew over for the funeral, and the man next to me in the church was introduced as Claude Lelouch. The French gave Gance an impressive funeral, with a guard of honour from the Garde Républicaine. French TV subsequently ran *Austerlitz* and *Bonaparte et la Révolution*. Many of Gance's former associates saw *Bonaparte* and told me they thought it 'shameful'. Ironically, they blamed Lelouch for destroying a masterpiece.

That an artist can so damage his work in an attempt at reviving it is a paradox that will probably never be explained. All we need to know, however, is that Abel Gance made the original *Napoleon*. While he earned virtually nothing from the original release, he did make some money out of the reconstruction. Images cabled him $10,000 from the Radio City show. Thames TV sent him a cheque from the London presentation and members of the audience contributed generously too. As a direct result of these events he received a French Academy award; an award from the British Film Institute; the highest honour that the British film industry can bestow, a Fellowship of the British Academy; a mass of fan mail and the finest reviews any film-maker could hope to read.

Happily, Michelle Snapes of the British Film Institute had recorded Abel Gance's last message to the audience:

'What can I say to all these friends in London and New York, the men and women who share the great emotion I feel in talking to them? They have allowed me to rediscover through cinema my true language and I shall never forget it. You are the luckiest of spectators to have been able to see the film in the way I had created it — that is to say with the same feeling I had. I am deeply moved by the knowledge that I am not forgotten and to see the importance my message can have across time.'

The *Napoleon* bandwagon rolled across the United States, staging live performances in sixteen cities, bringing the name of Gance to thousands who had never heard it before.

In Britain, *Napoleon* continued its success story; it was requested for the Royal Film Performance, 1982. A new British picture was the main event, but Thames TV and the BFI presented the triptych sequences with Carl Davis conducting the Wren Orchestra. I was amused by the spectacle of royalty applauding Bonaparte's invasion of Italy to spread the French Revolution.

Claude Lelouch announced that the version to be shown in Paris on July 14th would be the Coppola version. When I interviewed him for this book, he admitted that he disliked *Bonaparte* but said he thought that some time or other all the versions should be shown — 'they all show an aspect of Gance.' I was determined that when the film went home to France, it should be the longest version seen since 1927 — longer even than that shown in London.

Then came a series of surprises. Claude Lelouch unexpectedly donated his rights for France to the French government. In a letter to Jack Lang, he said he did not feel it was right 'to speculate on the death of a brilliant film-maker. I was very happy to have served as Gance's last producer in the most difficult period of his life. Now that only his fame remains to be defended, I believe that it is a matter for the entire French cinema.'[4]

Unkind gossips suggested that Lelouch knew he would have to finance the event himself. In any case, he held on to his world rights. If only he had returned his rights to Gance in his lifetime — what a gesture that would have been!

This created a difficult situation for the French. Jack Lang had promised Coppola that his version would be shown in Paris on July 14th. But now that the Cinémathèque owned the rights on behalf of the government, they were anxious to have the most complete version possible. André-Marc Delocque-Fourcaud was the new head of the Cinémathèque, and he invited me to Paris to examine all the *Napoleon* material they held. This was a dramatic moment; it gave me my chance to repay my debt to the Cinémathèque.

When I entered the viewing room, the first person I saw was Marie Epstein. I greeted her warmly, but she remembered my past behaviour and refused to speak to me. I spent several days viewing and found a great deal of fresh material. I also found 35mm footage to replace the 17·5mm blow-up which had served us so well for so long. I was very excited by a sequence of the family escaping from Corsica ... a scene of Salicetti and Pozzo di Borgo, planning to finish Bonaparte's career ... extra shots for Toulon, of an English garrison battling the French at La Grosse Tour. As I examined the prints, I became aware of mistakes I had made in the reconstruction — the occasional sequence in the wrong order, the odd title mistranslated. All these I was able to correct.

To make the French version as close to the original as possible, I asked the Cinémathèque if they were willing to pay for the titles to be made in the style of the *version définitive*. Delocque-Fourcaud agreed, and Stuart Lacock of Frameline Productions re-created the hand-lettered, eighteenth-century typeface. I set about cutting in all the new material, and making both a French and a new English version. The work took an astonishingly long time — it took over an hour just to rewind the film — and quite apart from *Napoleon*, I was working with David Gill on a television series, *Unknown Chaplin*. Thames thus continued their support for the project, but still could get no clarification of the rights position. Images provided explanations, but after eighteen months the BFI still had nothing to confirm their rights. This put the whole French operation in jeopardy, as Thames could hardly extend a budget for a project they didn't officially have. Nevertheless, they came to the rescue again with an advance to cover the extra music which Carl Davis had to integrate into the score — another marathon task. For the film was now twenty-three minutes longer.

Images and Zoetrope concluded their deal with the Universal Picture Corporation (a company which had burned its silent negatives in 1947). Once more, *Napoleon* fell into the hands of a big distributor. One could hardly blame Images or Zoetrope for this decision; the live presentations could not go on indefinitely. Carmine Coppola recorded his score on six-track Dolby stereo and the picture was transferred to 70mm. The BFI, against their better judgment, and the Cinémathèque made available the good-quality material to replace the 17·5mm blowup. I wish I had been given the opportunity to check the print, and especially the tinting, but as always with these things, no one ever has enough time.

Universal decided to open in the middle of July in Los Angeles—a town which had already had three return engagements of the live presentation. They gave it minimal publicity, feeling, presumably, that it had already had enough. Result; it did such poor business that not even *Variety* could bring itself to comment on it. They buried the takings in their 'LA Roundup' column, with the three letters 'NSG' (Not so good). And what was the reason for this débâcle? According to a Universal executive, 'The picture's no good.'

It struck me that had a major company like Universal picked up the picture after Telluride, it might have had a week's run at an art house, and that would have been the last anyone would have heard of it.

Once the picture was properly handled, under Bob Harris's supervision, business picked up spectacularly.

Eventually, the BFI received confirmation of their rights—although the full version is still restricted to the UK. But Bob Harris began to talk of the possibility of bringing it to the United States—with the Carl Davis score—and perhaps showing it in other countries.

The film has grossed the incredible figure of $7·5 million. Expenses have eaten into most of it, of course, and some of the profits were used to pay Zoetrope employees when the company was in trouble. I profoundly hope that one day the National Film Archive will be rewarded for their faith in the picture, let alone their huge (and continuing) investment. And I hope Claude Lelouch will consider giving some of what he has made to the rescue of other French silent films. For *Napoleon* is not the only great film from that era—there are other extraordinary pictures awaiting restoration, whose chances diminish every day. Many of these are in the vaults of the Cinémathèque Française, who are struggling against a severe lack of funds to preserve whatever they can.

The Cinémathèque had ambitious plans for *Napoleon*'s return to Paris on July 14th—they considered the Opéra, Palais de Chaillot, Palais des Congrès, and, most ambitious of all, Les Invalides. There was talk of roofing over the inner courtyard and bringing in 5,000 seats and the largest screen ever seen in France. It was an enormous challenge, and it proved too complex.

July 14th came and went, and there was no Paris show.

But the film *did* go home to France. And there *is* a happy ending, although it is unlikely that this story will ever end.

The enterprising administrator of a new cultural centre at Le Havre, Christopher Crimes, asked the Cinémathèque if *he* could open with the new version of *Napoleon*. Knowing of the new socialist government's support for regional activities, Delocque-Fourcaud agreed to an *avant-première*.

I flew over with Carl Davis and the Wren Orchestra in a chartered aircraft. Charles Beddow and Billy Bell, veterans of all the English presentations, brought over their special 20 fps projector. Cinélume of Paris provided the three machines for the triptych.

What an event it was! The picture captured the audience at once. They responded to incidents and titles which had passed over our heads. For this was *their* history. I felt even stronger waves of emotion from the people around me than in England or America.

At the end, the audience broke into applause as the triptych burst upon them, sixty feet wide. They gave a ten-minute standing ovation to the film, Carl Davis and the Wren Orchestra, and the projectionists.

Abel Gance's daughter, Clarisse, was so deeply moved she couldn't say anything.

Afterwards I met André Cerf, who had played in the film. 'I was at the Opéra,' he said. 'But it did not impress me nearly so much as this.'

And the next morning, the newspapers carried the headlines of my dreams:

PART THREE
APPENDICES

Cast and Credits

Note: This is intended to be the most accurate list of cast and credits assembled so far — from such sources as the original Opéra programme, the trade press and from interviews with the technicians themselves. Please let me know, care of the publishers, should you spot any errors.

Première: April 7th, 1927, at the Théâtre National de l'Opéra, Paris
Orchestra under the direction of M. Szyfer
Napoleonic drum-rolls and fanfares reconstituted by Charles Gourdin, ex-drummer of the Garde Républicaine

ABEL GANCE'S COLLABORATORS:

Assistant directors

Henri Andréani
Pierre Danis
Henry Krauss
Anatole Litvak (short period only)

Mario Nalpas
Viacheslav Tourjansky
Alexander Volkoff

Chief cameraman
Jules Kruger

Cameramen (*principals)

Fédor Bourgassoff
Paul Briquet (Triptychs)
Léonce-Henry Burel*
Eyvinge
Roger Hubert*

Lucas*
Monniot
Jean-Pierre Mundviller
(Brienne, Corsica)*
Émile Pierre*

Editing
Marguerite Beaugé

Art direction

Alexandre Benois (designer)
Pierre Schildknecht (chief art director)
Lochakoff (short period only)

Jacouty
Meinhardt
Pimenoff

Chief technical director
Simon Feldman

Studio manager
Michel Feldman

Casting director and production manager
Louis Osmont

Financial administration
Édouard de Bersaucourt   Noë Bloch

Production manager
William Delafontaine

Production staff
Constantin Geftman   Pauly
Hoden   Pironet
Komerovsky   (also catering and propmaster)
Georges Lampin   Rufly
Metchikoff   Michel Scripnikoff

Script girl and M. Gance's secretary
Simone Surdieux

Negative cutting
Henriette Pinson

Special effects
W. Percy Day   Eugen Schüfftan (short period only)
Edward Scholl   Wilky

Projection
Bonin

Stunt men and doubles
Pierre de Canolle   Robert Guilbert
Engeldorff

Nurse
Mme Marthe Mélinot

Engineer for André Debrie
Maurice Dalotel

Stills
Desboutins   Lipnitzki
Gedovius

Makeup
Wladimir Kwanine
Boris de Fast

Cast and Credits

Armourer
Lemirt

Weapons supplier
Mauger

Explosives supplier
Ruggieri

Wigs
Pontet-Vivant

Electricians
Albinet   Graza
Doublon

Costumes
Charmy   Mme Augris
Sauvageau   Mme Neminsky

Joséphine's costumes designed by Jeanne Lanvin
Costumes supplied by Muelle et Souplet
Footwear supplied by Galvin

Music
Accompaniment arranged and special pieces composed by
Arthur Honegger

Stagiaires (trainees)
Jean Arroy   Sacher Purnal
Jean Mitry

Distribution
Gaumont-Metro-Goldwyn
M-G-M
UFA

CAST

J.-J. Rousseau/staff officer, Toulon	ALBERTY
Fouquier-Tinville	Paul AMIOT
General Henriot	ANGELI
Captain Desaix	Robert de ANSORENA
Marat	Antonin ARTAUD
General Hoche	Pierre BATCHEFF
Santo-Ricci	Henri BAUDIN
Beaumarchais	BEAULIEU
Cromwell	BENEDICT

General Dugommier/Collot d'Herbois	Alexandre BERNARD
Jean-Jean	Armand BERNARD
Guillotin/Lomon	BEUVE
Calmelet	BLIN
Talma	Roger BLUM
General Menou	BONVALLET
La Fayette	BOUDRÉAU
Monge	Albert BRAS
Robespierre-le-jeune	Daniel BURRET
Vicomte de Beauharnais	G. CAHUZAC
Gasparin/Ricord	CAILLARD
Captain Marmont	Pierre de CANOLLE
Lucien Bonaparte	Sylvio CAVICCIA
Pozzo di Borgo	Acho CHAKATOUNY
Jérôme Bonaparte	Roger CHANTAL
General Carteaux	Léon COURTOIS
General du Teil	DACHEUX
Muiron	Pierre DANIS
Admiral Hood	W. Percy DAY
Captain Suchet	Jean DEMERÇAY
NAPOLEON BONAPARTE	ALBERT DIEUDONNÉ
Laurent-Basse	ENGELDORFF
L'Oeil-Vert (Bonnet)	Boris FASTOVICH-KOVANKO (Boris de FAST)
Fouché	Guy FAVIÈRE
Carnot	FLEURY
Marcellin Fleuri	Serge FREDDY-KARLL
Louis de Saint-Just	Abel GANCE
Tallien	Jean GAUDRAY
Corsican shepherd	Felix GUGLIELMI
Captain le Marois	Robert GUILBERT
The archer	Joë HAMMAN
Member of Bonaparte family	HAZIZA
Eugène de Beauharnais	Georges HENIN
Sergeant Junot	Jean HENRY
Salicetti	Philippe HÉRIAT
Montesquiou	JACQUINET
Tristan Fleuri	Nicolas KOLINE
Danton	KOUBITZKY
Moustache	Henry KRAUSS
Rouget de Lisle	Harry-KRIMER
Joseph Bonaparte	Georges LAMPIN
Dutheil	Georges LECLERCQ
Fabre d'Englantine	Raphäel LIÉVIN
Hérault de Séchelles	LOMON

Cast and Credits

Voltaire	MARTIN
General Schérer	MATHILLON
Washington	Ernest MAUPIN
Barras	MAXUDIAN
Fréron	Daniel MENDAILLE
Augereau	METCHIKOFF
Captain Murat	Genica MISSIRIO
Staff officer	Laurent MORLAS
Louis Bonaparte	Fernand RAUZENA
Diderot	RÉGNIER
Favière	Joachim RENEZ
Brissot	Émilien RICHAUD
Peccaduc	ROBLIN
General Masséna	Philippe ROLLA
Napoleon as a boy	Wladimir ROUDENKO
General O'Hara	Jack RYE
The painter, David	SAINT-ALLIER
Louis XVI	Louis SANCE
Volontaire de l'Ardèche	André SCHÉRER
Robespierre	Edmond van DAËLE
Franklin	VASLIN
Phélipeaux	VIDAL
Camille Desmoulins	Robert VIDALIN
Couthon	VIGUIER
Boissy d'Anglas/Staff officer	Raoul VILLIERS
André Chénier	VONELLY
La Bussière	Jean D'YD
Violine Fleuri	Mlle ANNABELLA
Marie-Antoinette	Mme Suzanne BIANCHETTI
Laetitia Bonaparte	Mme Eugénie BUFFET
Mlle Lenormant	Mme Carrie CARVALHO
Mme Danton	Mme Florence DALMA
La Marseillaise	Mme Maryse DAMIA
Élisa Bonaparte	Mme Yvette DIEUDONNÉ
Charlotte Corday	Mme Marguerite GANCE
Pauline Bonaparte	Mlle Simone GENEVOIS
Caroline Bonaparte	Mlle Pierette LUGAN
Joséphine de Beauharnais	Mme Gina MANÈS
Mme Marat	Mlle Noëlle MATÔ
Lucile Desmoulins	Mme Francine MUSSEY
Hortense de Beauharnais	Mlle Janine PEN
Madame Elisabeth	Mme Georgette SORELLE
Thérèsa Cabarrus/Mme Tallien	Mme Andrée STANDARD
Louise Gely	Mme TALMA

262

Madame Royale   Mlle THOMASSIN
Madame Recamier   Mme Suzy VERNON

Small roles

Jean Arroy (sans-culotte at Toulon, member of Convention), M. Pèrès, Pierre Ferval, Edmond Gréville, Michel Zahar (Cordeliers), de Bourgival (Cordeliers), Floquet (Convention), Robert Arnoux (Convention), André Cerf (soldier), Francis (soldier), Wells, Médus, Jean Mitry, Jean Dréville, Maggy Pironet.

The Board of Directors of the Société Générale de Films:
(Alexander d'ARBELOFF Original President)
Henri de CAZOTTE President
le Duc d'AYEN
Charles PATHÉ
le Comte H. de BÉARN
le Comte J. de BRETEUIL
E. KARMANN
C. LEMOINE
J. GRINIEFF
de la ROZIÈRE

'Heartfelt thanks to the following, for bringing their valuable assistance to the making of *Napoleon*: Duchesse d'AYEN, Princesse Edmond de POLIGNAC, Comtesse Charles de POLIGNAC, Mlle S. GUGGENHEIM, Comte de CHEVIGNE, Comte Jean de POLIGNAC, Duc de GRAMONT, Baron Paul de THOISY, Baron FOY, MM la CAZE, Marcus et Arthur LOEW, Léon GAUMONT, RUBIN, E. COSTIL, Ludwig LAWRENCE, Dr BRAUSBACK, Rudolph BECKER, Paul BRUNET, Antonio MOSCO, LUCHAIRE, Georges D'ESPARBÈS, Élie FAURE, Pierre ROCHÉ, René DÉLANGE, N. BLOCH, André DEBRIE, Michel FELDMAN, H. NIÈPCE, FREDERIX — and also to those who, by their understanding, their assistance and their labour have added a building block to the construction of the film.' — A.G.

Synopsis

Note: This synopsis is taken from Gance's original scenario, published in 1927 by Librairie Plon, Paris. It contains all the sequences described in the scenario, but does not include the variations of existing scenes between script and screen. Missing sequences are italicised. (Other scenes cut from US version.) Unless otherwise stated, quotations are from the film titles.

PART ONE
The Boyhood of Napoleon

Brienne

A wall of snow. Little by little, the famous hat emerges. There is a shower of snowballs and the hat is knocked off. The young Napoleon is commanding a snow fortress — twenty comrades against sixty.

The monks in charge of Brienne College, the Minim Fathers, encourage these battles, but as soon as they venture on to the battlefield they are scattered by snowballs and return to watch from the safety of a doorway.

The opposing leaders, Phélipeaux and Peccaduc, are personal enemies of Napoleon at Brienne. They creep stealthily up to Napoleon's fortress.

Tristan Fleuri, the scullion, watches the battle and cries out: 'Look out, Napoleon! Phélipeaux is putting stones in his snowballs!' Too late — Napoleon is already struck and injured. But now he knows the culprit, he leaps angrily over the parapet and races towards the enemy camp, falling among them like a bomb and seizing Phélipeaux. He drags him over the wall of the fort and takes on Peccaduc as well. The teachers laugh and applaud behind the window panes.

Napoleon thanks Tristan Fleuri then returns to his fort to resume command. Now a battle royal breaks out. Napoleon rallies his troops and issues orders with calm confidence. The battle rages more and more fiercely until, at the moment of victory, a smile breaks on his lips. He leads his troops in a final victory charge and plants his flag upon the enemy position. Fleuri cheers with such delight that Phélipeaux silences him with a snowball.

The teachers emerge, and Pichegru asks the name of the victor. With his Corsican accent, Napoleon pronounces his name 'Nap-eye-ony'.

'What did you say? Paille-au-nez — straw in the nose?'

The other boys burst out laughing. Napoleon wheels round. The laughter stops abruptly.

'My boy, you will go far. Remember that it was Pichegru who said so.'

The boys form a crocodile and return to their classes.

'A geography lesson: a study of the climate of islands.'

In the schoolroom, a teacher is dictating as he draws an island:

'As for Corsica, that half-civilised island ...'

Napoleon rises to his feet, pale and angry. The boys make fun of him. He sits down again and writes in his exercise book, 'As for Corsica, the most beautiful island in the world ...' Phélipeaux and Peccaduc, sitting either side of Napoleon, give him surreptitious kicks. The teacher is about to conclude the lesson when he remembers: 'A little island lost in the ocean ... ' He draws an island on the blackboard and adds its name: St Helena. Napoleon writes it down, and falls into a reverie, ignoring the kicks from either side.

'Both masters and pupils felt the same antipathy for this proud, fierce child, who lived in a kind of savage isolation.'

In the dormitory, Napoleon writes of his unhappiness in a letter. Phélipeaux reports the fact that he is hiding letters in his bed to a monk, who tears the letter up, to Napoleon's fury.

His one consolation, his proud companion in misfortune, is kept in Tristan Fleuri's garret — a young eagle. Napoleon speaks lovingly to it, and caresses its magnificent head. When he goes to fetch it water, his two enemies seize their chance and set it free.

Enraged, Napoleon returns to the dormitory and demands to know who released his eagle. No one admits to it. 'Then you're all guilty!' Napoleon hurls himself upon them, dashing from bed to bed with the speed of lightning. Pandemonium. Pillows are flying and bursting and the feathers whirl in the dormitory like the snow which is still falling outside. The Minim Fathers have great difficulty in breaking up the epic battle. But eventually they pick Napoleon off the floor.

'Who d'you think YOU are?' demands one.

'A man,' replies Napoleon.

The teachers grab the boy, who struggles fiercely, and throw him out into the snow. Napoleon lies on the limber of a cannon, weeping. Fleuri sneaks out with his cloak and hat. Suddenly, Napoleon catches sight of his eagle, in a tree. He speaks to it through his tears, and the eagle flies down and perches on the barrel of the cannon. Napoleon smiles, and caresses it.

Napoleon and the French Revolution

Nine years later, at the Revolutionary Club des Cordeliers. 'Death to Tyrants' reads the legend tattooed on the chest of a sans-culotte who guards a door, refusing entry to everyone. Hundreds of people pack the vast hall. Danton's secretary, Camille Desmoulins, is made aware of a song, the sheets of which have just arrived with a printer. He reads it and questions the printer, who points out a young captain. He tells them to wait, and hurries to the door. This time, the sentries draw respectfully aside and open up. Desmoulins steps inside, then retreats.

'The three gods.'

Inside what was once the sacristy are the leaders of the Revolution — Danton, shaking with Homeric laughter, Marat, sallow and ill-looking, and Robespierre, pale, cold and sinister.

Desmoulins at last plucks up the courage to interrupt Danton.

'Your friend Dietrich has sent you a Captain of the Rhine Army with a song called the Marseillaise — can they distribute the copies while they wait for the meeting?'

Danton reads it and his concentration is intense. He strides out into the hall, and the assembly rises and applauds. After surveying them, and enjoying the adulation, he orders them to be seated, and to listen. He and the young Captain mount a pulpit, and with great passion, the Captain sings the song for the people. It receives a fantastic ovation. Danton embraces him and asks his name. 'Rouget de Lisle.' Danton orders the song to be distributed, and people scramble for the sheets. De Lisle teaches them the words. When the crowd reaches unison, Danton takes the stage and de Lisle slips away. On the edge of the crowd, a young artillery lieutenant stops him.

'I thank you on behalf of France, Monsieur. Your hymn will save many a cannon.'

'Thank you, lieutenant — tell me your name so I can remember it.'

'Napoleon Bonaparte.'

At the Tuileries, the same evening, in a setting of extreme wealth, Louis XVI sits with his Minister of War, signing commissions. A storm rages outside. His hand is poised over one commission, but the ink falls and a blot obscures the name. He can read BUO and TE on either side of the blot. 'What name is this?' he asks his Minister.

'Bonaparte, sire.'

Louis begins to rewrite it, and the storm brings the branch of a tree crashing to the balcony. The King starts, and remarks on the fierceness of the squall.

On the embankment, the wind is still blowing, but two shabbily dressed young men are examining the stalls of food and books. They argue as they pool their money. Talma, future king of the stage, wants to buy sausages; Napoleon wants to buy the tragedy Cinna *by Corneille. Napoleon wins, but their argument has been overheard by a woman who is touched by their predicament and buys the sausages for them. The problem for her now is how to present them without causing offence. Talma is correcting Napoleon's faulty pronunciation and adjusting his gestures when she approaches. Napoleon is at the peak of lyrical fervour when she offers him her sausages on a greasy paper. Napoleon is not easily surprised, but he is nevertheless surprised. She departs hastily, and Talma calls after her for her name: 'Madame Sans-Gêne!'*

The two friends forget Cinna *for their sausages. As they walk past a brightly lit window, Bonaparte suddenly gestures to Talma. A child of ten, song sheet in hand, is teaching the Marseillaise to his blind grandfather of eighty. Bonaparte grips Talma's arm briefly in emotion.*

In a Poor House

Two Corsicans, Pozzo di Borgo and Salicetti, hide behind a door as Violine Fleuri climbs the staircase, Salicetti jumps out and blocks her way, but Violine scurries to safety while Pozzo laughs. They place bets as to who will be the first to succeed with their attractive neighbour.

'Violine's fear of her neighbours on the right was compensated by a secret passion for her neighbour on the left.'

Bonaparte lives in a state of utter poverty. He puts on a boot which is so weak at the seams that his foot goes right through it. Realising he can't go out in such a state, he decides to seek help from his Corsican neighbours. They dislike Bonaparte, however, and refuse to help. They even hide a steaming tureen of soup under the table. Bonaparte manages to upset it before he leaves.

Back in his room, he makes a boot out of cardboard.

The two Corsicans make another attempt to ensnare Violine, but they are interrupted by Bonaparte. Violine stammers her thanks. With a cool little bow, Bonaparte withdraws. She kisses the spot where he was standing. Pozzo di Borgo leaves a note: 'Until death, Napoleon. Pozzo di Borgo.'

The Enrolments of 1792

A poster proclaims the danger; '300,000 bayonets are turned against us. The Royalists are plotting. The entire Vendée groans under arms. France is suffocating in the clutches of the foreign war while the fires of civil war consume her. The Nation is in danger! Citizens, to arms!'

Unusual faces, filled with heroic exaltation. A hundred—a thousand, all moved by the same feeling. They dissolve into a single immense head which synthesises them all. It is the face of France in 1792.
Rapid-cut sequence of trumpeters on the march; cannon on the Pont-Neuf; the announcement 'The Nation is in danger!'

At the Pont-Neuf, a vast enrolment booth. Intercut with drum rolls, a sequence of men and women signing up—old men, boys, invalids, girls. Bonaparte and his sister, Elisa, watch. 'His soul is open, his face impenetrable. Groundswell, in bursts, around them. He watches, he analyses. His eyes plunge into the present in order to deduce the future. His impassiveness contrasts with the universal ardour.' (Scenario.)

Danton climbs on to the enrolment table: 'Do away with ink, citizens. You should be signing in your own blood!'

The National Guard is leaving for the north. 'Enthusiasm gives way to a sort of collective madness. Strangers kiss. The most epic soldiers that France has ever possessed are all there. Tristan Fleuri watches; his heart overflows. He is in ecstasy, caught by the demon of war.' (Scenario.)

After an elaborate montage of rapid cutting — cannons, bells, drums, Danton — Bonaparte is transfigured. A great sense of purpose has awoken within him. 'I believe,' he says to Elisa, 'that one can do miracles with a people like that.'

Tristan Fleuri, father of Violine and Marcellin, has just been appointed Public Water Sprinkler to the King. He and Marcellin harness themselves to their water cart. When their overseer refuses to wear a revolutionary cap, sans-culottes string him up. Fleuri does not make the same mistake, and carries two hats to suit whichever side he encounters.

In a narrow street, Fleuri's water cart passes Bonaparte and sprays his cardboard boot, which falls to pieces. At the same moment, a carriage, containing, among others, Joséphine de Beauharnais and Paul Barras, draws to a halt outside the house of the famous palmist, Mademoiselle Lenormant.

Joséphine catches sight of Bonaparte and laughs at his predicament. Bonaparte watches as the group enters the house. Inside, gathered round a glass table above which an owl hovers, the group listens to the palmist as she tells Joséphine: 'An amazing fortune ... you are going to be QUEEN, Madame!'

Barras throws himself down, and mimicking the affectation of a courtier says, 'Yes, Joséphine. Queen of my heart!'

Outside, Bonaparte picks up a wreath of roses, dropped by Joséphine. *He goes to a pawnbroker, and pawns his watch for three francs. He returns to his room and finds a lily, left by Violine. He throws it out on to the landing, disappointing both Violine and her father, who was about to approach Bonaparte to remind him of Brienne.*

The night of August 10th, 1792. A Revolutionary mob in the street outside casts its sinister shadows on to the ceiling of Bonaparte's room. In the National Assembly, the Monarchy is undergoing its death throes. In a blacksmith's forge, Danton cracks a horseshoe before the crowd; 'This is what you have done today to the Monarchy.'

Bonaparte watches, impotent, as the mob hangs a man outside his window. 'How cowardly and vile men are,' he writes. 'Each man seeks to advance his own interests and works to use horror as a means to success.' But from second to second, as the Monarchy crumbles, Napoleon has the vague feeling of a source of light growing within him.

Pozzo di Borgo sends Violine a present — a superb court dress. He then rushes out and tells some tricoteuses that a blue-blooded aristocrat is hiding in the house. *Violine is seized by the women and dragged off to prison. Marcellin tells Tristan, who converts his water cart into an offensive weapon, with a bayonet concealed in the shaft. He then charges like a thunderbolt to the prison of La Force. As soon as a hostile crowd surrounds him, he opens his valves and triggers his bayonet and the sans-culottes fall back. And when he rescues Violine, and the tricoteuses realise she is his daughter, they perform a complete volte-face and shout 'Save her!' Marcellin has his revenge on Pozzo, thanks to the bayonet, and Violine and Fleuri are borne in triumph on the watercart, pulled along by the singing crowd.*

In the Tuileries, some sans-culottes discover a terrifying figure playing Dies Irae *on the organ — the Marquis de Sade 'burying the Monarchy'.*

'Marcellin, too, was overthrowing the Monarchy!'

A dozen urchins, from two to nine years old, some dressed as sans-culottes, others as aristocrats, restage the storming of the Bastille, using Fleuri's precious model as the focal point. They shatter it and Fleuri, furious, punishes his small son.

In Corsica

'Until now the axis of the dramatic action has been the crowd and the main character the Revolution. Bonaparte has been no more than a drop of water lost in the turbulent ocean, but a drop of water with the gift of independent thought and capable of resistance when all others were obeying the blind thrust of their passions. His character has been tempered. The crystallisation of his spirit has taken place amid the collapse of the Monarchy, and from now on he will have but one idea; to impose order upon this chaos.' (Scenario.)

'Bonaparte, who has not been back to Corsica for several years, arrives in Ajaccio with his sister Elisa in an attempt to reawaken national feeling.'

Mother Laetitia cannot believe the figure standing before her is her son. There is a joyful reunion at her home, Les Milelli, with the whole family.

The family has a close friend in the shepherd Santo-Ricci. He interrupts the joyful reunion to tell Bonaparte of some grim news — 'Paoli, our old and great Paoli, the revered father of us all, is about to sell us to the English.' Bonaparte, appalled, seeks confirmation from his family. Then he declares, 'As long as I'm alive, Corsica shall never be English.'

Bonaparte rides through his homeland, and, visiting the grotto of Casone, which had witnessed his youthful dreams, he reflects upon the fate of his little country.

In the tranquillity of the garden at Les Milelli, he considers whether to return to family life, or to sacrifice his individual happiness by entering the political arena. As the official representative of France, he sees the people drawing away from him — towards Paoli and English domination. The sworn enemy of the Bonaparte family, Pozzo di Borgo, has become Paoli's deputy, and he demands death to Napoleon. Aroused by his words, a mob pours through the narrow streets of Ajaccio and masses outside the

Bonaparte's town house. Napoleon steps out and silences them with his piercing gaze. As they fall back and begin to disperse, a flicker of a smile plays on his lips.

Ignoring the wise advice of his family, who warn him to flee the hatred of his people, Napoleon comes every day to the deserted headland of the Sanguinaires. Gazing at the horizon from the top of a favourite rock, he takes up the pose he will adopt at St Helena at the end of his life.

Pozzo di Borgo persuades Paoli to sign a death warrant for Bonaparte.

A secret meeting of old shepherds is held in the mountains, at which they, the last supporters of the persecuted Bonaparte family, swear to defend it until death.

At the Moulin du Roy inn, a hotbed of political dissent, two Corsican gendarmes put up a proclamation offering a large reward for Napoleon's capture, dead or alive.

Napoleon's brothers, Lucien and Joseph, set out in disguise for Calvi to seek help from the French authorities. And Napoleon decides to take action himself.

At the inn, an argument is raging between supporters of Spain and Buttafuaco, Italy and the Duke of Savoy, and England and Paoli. All are united in their desire for the death of Bonaparte. To their stupefaction, Bonaparte himself appears, daring to speak out at the very moment when a price is on his head.

'Our fatherland is France … with me!'

The nobility of the gesture momentarily disarms all hatred. The crowd subsides as they listen to his argument. 'Believe me, a man will come who will unite all the hopes of the nation, and then … '

Paoli's gendarmes burst in, led by Pozzo. The crowd panics.

The shepherd Santo-Ricci sees the gendarmes capture Bonaparte and he orders the other shepherds to hide in the shadows. Bonaparte is tied up and Pozzo announces that he is to be shot in the courtyard. Santo-Ricci manages to free him. The shepherds divert the gendarmes while Bonaparte makes his escape.

Bonaparte leaps from the roof of the inn to his horse, pursued by forty gendarmes.

At Paoli's office in the town hall of Ajaccio, the insurrectionary council declares war on France. Yet the tricolor still flies outside the window. Suddenly, the flag is torn from its pole. Bonaparte clambers over a balcony and declares, 'I am taking it away. It is too great for you!' He vanishes as swiftly as he appeared. Pistols are fired from the window. Too late.

Blazing with anger, Paoli orders exile for the Bonaparte family and gives power of life and death to every Corsican patriot over the members of his family.

At Les Milelli, the shepherds have prepared defences. Bonaparte rides up and tells his family to leave immediately — they will meet at the beach at Aspreto. He disappears again. Mother Laetitia refuses to leave until Santo-Ricci tells her, 'Flee for Napoleon's sake. Think of his despair if he has to blame himself one day for the death of all his family.' That thought overcomes Laetitia's resistance.

Bonaparte gallops across a stream. Close on his heels, the gendarmes open fire, but miss him. Pozzo decides to cut off his retreat, and taking a long mountaineering rope from one of the gendarmes, he stretches it across the road, securing it round two sturdy trees. Bonaparte heads for the trap, but he draws his sabre and slices the rope, confounding the waiting gendarmes.

He rides into a wood. Slashing his way out with his sabre, he encounters a precipice. He is shot at by a gendarme and falls, but he is not harmed, merely pretending, and he leaps upon his assailant, succeeding in pushing him over the edge. He grabs his victim's cloak and rides off on his horse.

Bonaparte is now in pursuit of himself. He shouts, 'I've just seen him dive into the sea!' He sees a small boat, moored to a rock.

He climbs aboard, to find it without oars or sail. He unwraps the great flag from the town hall and converts it into a sail. As he sails away, he shouts, 'I shall bring it back to you!'

Les Milelli is in flames. Corsicans feed the blaze. The shepherds urge Laetitia to begin her flight. A storm builds up. The little party struggles through the maquis. *The pursuers torture an old shepherd to find out the fugitives' route.*

In his small boat, Bonaparte is drawn at giddy speed towards the open sea, about to begin an epic battle with Fate.

'That same night, at the same time, another mighty storm was unleashed at the Convention.'

Robespierre demands a public indictment of all Girondins.

Bonaparte desperately battles against the storm, manoeuvring his sail. Lightning blinds him.

The fugitives on the run. The wind is blowing twice as violently as before, and they have to cross a raging torrent.

The Girondins try to escape. They rush forward, to be repulsed by waves.

The Convention itself begins to roll as though at the mercy of the waves.

The exhausted fugitives have collapsed in the downpour to wait until the storm abates.

Napoleon struggles to bale out his dinghy, which tosses crazily.

'Thus all the giants of the Revolution were swept, one after the other, into the raging whirlpool of the Reign of Terror. And a man, the defiant sport of the Ocean, his tricolor sail opening to the wind of the Revolution, was being triumphantly carried to the heights of History.'

The sea has grown calm. Aboard the sailing ship *Le Hasard*, Joseph and Lucien spot the small, storm-battered dinghy. They alter course. As they bring the dinghy in with grappling hooks, they are astonished to see Napoleon, unconscious in the bottom of the boat, clutching the torn tricolor.

The exhausted fugitives, in a pitiful state, drag themselves along. Suddenly, their faces light up, for before them … the Aspreto beach!

Bonaparte stares about, as if waking from a nightmare, sees the tricolor in his clenched hand, remembers and cries, 'Quickly — to Aspreto beach!' The ship changes course once more.

A cove at Aspreto — wild delight as Laetitia's family see the ship approaching from the horizon. But the townspeople are in hot pursuit with scythes and hammers. As the boat draws near, they open fire. Santo-Ricci is hit, but he sees the family board the ship before he dies. The townspeople retreat under fire from the ship.

As it sails towards France, Napoleon declares, 'And now the Bonapartes have one country and one country only — FRANCE!'

A cruising English sloop, the *Agamemnon*; a young officer is peering intently through his telescope. 'Captain,' he says, 'permit me to sink that suspicious-looking vessel.'

'No, Nelson,' says the Captain. 'Don't waste powder and shot on such an insignificant target.'

Napoleon's boat draws farther and farther away.

'Caesar and his destiny. A future Emperor, three kings and a queen on a few square metres between sky and sea.'

Bonaparte takes the helm, and an old pilot murmurs: 'That young captain is amazing. I have been watching him for two hours now. He is making straight for France without ever looking at the compass.'

An eagle flies down to alight on the pole of the flag flying at the top of the mainmast.

PART TWO

'Charlotte Corday, a fanatical admirer of the Girondins, has dreamed since their fall of avenging them on the person of the bloodthirsty Marat.'

Concealing a knife in her bosom, she calls upon Marat, who receives her in his bath. She pretends she has a list of suspects, and says she cannot talk in front of witnesses. The housekeeper is expelled. Suddenly, Corday dashes through the curtains, and the dying Marat is revealed, a knife in his chest. Corday is quickly arrested.

'In September 1793, the port of Toulon, where 20,000 English, Italians and Spaniards were entrenched, was besieged by a French army under the command of General Carteaux.'

Tristan Fleuri, Violine and Marcellin escape the September massacres by running an inn on the outskirts of Toulon. They soon realise the provinces are not escaping the fury of the extreme factions. French troops are retreating everywhere. In Violine's room is a hiding place with some mysterious books and pictures — even a crusader's sword. Fleuri's room is a miniature arsenal, where he indulges in bayonet practice, with Marcellin as drummer boy. Fleuri sees Violine praying, surrounded by books about Joan of Arc. Embarrassed at being discovered, she throws herself into her father's arms and says, 'At all costs, papa, someone must save France!'

Bonaparte discovers the army in a terrible state. Soldiers use mortars as a press to make rough wine. Others play 'boules' with shot. There is a complete lack of discipline. Bonaparte can stand it no longer, and leaves.

Fleuri has read that Caesar slept with lead weights on his chest and instructs his children to load fire dogs on to his groaning body.

Carteaux and his staff come blustering into Fleuri's inn. His staff never stop bowing and scraping obsequiously around him. Bonaparte appears — Violine is shocked, but delighted. Bonaparte marches up to Carteaux who is taken aback by the intrusion of a junior officer into this dazzling conclave of generals.

'What have you come here for, young man?'

'I have come as second in command of the siege artillery, sir.'

A laugh on Carteaux's face, then an ironic pout. 'Artillery? Why, we don't need any. We shall take Toulon with the sword and the bayonet!'

Bonaparte smiles slightly and prepares to leave, but Carteaux calls him back. 'If you were in my place, what would you do?'

Bonaparte explains his strategy.

'Well, Captain Cannon, one can see you are not good at geography. Remember this: firstly, artillery is useless, and secondly … '

A red-hot cannonball crashes into the room. Everyone takes to their heels in confusion. Carteaux sits on the ground, like a great, terrified child. Bonaparte kicks the cannonball into the ashes of the hearth and says, 'Secondly, it is most unpleasant.'

With the inn cleared, Bonaparte sits down to examine a plan of Toulon. Fleuri summons up his courage and begins, 'Captain, I was … '

Napoleon snaps: 'Bread, olives and silence!'

Fleuri, struck dumb, backs away, falling over himself.

Marcellin has surreptitiously taken Bonaparte's hat and put it on, along with his sword, and as Bonaparte paces the floor, Marcellin walks thoughtfully behind him, copying his movements. Fleuri plucks him away like a chicken.

'Carteaux, being found incapable, was replaced by General Dugommier.'

In an elegant office, a council of generals is presided over by Dugommier. Outside, in the barrack square, Bonaparte is training horses and their handlers for the artillery. Deafening noise and smoke. Dugommier asks him to come inside and join the conference.

Fleuri is mobilised, and imagining military glories he is filled with pride — until he learns he is to be a cook, when he is overcome with disappointment.

Bonaparte arrives at a bastion to discover the cannon being withdrawn. He orders the troops to replace the cannon. 'Impossible, Captain,' they reply.

'Impossible is not French.'

The cannon is replaced, and Napoleon fires the shot that returns it to action. But he encounters bitter opposition from Salicetti.

Synopsis

Bonaparte turns the bastion into the 'Battery of Men Without Fear', with
the help of Junot, a pot of paint and a brush. The soldiers rally, and French
courage blossoms once more. Vying with one another, they all rush to be
first at the breach into the bastion. Dugommier promotes Bonaparte
commander-in-chief of the artillery.

*Fleuri is cooking for the armies of the republic and he is very gloomy.
Marcellin rejects him, and Fleuri weeps, his tears dripping one by one into the
sauce he is stirring.*

*It is 6 a.m. A surprise sortie by English troops under the leadership of General
O'Hara, while Sidney Smith keeps watch on the French fleet imprisoned in the
anchorage. The French retreat under terrible artillery fire. Dugommier is
wounded and fights as he retreats. Bonaparte watches in anxiety and, as
Dugommier is brought in, whispers, 'You left without an order from me, Papa
Dugommier.'*

Dugommier admits it. 'You command.'

*Bonaparte: 'Order the retreat and call a council of war for this evening.'
Shame on all sides. Dugommier weeps with rage, but gives the order.*

At the council of war, Dugommier, discreetly prompted by Bonaparte,
explains his strategy.

'The enemy council of war was a veritable Tower of Babel.'

Bonaparte calls for an attack at midnight, and 'order, calm, silence'.
Three old soldiers gaze through the window with renewed confidence at the
figure of Bonaparte standing by the fireplace. He notices them, and smiles
to himself.

During the preparations for battle, Marcellin joins the troops as a
drummer boy. He asks the veteran Moustache: 'How old was the little
drummer boy Viala when he died?'

'Thirteen.'

'What luck! That means I've six years left to live.'

Midnight; the rain is falling and the wind howling, but Bonaparte gives the
artillery the signal to attack. At the fort of Little Gibraltar, the French are
checked, and retreat under the withering fire of the English.

*Bonaparte orders the Ardèche volunteers, new recruits, brought up as
reserve. When ordered into action they appear clumsy and stupid. They allow
themselves to be massacred without firing a shot in return, although no one runs
away. Bonaparte grabs one of them: 'This is outrageous! Not one of you has
fired a single cartridge!'*

*The young soldier replies, 'We don't know how to load our guns, m'sieu.
We've been soldiers only since last night.'*

Bonaparte is shocked. 'But ... that is impossible!'

Moustache answers, 'Impossible is not French, Captain.'

*Bonaparte embraces the young soldier, then makes a lightning decision and
orders a charge. He sets off at a gallop, followed by a hundred cavalrymen. As*

274

they reach the main position of the Ardèche volunteers, Bonaparte takes off his hat to them—and the cavalrymen do the same.

At this moment, the members of the Convention decide to call off the assault. Says Salicetti, 'Bonaparte has just committed the greatest crime in history. An assault on a night like this—it was such folly that even his head cannot pay for it!'

Dugommier issues instructions for Bonaparte to call off the attack.

Bonaparte looms through the rain and utters a single word of contempt: 'Speechmakers!'

Dugommier and Bonaparte talk together, then Dugommier once more assumes his air of leadership, and takes personal responsibility for continuing the attack. The members of the Convention are furious, but Dugommier silences them.

Prodigious but useless feats of courage by the French as they attack Little Gibraltar—a wide ditch of water prevents their crossing. A human ladder is organised—twice, men are pitched into the ditch. Napoleon is wounded in the thigh. The British defence seems indomitable.

'Never does Bonaparte show such fearlessness. He is everywhere, sees everything, and is equal to everything. Lightning from the sky and flashes from cannon encircle him. He is in the thick of fire, in his element.'

The English gunners are hacked to pieces around their guns. Of all those who defend the redoubt, not one escapes unwounded. Amid the cries of the wounded and dying, the firing stops and hand-to-hand fighting begins. Swords are the only weapons left.

At the English council of war, Admiral Hood orders the destruction of the French fleet by fire.

On shore, the frantic defenders of Toulon begin to embark on the British and Spanish ships. Women and children are crushed in the rush.

Sidney Smith orders oil and pitch to be emptied over the French ships and fuses to be laid. One of the most formidable fires in history flares up—this and the fire of Moscow are the two most vividly imprinted on Bonaparte's mind.

Sans-culottes swarm down the hillside like demons in the glow of the flames—the English, Spanish, Sardinian and Neapolitan troops try to counter-attack but they are scattered like spray. Final, apocalyptic battle in the wind and the flames. The English ships fire one hundred shots a minute. Admiral Hood, aboard the Victory, *weeps, his head in his hands. There are no more boats and the remaining civilians are shot down by the sans-culottes. Bonaparte looks on without moving. Everything is ablaze.*

'At dawn, the Commissioners of the Army who come to bring him the rank of brigadier-general by way of an apology, find him asleep with his head on a drum.'

Dugommier points: 'This is the victor of Toulon.'

On to a tree, beside Bonaparte, flutters the eagle.

PART THREE
The Terror

After the capture of Toulon, Fleuri is instructed by Salicetti to prepare a dinner for the Commissioners of the Army.

Fréron administers exemplary punishment to the citizens of the town for having assisted the English. Some eight hundred hostages have been rounded up indiscriminately—including old men, women and children.

Salicetti confronts Violine and shows her her name on the list of hostages. 'If you call out, I shall add your father to the list.' She resists, and Salicetti orders her to be taken away with the others.

Fréron announces the name of Toulon will be abolished, to be replaced by that of City of Shame. The whole town will be razed to the ground. He then remembers one last detail—hostages to the number of eight hundred will be shot en masse on the spot.

Salicetti calls upon the commander of artillery, Bonaparte, to put the sentence into execution immediately.

'Am I a butcher?' protests Bonaparte. 'I refuse!'

Salicetti promises that his refusal will be reported to Robespierre, and assigns the job to the aged General du Teil. Bonaparte rides away to avoid witnessing the massacre and Violine is frantic that he fails to do anything to save the hostages.

Du Teil takes command of the firing squad, in tears. The soldiers drink to boost their failing courage. Marcellin runs after Bonaparte, who agrees to ride back to rescue Violine—but he is too late. A hundred guns open fire. Those victims who survive, though wounded, are spared death—and among them is Violine, who is reunited with Fleuri.

Bonaparte sets out again, reading.

Salicetti comes to Robespierre to beg the favour of putting Bonaparte on trial. To his surprise, Robespierre says, 'Let General Bonaparte be offered the command of the Paris garrison in place of Henriot.' He adds, 'He is a man of strength, such as we lack in Paris, this Bonaparte. If he refuses, then I will give him to you.'

In March 1794, Robespierre has attained the height of his power, and has assumed complete control of the policy of the Revolutionary government. He is supported by Couthon and Saint-Just. Saint-Just is the most awe-inspiring figure of the Terror.

On Robespierre's orders, Danton is arrested and condemned to death for conspiracy against the Republic. The tumbril passes Robespierre's office, and Danton calls out, 'Infamous Robespierre! The scaffold is calling for you! You will follow me!'

The crowd cries out for mercy for Danton. Robespierre, hiding behind half-drawn shutters, makes no move.

Salicetti returns to inform Robespierre that Bonaparte refuses the command of the Paris garrison. 'He does not wish to support a man like you.' Robespierre orders his arrest.

Saint-Just denounces Viscountess Joséphine de Beauharnais — 'She would seduce the most virtuous.'

Bonaparte is imprisoned at Fort Carré, Antibes, and Joséphine is thrown into the prison at Les Carmes. She sobs distractedly as her children are taken from her. She is allowed her little dog. There is blood on the walls. A young man takes pity on her, and introduces himself as General Hoche.

Passing through Antibes, Salicetti comes to provoke Bonaparte. 'Are you preparing your defence?' he asks. Bonaparte, absorbed in his work, replies, 'No, I'm working out a route to the East, by way of a canal at Suez.'

In the prison at Les Carmes, reading out the roll-call of the condemned, is Fleuri, the sweat standing out on his brow. 'De Beauharnais.'

A cry. Joséphine staggers to her feet, supported by Hoche. She reaches Fleuri at the same time as a tall man of aristocratic bearing. The Viscount de Beauharnais, divorced from Joséphine two years earlier, has also to pay the price of his noble birth.

'What, two of you?' says Fleuri. 'Well, work it out yourselves. I only need one head.'

'For once, madame,' says the Viscount, 'allow me to take precedence.'

He kisses her hand, and a tipsy woman mimics the hand-kissing with a fat sans-culotte. Joséphine faints.

'The thermometer of the guillotine.'

A little chapel, with a stained glass rose-window. A tall filing rack is marked: 'On Trial — Next batch — Beheaded — Innocent'.

The last compartment, being empty, provides a contrast to the others. A sort of cyclops, a one-eyed man called Bonnet, has charge of these bloody archives. He hands over a pile of dossiers, and La Bussière and Fleuri settle down to work. La Bussière gives a quick glance around him, pulls out a dossier, tears a piece off and begins to eat it. Fleuri is astonished. He looks at the name on his next dossier, sees 'Napoleon Bonaparte', and tries to make La Bussière eat that one, too. In mime, La Bussière indicates he would suffocate. However, he chews up the dossier on Joséphine de Beauharnais, his eyes darting about to make sure no one is watching. Fleuri makes pellets of the Bonaparte dossier and stuffs them into his clothes.

Suddenly, they both duck behind a pile of dossiers, for Saint-Just enters. They are frozen with fear. Saint-Just passes and contemplates with great satisfaction the sinister filing racks.

At Antibes, Salicetti cannot understand the strange delay in the arrival of Bonaparte's file. 'Another must be made up here and he must be shot within three days.'

Thermidor
The Convention is a seething volcano. The galleries are full to bursting; in one

of them, Violine with Marcellin. Robespierre mounts the rostrum. Every voice seems opposed to him: 'Death to Saint-Just! Death to Robespierre!' Tallien runs forward, brandishing a knife. 'I have armed myself with a dagger to pierce the breast of this new Cromwell if the Convention lacks the courage to indict him.' Robespierre reaches the spot where Danton used to sit. A shout: 'The blood of Danton is choking you!'

Robespierre walks up the benches of the right, which stand empty.

'You're walking on the graves of the Girondins!'

Saint-Just leaps to the tribune and shouts 'Jackals!' The house suddenly falls silent. Violine produces a pistol. Nobody notices her.

Saint-Just says, 'Yes, we had to have victims, but is not the Revolution a great beacon lit upon tombs?'

As he talks of the Terror, which he admits dulled the sense of crime, we see a kaleidoscope of shots—the Nantes drownings, the bottom of a boat giving way, children sinking into the water; a bell ringing in a raging hurricane; the wheels of a tumbril; the Lyons massacres, hundreds of prisoners shot by cannon at point-blank range; the seething crater of a volcano; a burst of brutish laughter.

'Have you not forgotten that during this time we have created for you a France that is new and ready to be lived in? ... passed 12,000 decrees of which two-thirds were dedicated to human ends?'

Another hail of images—flowers, sunshine, grape-harvesters on a bright road—and a series of animated words—equality, abolition of slavery, primary schools, hospitals, Blind Institutes, Zoological Gardens, THE RIGHTS OF MAN ...

Saint-Just descends from the rostrum and rejoins Robespierre, who embraces him. The deputies begin yelling as before. Violine replaces her pistol. 'They are too great for us.'

The grim archives in the chapel—La Bussière is still eating. An officer rushes in and hands Bonnet a list. To be guillotined tomorrow: Robespierre, Couthon, Saint-Just ...

Bonnet looks up with a bewildered eye and says, 'What a mess.'

Celebration outside Les Carmes. Joséphine and her children are reunited. Bonaparte, too, is released.

'The following year, Bonaparte, in spite of his poverty, refuses the post of a general of infantry in the Vendée, offered him by Aubry, the War Minister.'

General Hoche asks if he finds it inconvenient to fight under his command. Bonaparte replies that when 200,000 foreigners are violating our frontiers, it is certainly inconvenient to go to war against Frenchmen. However, they shake hands—although Bonaparte is struck off the list of officers holding commissions.

Outside Aubry's office, he sees Joséphine once more.

He returns to his shabby room, with Talma, Junot, Marmont. They haven't a sou between them. They empty their pockets of all they possess—knives, keys and trinkets, and Bonaparte adds his watch. Junot goes off with the lot, tied up in a table-cloth.

Bonaparte explodes. 'I am suffocating in this cage.'

'What cage are you talking about?'

'Why, France, of course.'

He begins to talk of founding an Empire.

'In his search for some way of making a living, he believed he had found a new path open to him.'

Bonaparte works in a bookseller's premises, crating books. But he shows such astonishing clumsiness that he walks out.

Reinstated to his rank, but given an obscure post in the Army topographical office, Bonaparte brings to Pontecoulant his plans for the Italian campaign. Pontecoulant, being shaved, is so impressed he forgets the soap on his chin, and writes a recommendation to General Schérer with the Army of Italy. But Schérer laughs until the tears roll when he receives the plans at Nice. He writes on one corner: 'These plans are the work of a madman. Let the fool who wrote them come and execute them — Schérer.'

At his lodgings, Bonaparte receives his plans back while he is in the middle of some cooking. He is about to add them to the fire when he changes his mind. He goes to the window. The snow is driving in through a broken pane. Bonaparte glues the plans to the window frame.

France, in agony, is facing starvation. Distress beyond all imagination is making the people drift away from the Republic. Bonaparte and Junot walk in the snow past a queue at the door of a baker's shop, and they pause at the window of Mme Tallien's town house. Everywhere gold, lights, a swirl of voluptuousness.

'If in eight days the Revolution has not found its leader, France is lost,' declares Bonaparte.

For two months, under the cloak of anarchy, Paris has been filling up with émigrés who exploit the people's misery. Pozzo di Borgo and Salicetti also stir up the crowd against the Convention. Royalist Sectionnaires occupy the Pont-Neuf.

At Joséphine's house, Barras looks down into the street. 'I need a man,' he says. She suggests that droll young Buona … Buonaparte. And uses her charms to insist … Barras overcomes his jealousy and agrees to consider the idea.

'And on the 12th of Vendémiaire … '

The Convention is in uproar.

Bonaparte is in the public gallery.

Barras calls out for a general to put down the royalist insurrection. 'I propose the victor of Toulon, Bonaparte.' Assent. 'Does anybody know where he lives?'

With Junot, Bonaparte leaves the Convention and returns to his room. In a reverie, in the space of forty seconds, the whole Revolution passes before his eyes. The window panes burst into fragments. Only the plans for the Army of Italy, forming one of the panes, remain in place.

Barras enters Bonaparte's room and asks for a decision in three minutes.
'Without a hand of iron, the Convention is lost.' He returns to the landing.
Bonaparte, alone, goes to the stove and takes out a small live coal with some
tongs, and summoning up all his will-power, places it in the hollow of his hand.
The coal burns the flesh.

When Barras returns, Bonaparte accepts. 'I have no liking for those I
shall be serving, but when territory is threatened, the first duty is to rally to
those who hold the reins of government.'

Outside, a poor woman sobs in the doorway. She has six hungry, wailing
children. Bonaparte gives her all he has and forces Barras to do the same. Then
they enter the carriage.

Bonaparte arms the Convention with 800 guns, and sends a young major
called Murat to recapture the cannon in the hands of the Sectionnaires.
These he places in strategic positions at the Tuileries, the Place du Carousel,
the Pont-Royal.

At the Church of Saint-Roch is Tristan Fleuri, who is delighted when
Bonaparte pauses, albeit briefly, on his way to the wretched prospect of fighting
Frenchmen.

Bonaparte orders his artillery to fire blanks. The infantry use live rounds
when fired upon. The Sectionnaires lose ground, and take refuge in the church.
They soon surrender.

Pozzo di Borgo aims a shot at Bonaparte, but it misses. Fleuri, wondering
where the shot came from, accidentally discharges his musket, and the ball
strikes Pozzo on the cheek.

A few moments later, the crowd unmasks Salicetti, disguised as a
coachman and preparing to flee. Bonaparte orders the release of Salicetti
and Pozzo: 'I can forgive them easily, but I shall not forget.'

Though important politically, Vendémiaire has been limited to a few
skirmishes, and the large majority of Parisians remain totally ignorant of
the event. When Joséphine asks, 'What's the noise, M. Fouché?' he replies,
'It is Bonaparte entering history again, madame.'

Bonaparte returns to the Convention as the Saviour of the Revolution.
Barras proposes that he be nominated General in Chief of the Army of the
Interior. Crowds gather outside his lodgings. Bonaparte's aides de camp try
to hold back the delirious people, but it is hopeless. They scream and shout
and shove. Bonaparte exchanges his hat and cloak with Sebastiani, and he
and Junot plunge through the crowd without being noticed.

They go to the Zoological Gardens, one of Bonaparte's favourite walks. As a
newsboy runs past, the headline of his news-sheet reads 'BONAPARTE SAVIOUR OF
THE REVOLUTION'. *Bonaparte meditatively approaches an eagle. He caresses it*
as he used to do at school.

Mother Laetitia, her children clustered round her, reads a letter:

My dear Mama
*   You will have learned from the public newsheets everything that concerns*

me. I have been nominated by decree General of the Army of the Interior. We have vanquished, and all is forgotten.

Mother Laetitia: 'Let us hope that it lasts!'

The Reaction

At the prison of Les Carmes, Fleuri reads the roll-call once more. Same despair, same tragedy in the faces. But there is dancing — and the guests are vastly amused at the re-enactment.

'In this feverish reaction of life against death, a thirst for joy seized the whole of France. 644 balls had taken place in the space of a few days over the tombs of the victims of the Terror.'

Three beautiful women attend the Ball, and their charm eclipses Bonaparte's sudden fame — Mme Tallien, Mme Recamier and Mme de Beauharnais. Bonaparte strides up to the group of her admirers, completely fascinated. While Joséphine watches, General Hoche plays chess with Bonaparte — and loses. 'You're decidedly a better general than I,' he says, retiring gracefully. Joséphine sets out to captivate Bonaparte, and hypnotises him with her fan. 'What weapons do you fear most, General?' she asks.

'Fans, madame,' he replies.

Bonaparte notices a group of poor people outside. Throwing his purse to a maître d'hôtel, he says, 'Set up a buffet outside.' The poor are delighted. The rich, at first askance, begin to dance with the poor.

The Ball becomes more and more licentious until the girls are dancing without any clothes at all.

Having ordered all arms seized from private citizens, Bonaparte receives an unexpected request. Eugène de Beauharnais, aged fourteen, pleads to be allowed to keep the sword of his late father. Bonaparte agrees, and next day, to thank the general, comes Joséphine.

Bonaparte cancels all his appointments, and turns his attentions solely to Joséphine. He behaves awkwardly — nothing he does seems right, and Eugène is greatly amused.

Two hours later, the general staff are still waiting outside the door …

Realising his deficiencies, Bonaparte decides to polish up his love-making. Down on one knee, he is making ardent vows of love to his friend Talma, who is giving him lessons. Suddenly, he embraces a globe.

'Are you kissing Paris?' asks Talma.

'Paris? It's Joséphine's mouth!' replies Bonaparte.

He comes every day to see Joséphine — and the little shadow of Violine comes too, deeply distressed.

Realising that Barras wants her off his hands, Joséphine agrees to marry Bonaparte on condition that Barras appoints him Commander of the Army in Italy. While discussing this matter, Joséphine is horrified to see that Bonaparte has arrived, and is playing Blind Man's Buff with her children. No escape for Barras! But Bonaparte has a handkerchief over his eyes — she sends Barras out, and hopes for the best. When she tries to remove the blindfold, Bonaparte smiles.

'In love, my dear Joséphine, one should not see more clearly than this!'

That evening, the unconscious form of Violine is brought upstairs — she has a small, half-empty bottle in her tightly-clenched hand. Joséphine and Barras are there — the first sight that Violine sees as she recovers consciousness. She closes her eyes again. The doctor announces she is saved.

Bonaparte is officially appointed Commander of the Army of Italy. Junot rushes to his lodgings to impart the news. Bonaparte is unmoved. He finishes a mathematical problem on a blackboard. Then he goes to the window and peels off the plans for the Army of Italy, and reads Schérer's note: 'These plans are the work of a madman … '

'AT LAST!'

Joséphine tells Fleuri that she is taking Violine into service so he will be able to join the army without worry.

Bonaparte bursts into Joséphine's boudoir and announces, 'We must get married, madame. Quick — a notary, the banns, the certificates!'

Now it is Joséphine's turn to exercise her organisational abilities. Servants run in all directions.

At the wedding, on March 9th, 1796, Bonaparte is late. The guests wait patiently, while the registrar nods off.

In Violine's tiny room; as soon as Fleuri leaves, she bolts the door and begins to sew large white veils from a drawer with great care and skill.

At the end of two hours, Joséphine drums her heels with irritation. Her lawyer Calmelet goes out in search of Bonaparte. He finds him in his room, surrounded by maps of the Italian campaign. 'And your marriage, sir?' Bonaparte is shocked. He leaps to his feet and grabs his uniform, becoming hopelessly muddled as he hurries to put it on.

Like a whirlwind, Bonaparte bursts into the room where everyone awaits him, and slams his hand on the desk to wake the registrar.

The civil service begins. 'Faster, monsieur!' orders Bonaparte.

The frightened registrar continues, more quickly. 'Skip all that,' says Bonaparte.

'In the name of the law, will you take … '

'YES!'

Joséphine whispers to Barras: 'He frightens me, your Buona-parte.'

Violine arranges her hair like Joséphine. For she is also to be married that evening. She dresses herself in her veils, kneels on the bed, and produces from a locked cupboard a little shrine to Napoleon — one of his gloves is in there, a plume, and a little wooden statue.

It is the first of many altars to be erected by the people in their homes in homage to the new Alexander.

Joséphine moves almost shyly towards Bonaparte beside the wedding bed, and as they embrace the screen becomes gradually more opaque.

Violine moves to the wall, where the shadow of Bonaparte appears, as large as she. It is the little doll, the five-sou 'god of the day' that creates the shadow. Violine slowly kisses the cherished shadow.

Mother Laetitia with her three daughters. Sunshine. She finishes reading a letter. 'Married! Let us hope it lasts!!'

And in the night of 21 Ventôse, Year IV ... with a paltry 40,000 francs to divide among his Italian army ... Bonaparte leaves Joséphine, forty-eight hours after his marriage, and sets out for the conquest of the world.

He does not want to leave Paris without acquiring new strength inside the walls of the Convention. He opens one of the great doors and takes a step forward. Moonlight floods the arena. Nothing stirs. The heavy door swings shut behind him. He is startled by the noise. He climbs the rostrum and gazes at the empty seats. Gradually, the hall becomes peopled with phantoms. Fearing this hallucination, he tries to leave, but the gigantic figure of Danton rises from the closed door and advances.

'Listen, Bonaparte. The French Revolution is about to speak to you.'

The shades have a unity in death they lacked in life.

'We have realised that the Revolution cannot prosper without strong authority. Will you be its leader?'

Bonaparte replies with a nod.

Saint-Just rises and says, 'On the word of Saint-Just. If you one day forget that you are the direct heir of the Revolution, we shall turn ferociously against you. Will you remember?'

And Bonaparte is asked his plans.

'The liberation of oppressed people, the fusion of great European interests, the suppression of frontiers ... and ... THE UNIVERSAL REPUBLIC. Europe will become a single people, and anyone, wherever he travels, will always find himself in a common fatherland. To achieve this sacred aim, many wars will be necessary, but I proclaim it here for posterity, victories will one day be won without cannon and without bayonet.'

A gigantic ghost dressed in the style of the English of the seventeenth century: 'Do not give way to the temptation of power.'

'Who are you?'

'Cromwell.'

A lone man with an austere, foreign-looking face, says, 'Follow my example.' It is George Washington.

The great revolutionaries, in close, affectionate ranks, break into the Marseillaise.

En route to Nice, where he will join the Army of Italy, Bonaparte sits in his coach writing despatches and handing them to despatch riders who thunder past outside. He writes, too, intensely emotional letters to Joséphine.

Joséphine comes to Violine's room with some sewing, and surprises her praying at her shrine. Violine is desperately upset, but Joséphine calms her and they pray together.

Bonaparte finds the carriage too slow for him; he continues the journey on horseback. The generals awaiting him at Albenga are highly resentful. They regard Napoleon as an upstart, and they are determined to demonstrate their feelings.

The soldiers are in an even worse state than at Toulon. When one produces a crust of bread, he has to defend it at sword point against his comrade, only to lose it to an officer. When Bonaparte arrives, the generals turn their backs on him. Bonaparte loosens his belt and throws his sword on the table. The noise causes the generals to whirl round in surprise. Bonaparte obliges them to remove their hats simply by staring at them. He then replaces his and takes his seat to discuss plans for the forthcoming campaign. The generals are apoplectic when he announces the Army of Italy will take the offensive. They are even more dismayed when he announces a review of the army in just two hours.

The TRIPTYCH opens with an unbroken panorama of the Albenga camp. The entire, ragged army is lying on the ground. Bonaparte appears, and gives the command 'ATTENTION!' The whole army is on its feet in an instant. A central aisle is formed. Bonaparte gallops up and down in each direction and his eagle gaze gradually electrifies this crowd. A sudden, extraordinary wave of infatuation spreads from soul to soul. The leader has arrived. Bonaparte leaves the field, followed by his staff.

One hour later, the entire Army of Italy appears, drawn up impeccably for review by the new commander.

(The following scene belongs to the non-triptych, single-screen ending.) Tristan Fleuri is standing among the ranks, beside himself with excitement at meeting Bonaparte, and determined to remind him of Brienne. As he rides up, Fleuri takes two paces forward and says, 'General, I was at Brienne.' Bonaparte stares at him for a brief moment, then shouts: 'Two paces forward – march.' The troops absorb Fleuri in line once again and Bonaparte rides off. Poor Fleuri all but collapses with disappointment.

'Within a few hours, Bonaparte was to find a sudden, almost unparalleled enthusiasm growing around him. Miraculously, order was restored.'

Bonaparte takes off his hat and salutes his army, as they cheer him. That night, for the first time, the Army slept confidently. The next morning, April 11th, 1796, the ragged crowd awakens with the spirit of the Grand Army. The drummers sound reveille, and Bonaparte addresses his troops from the top of a jagged rock.

'Soldiers! You are naked and ill-fed. The Government owes you much, but it can give you nothing. The patience and the courage you display amidst these rocks are admirable, but they do not win you glory. I want to lead you into the most fertile plains in the world. Rich provinces and great towns will be in your power. There you will find honour, glory and riches. Soldiers of Italy, will you lack courage or constancy?'

A great storm of corporate enthusiasm is unleashed. Waves of jubilation run through this crowd of wretched men. They already feel themselves capable of vanquishing the world.

'Two hours later, by a miracle of speed, the great Army was on the march.'

'The troops move forward towards Italy in a true triptych — two absolutely identical armies descend at the same pace towards the bottom of the central screen, forming a flowing, curving pattern which harmonises amazingly with the central image in a play of strictly symmetrical photogenic masses.' (Post-production script.)

'Forty-eight hours later, at Montenotte, Napoleon laughingly opened the gates of Italy.'

The soldiers of the Republic rush pell-mell through the disembowelled houses, and the Austrians are gripped with fear in the face of this incredible army of madmen, practically unarmed.

'And through the open door swept the strongest and richest torrent of human power that history had ever seen unleashed.'

On the flanking screens is Napoleon, in a fantastic ride past the columns on the verge of the road, while in the centre, the Old Guard march on, accompanied by pretty French girls from home, and beautiful Italians picked up along the way.

'On April 16th, 1796, having outstripped his entire army and staff, he was on the heights of Montezemolo, at an altitude of 2,700 ft.'

Sweeping prospect of Alpine peaks. The solitary silhouette of Bonaparte stands out on the central screen, between heaven and earth. On to the screens appear in fluid superimposition his dream armies, the battles of the future, and the obsessional image of Joséphine.

'While the Beggars of Glory, their stomachs empty, but their heads filled with songs, leave history to pass into legend … '

The ragged troops are interrupted in their rhythm by the sight of a shadow on the road before them. The eagle! It stretches its wings across all three screens, and the great advance picks up its impetus. As the images become faster and faster the triptych becomes one gigantic tricolor flag, and the *Chant du départ* is succeeded by the Marseillaise. 'A maelstrom fills all three screens. The whole Revolution, swept on at delirious speed towards the heart of Europe, is now one huge tricolor flag, quivering with all that has been inscribed upon it, and it takes on the appearance of an Apocalyptic, tricolor torrent, inundating, enflaming and transfiguring, all at one and the same time.' (Post-production script.)

The Different Versions
of *Napoleon*

1 Opéra, April 1927. 35mm tinted and toned.
    Length: 5,600m. Première: April 7. Music: Arthur Honegger. With triptychs.
2 Apollo, May 1927. 35mm tinted and toned.
    Length: 12,800m. First showing of definitive version, but without triptychs. Shown in two parts, twice only: May 8–9 for trade, May 11–12 for press.
3 German version, Oct. 1927. 35mm tinted and toned.
    Length: under 3 hours. Distributed by UFA. Première: Oct. 11. Music: Werner Heymann. With Triptych. (UFA used this version for Central Europe.)
4 Marivaux, Nov. 1927. 35mm tinted and toned.
    Opéra version adjusted by Gance. It could be seen in two episodes. Matinée: Brienne, Toulon and Italy (triptych) only. The evening performance included the remainder of the Opéra version, repeating Italy (triptych). Released by Gaumont-Metro-Goldwyn.
5 Version released to provinces, winter 1927–8. Several versions were circulated. The Opéra version was occasionally shown in the same city at the same time as the definitive version, with or without triptych. At Nice, the Apollo version was shown in several parts. At Boulogne, a version of 10,000m. Exhibitors elsewhere reduced the long version to suit themselves.
6 Definitive version as sent to USA. Edited down to 29 reels.
7 Gaumont-Palace, March–April 1928. 35mm black and white.
    New version, not edited by Gance. Part One: March 23–9, Part Two: April 6–12. Total length: probably about three hours.
8 British version, June 28, 1928. 35mm tinted and toned.
    Length: 11,400 ft. Released by Jury-Metro-Goldwyn. With triptych.
9 American version, Jan. 1929. 35mm black and white.
    Length: 8 reels. Released by Metro-Goldwyn-Mayer. No triptych.
10 Pathé-Rural version. 17·5mm tinted and toned.
    Length: 17 reels. French/English titles. No triptych.

11 Pathé-Baby version, 1928. 9·5mm black and white.
   Length: 9 reels. Notched titles, French. No triptych.
12 Pathescope version. 9·5mm black and white.
   Length: 6 reels. Notched titles, English. No triptych.
13 *Napoleon Bonaparte* vu et entendu par Abel Gance, 1935. 35mm black and white, sound.
   Length: 13 reels, later cut to 10 reels. Music: Henri Verdun. No triptych.
14 Film-Office version. 16mm/9·5mm/8mm black and white.
   Length: 5 reel abridgment of 1935 sound version. Subtitles over the picture. No triptych.
15 Studio 28 version. 35mm black and white, sound.
   Napoleon Bonaparte (1935) plus synchronised triptych.
16 *Bonaparte et la Révolution*, 1970. 35mm black and white, sound.
   Gance's own reworking of silent and sound *Napoleon*.
   Length: 4 hours 45 minutes with additional shooting, later cut to 4 hours at 24 fps. No triptych.
17 Kevin Brownlow reconstruction of the silent *Napoleon*. 35mm black and white.
   Length: 4 hours 50 minutes at 20 fps. Music: Carl Davis. With triptych.
18 'Coppola version'. 35mm toned.
   Shortened version of no. 17.
   Length: 4 hours at 24 fps. Music: Carmine Coppola. With triptych.
19 Kevin Brownlow reconstruction for Cinémathèque Française. 35mm black and white.
   Length: 5 hours 13 minutes at 20 fps. Music: Carl Davis. With triptych.

Notes

Throughout the Notes, the letters AG/CNC refer to the Abel Gance papers in the Centre National de la Cinématographie, Paris.

Preface
1 Abel Gance wrote, 'That he was the most tragic character in history is proved to me by these words of his: "All my life I have sacrificed every-thing—peace of mind, happiness, my future."' Quoted in M-G-M publicity for *Napoleon*, 1928.
2 Interview, Robert Vidalin to Veronica Bamfield, Paris, 1981.
3 Steven Kramer and James Welsh, *Abel Gance*, Twayne, Boston, 1978, p. 13.

Part One: The Making
1 The Fuse Is Lit
1 *Bioscope*, July 4, 1928, p. 44.
2 Maurice Bardèche and Robert Brasillach, *The History of Motion Pictures*, W. W. Norton & Co. and Museum of Modern Art, New York, 1938, p. 231. Published in Britain as *The History of the Film*, in France as *Histoire du cinéma*.
3 Paul Rotha, *The Film Till Now*, Cape, London, 1930, p. 233.

2 Chasseur d'images
1 Maurice Bardèche and Robert Brasillach, *The History of Motion Pictures*, W. W. Norton & Co. and Museum of Modern Art, New York, 1938, p. 163.
2 Roger Icart, *Abel Gance*, Institut Pédagogique National, Toulouse, 1960.
3 Abel Gance, *Prisme*, Éditions de la NRF, Gallimard, Paris, 1930, p. 162.
4 Léonce-Henry Burel to René Prédal, microfiche, Éditions l'Avant-Scène, Paris.
5 Ibid.

6 Gance, op. cit., p. 158.

7 Bardèche and Brasillach, op. cit., p. 164.

3 Pictures in the Fire

1 Gance later hired the set designer of *Orphans of the Storm*, Edward Scholl, to work on *Napoleon*. According to the *New York Times*, 'Edward Scholl is a New York portrait painter who has devoted much thought and study to the art of the screen as designer of settings for special effects. In America, his talents have been used by such directors as D. W. Griffith and the late Thomas Ince. Scholl worked for many months on the scenes for the battle of Toulon. Models of ships were built by the dozen, drawings made and plaster models taken in the famous marine museum of the Louvre. Contemporary prints were studied for likenesses of Lord Hood and others — all this for a few brief flashes on the screen.' *New York Times*, June 5, 1927, VII, 5:6.

2 Griffith historian Russell Merritt feels this was simply a gesture in the spirit of *noblesse oblige*; he has discovered no documents on a Napoleon project among the Griffith papers at the Museum of Modern Art, nor has their curator, Eileen Bowser. A year or so later, Griffith announced an episode film à la *Intolerance* entitled *Christ and Napoleon*, but Merritt thinks this was just another of the grandiose ideas which kept Griffith's name in the public eye.

3 Gance also noted the strange box mounted on the front of Sartov's Bell & Howell camera. This accommodated gauzes in six positions and, with a special lens, was responsible for the 'soft focus' effects in Griffith's films. Gance took back to France two Bell & Howell cameras, together with lighting equipment, and following the Sartov example, acquired gauzes and soft focus lenses for use in *Napoleon*. (The original Sartov matte box and lens is in the author's collection.)

4 Asked his opinion of Gance, Griffith said, 'If Gance worked in the United States, it would mean an advance for the motion picture of fifteen years.' (*Ciné Miroir*, March 1, 1926, p. 139.) Griffith did his best to persuade Gance to work at his studio, and a project with Lillian Gish, *Joan of Arc*, was under consideration for a time. See p. 41.

5 Jean Dréville to Veronica Bamfield, Nov. 16, 1981.

6 Quoted in Sophie Daria, *Abel Gance hier et demain*, La Palatine, Paris, 1959, p. 82.

7 Gance *carnet*, AG/CNC.

8 Résumé, Sept. 25, 1923, AG/CNC.

9 *Paris-Soir*, April 16, 1927.

10 Jean Arroy, *En tournant Napoléon avec Abel Gance — souvenirs et impressions d'un sans-culotte*, Éditions la Renaissance du Livre, Paris, 1927, p. 34.

11 Gance *carnet*, AG/CNC.

12 Interview, Dagmar Bolin to author, Paris, March 1982.

13 Victor Hugo, *Ninety Three*, unidentified English edn, 1908, London Library, p. 158. Gance once planned to film this.

14 Quoted in Arroy, op. cit., pp. 35–7.

15 Résumé, op. cit.

16 Interview, Simone Surdieux to author (interpreter Bernard Eisenschitz), Rosureux, 1981.

17 D'Esparbès wrote *L'Agonie des aigles*, which was filmed by Bernard Deschamps for Pathé Consortium in 1922 with the star of *La Roue*, Séverin-Mars, as Napoleon.

18 D'Esparbès to AG, Aug. 30, 1924, AG/CNC.

4 The Sum of Recollection

1 'Sous l'aile du coq', unpublished ms. of Maud Pathé.

2 AG/CNC.

3 Résumé, Sept. 25, 1923, AG/CNC.

4 Ibid.

5 AG to Barattolo, Oct. 16, 1923, AG/CNC.

6 AG to Barattolo, n.d. 1923, AG/CNC.

7 Wengeroff to AG, Feb 7, 1924, AG/CNC.

8 AG to Wengeroff, Feb. 11, 1924, AG/CNC.

9 Unidentified newspaper, probably May 1924, AG/CNC.

10 Contract, May 1924, AG/CNC.

11 Westi was involved in several films apart from *Napoleon*. It bought *Miracle of the Wolves* for Central Europe. It contributed to *Michael Strogoff* of Tourjansky, *600,000 francs par mois* with Koline, *Vertige* of L'Herbier and German films. It joined forces with Pathé and formed an organisation called Pathé-Westi.

12 *Lichtbildbühne*, June 17, 1924, and Mussolini's letter of authority, June 23, 1924, AG/CNC. It was part of Gance's character that he was always trying to gain to his cause people with whom he had nothing in common.

13 *Éclair*, Aug. 15, 1924.

5 Unsung Heroes

1 Interview, Jean Mitry to author (interpreter Lenny Borger), Paris, 1981.

2 Jean Arroy, *En tournant Napoléon avec Abel Gance — souvenirs et impressions d'un sans-culotte*, Éditions la Renaissance du Livre, Paris, 1927.

3 Interview, Viacheslav Tourjansky to author (interpreter Bernard Eisenschitz), Paris, 1969.

4 Volkoff was perhaps the first film-maker to put Gance's revolutionary ideas of rapid montage into action, for *Kean* went into production shortly after the release of *La Roue*. 'When I shot my montage of dancing legs and all sorts of atmospheric details in the Coal Hole tavern, I was aware of the suspicion and even hostility which surrounded me. Yet when it was all cut together, everyone realised that the sequence stood as one of

the best in the entire film.' *Photo Ciné*, April 1928, quoted in G. M. Coissac, *Les Coulisses du cinéma*, Pittoresque, Paris, 1929, pp. 113–14.

5 Koline could hardly speak a word of French, nor could many of the Russian actors. Most of their careers came to an end with the arrival of sound. (Annabella told me that her makeup man on *Le Million* was Chakatouny, the Pozzo di Borgo of *Napoleon*.)

6 Handwritten draft, AG/CNC.

6 *Anything Possible*

1 Interviews, Simon Feldman to author, Paris, 1981/2.

2 Interview, Marcel David to author, Paris, 1982.

3 Interview, Claude Makovski to author, Telluride, Colorado, 1981.

4 Jean-Paul Mundviller took Gance to court for hiring him as *chef opérateur* and crediting him only as *opérateur*. Mundviller's lawyer, M. Paul Weill, pleaded his client's importance and stressed the dangers he faced. (The example he gave, of being knocked down by a cavalry charge, occurred on another picture, *Le Joueur d'échecs*.) The court found in Mundviller's favour and awarded him damages of 10,000 francs. *Le Figaro*, Dec. 21, 1928, *Le Journal*, Nov. 24, 1928.

5 *Photo Ciné*, April 1928, quoted in G. M. Coissac, *Les Coulisses du cinéma*, Pittoresque, Paris, 1929, pp. 113–14.

6 A device Burel credited to a cameraman on *La Roue*, Duverger.

7 Man Ray was the famous surrealist. H.-P. Roché was the author of *Jules et Jim*.

8 AG to J.-P. Mundviller, Aug. 28, 1924, AG/CNC.

9 *Paris-Soir*, quoted in *Cinéa-Ciné pour tous*, June 1, 1927.

10 Also known as *Ciné mitrailleuse facine*, patented June 14, 1922 (source J. Deslandes). The high speed camera was known as Camera GV — 'grande vitesse'.

11 Int., Marcel David to author.

12 In the First World War, the Aeroscope camera was used by front-line cameramen. It could be pumped up by compressed air and then hand-held. It was so unreliable, however, it was little used after the war.

13 It took its name from the firm for which it was manufactured, Société Française Sept, Avenue Kléber, Paris.

14 Jacques Brunius, *En marge du cinéma français*, Arcanes, Paris, 1954, p. 75.

15 Journalists continued to refer to flying footballs with cameras. When I took this up with Feldman he sighed: 'You are a journalist. You know what journalists write.' Even when Jean Mitry claimed to have thrown one, Feldman dismissed the idea absolutely.

16 For *The Last Laugh* (1924), the German film so celebrated for its moving camera work, cameraman Karl Freund had carried a heavy camera on a wooden tray, supported by shoulder straps.

17 Jean Arroy, *Photo Ciné*, May 1927, quoted in Roger Icart, *Abel Gance*,

Institut Pédagogique National, Toulouse, 1960, p. 125.
18 Alexander Volkoff, *Photo Ciné*, April 1928, quoted in G. M. Coissac, op. cit.

7 *The Search for Napoleon*

1 Fauchois was the author of *Boudu sauvé des eaux*, filmed by Renoir.
2 He was also a politician of the extreme right, one of the originators of the fascist coup of Feb. 6, 1934. During the Occupation he was shot down by the RAF on a flight to Beirut.
3 *Catherine*, or *Une Vie sans joie*, was directed by Dieudonné in 1924, from a scenario by Jean Renoir, who also appeared in it. It was not released until 1927, to exploit Dieudonné's success in *Napoleon*. The delay was partly due to legal wrangling between Renoir and Dieudonné.
4 Not to be taken too seriously! In 1964 Dieudonné told ORTF the same story with slight changes, indicating it was a party piece.
5 Mosjoukine to AG, July 4, 1924, AG/CNC.

8 *'On tourne!'*

1 Jean Arroy, *En tournant Napoléon avec Abel Gance — souvenirs et impressions d'un sans-culotte*, Éditions la Renaissance du Livre, Paris, 1927, pp. 46–7. No one but Arroy remembers this, least of all Feldman, who would have been involved. Nor do any photos of that day exist with Gance at a microphone.
2 Pierre Schildknecht became one of the top art directors in France under the name of Pierre Schild. He went to Italy and Spain in the Second World War, and worked there for the rest of his career.
3 Many reference books list Eugène Lourié among the art directors. When I met him in Hollywood he said, 'I worked on *Napoleon*, but not that one — the Sacha Guitry version.'
4 Blaise Cendrars's film about the making of *La Roue* exists at the Service des Archives du Film, Bois d'Arcy, together with a record of the 1930 film *La Fin du monde*. About two reels of *Autour de Napoléon* exist at the Cinémathèque Française.
5 Interview, Simon Feldman to author, Paris, 1981.
6 Louis-Antoine Fauvelet de Bourrienne, *Memoirs of Napoleon Bonaparte*, ed. R. W. Phipps, New York, 1891, 1:4–5, quoted in Steven Kramer and James Welsh, *Abel Gance*, Twayne, Boston, 1978, p. 96.
7 Arroy, op. cit., p. 49.
8 Interview, Henri Cointe to Veronica Bamfield, Briançon, 1982.
9 Interview, Gabriel Fornaseri to Veronica Bamfield, Briançon, 1982.
10 Int., Henri Cointe to Veronica Bamfield.
11 'Personal memoir of René Jeanne', in René Jeanne and Charles Ford, *Abel Gance*, Seghers, Paris, 1963, p. 56. I used his phrase 'the charm of dynamite' as the title of a film about Gance.

9 The Enchanted Isle

1 *Lectures pour tous*, Aug. 1925.
2 Interview, Simone Surdieux to author (interpreter Bernard Eisenschitz), Rosureux, 1981.
3 Since destroyed by fire.
4 Quoted in *A la recherche de la culture corse*, in *Le Mémorial des Corses*, Fernand Ettori, Ajaccio, 1979, vol. 4, p. 412.
5 None of the pit shots was used.
6 Interview, Simon Feldman to author, Paris, 1981/2.
7 *Lectures pour tous*, Aug. 1925.
8 *L'Éveil de la Corse*, May 6, 1925.
9 Unidentified article by 'Stephane Vernes' in Simone Surdieux's scrapbook.
10 *Lectures pour tous*, Aug. 1925. He was asked not to wear his hat in town.
11 *La Jeune Corse*, quoted in *A la recherche*, op. cit.
12 It was the end, instead, for Mabel Poulton. Completing her role in *Ame d'artiste*, she saw a strikingly pretty girl at the studio and was told it was Annabella, playing Violine. 'Why was I rejected? I was never sure. The producers said they wanted a French girl ...' Interview, Mabel Poulton to author, London, 1981. Gance had originally hoped Lillian Gish would play the part.
13 Napoleon adopted the golden bee as his personal emblem when he became Emperor.
14 Chiappe, a friend of Bonardi and also a Corsican, had been tested by Gance to play the older Napoleon.
15 A documentary-style film had recently been made by director Gennaro Dini, adding more lustre to Romanetti's reputation. The bandit was killed soon after his meeting with Gance.
16 Quoted in *A la recherche*, op. cit.

10 Entr'acte

1 Rudolph Becker to AG, March 22, 1925, AG/CNC.
2 AG to Becker, March 23, 1925, AG/CNC.
3 Unidentified newspaper, AG/CNC.
4 Sept. 26, 1925.
5 AG, confidential memo, June 21, 1925, AG/CNC.
6 Confidential report, n.d. but must be June 1925, AG/CNC.
7 Abel Gance, *Prisme*, Éditions de la N.R.F., Gallimard, Paris, 1930, p. 325.
8 *Le Figaro*, Sept. 28, 1925.
9 *Le Figaro*, Oct. 6, 1925.
10 Gance, op. cit., p. 324.
11 *Cinéa-Ciné pour tous*, April 1, 1925, p. 7.
12 Interview, Alexander d'Arbeloff to author, London, 1981.

13 D'Ayen had been responsible for the medieval fortress of Carcasonne, which had been the main location for *Miracle of the Wolves*.

14 'While everyone was concentrating on resuming the production of *Napoleon*, and organising its financing, this was the only thing that mattered and the settlement with d'Arbeloff, in relation to his 100 per cent ownership shares and his presidency of SGF, was left in abeyance. However, it was agreed that d'Arbeloff would remain legally president of the Société Générale des Films and owner of 100 per cent of its shares with its assets and rights on *Napoleon*'s production.' Correction by Alexander d'Arbeloff to manuscript, April 1982.

15 Int., Alexander d'Arbeloff to author.

16 Letter of agreement, Nov. 1, 1925, AG/CNC.

17 SGF were subsequently to finance Jean Epstein's *Finis Terrae* and Carl Dreyer's *La Passion de Jeanne d'Arc* and they released Maurice Tourneur's *Équipage* (production Lutèce-Films). Dreyer sued SGF in 1931.

18 Int., Alexander d'Arbeloff to author.

19 Photograph in the collection of the Cinémathèque Française.

11 The Siege of Toulon

1 Jean Arroy, *En tournant Napoléon avec Abel Gance — souvenirs et impressions d'un sans-culotte*, Éditions la Renaissance du Livre, Paris, 1927, p. 61.

2 Quoted, ibid., pp. 78–9.

3 AG/CNC.

4 Interview, André Cerf to Bernard Eisenschitz, Paris, 1981. (He is referred to as Henry Cerf in the publicity reports and in the Opéra programme.)

5 Arroy, op. cit., p. 86.

6 Dreyer was preparing *La Passion de Jeanne d'Arc* for SGF.

7 Quoted in *Cahiers du cinéma*, No. 124, Oct. 1961, pp. 32–3.

8 Interview, Robert de Ansorena to author, Paris, 1981. Still active in the theatre and television, he has changed his name, for reasons of pronunciation, to de Sorena.

9 Interview, Simon Feldman to author, Paris, 1981/2.

10 Mme Braquehaye to Bernard Eisenschitz, Dec. 17, 1981.

11 Int., de Ansorena to author.

12 Quoted in *Cahiers du cinéma*, op. cit.

13 Arroy, op. cit., p. 108. According to *Paris-Soir* (n.d., AG/CNC), 220 insurance declarations were submitted, of which fifteen were serious. Dreyer had casualties on the last scenes of his *Jeanne d'Arc*.

12 Cordeliers and Convention

1 Interview, Harry-Krimer to author, Saint Josse-sur-mer, 1982.

2 Interview, Robert Vidalin to Veronica Bamfield, Paris, 1981.

3 *Lectures pour tous*, Nov. 1926, p. 18.

4 *Le Temps*, March 19, 1926.
5 Int., Harry-Krimer to author.
6 Interview, Gina Manès to author (interpreter Bernard Eisenschitz), Abitain, 1981.
7 *Cinéa-Ciné pour tous*, Nov. 1, 1927.
8 Victor Hugo, *Ninety Three*, unidentified English edn, 1908, London Library, pp. 162–3.
9 Ibid., p. 116.
10 *Napoléon vu par Abel Gance*, Librairie Plon, Paris, p. 124.
11 Interview, Simon Feldman to author, Paris, 1981/2.
12 *Lectures pour tous*, Nov. 1926.
13 Jean Arroy, *En tournant Napoléon avec Abel Gance — souvenirs et impressions d'un sans-culotte*, Éditions la Renaissance du Livre, Paris, 1927, pp. 111–12.

13 Sweep of Empire
1 The Locarno peace treaties had been signed in December 1925.
2 General Vincent, who had commanded the troops used on *J'accuse*, temporarily replaced General Nogues, commander at Toulon. *L'Illustration*, April 2, 1927.
3 *Lectures pour tous*, Feb. 1927.
4 Alexander Lony to Bernard Eisenschitz, n.d. (Dec. 1981).
5 Gance dated this as Sept. 1922, but he was still working on the editing of *La Roue* until Dec. 1922; it is more likely to be around Aug. 1923.
6 His *carnets* show that he planned to project certain 'paroxystic' sequences on a tricolor triptych — an effect he reserved for the last scene. See p. 157.
7 Raoul Grimoin-Sanson encircled the audience with a panorama of Paris filmed from a captive balloon; his process required ten cameras and ten projectors. It was closed down because of fire risk.
8 Interview, Comte de Béarn to Bambi Ballard, Paris, 1982.
9 Rapport sur les origines du brevet secret 11035, Dec. 28, 1926, AG/CNC.
10 Bulletin AFITEC No. 27, 1967, quoted in Debrie catalogue, Établissements André Debrie, Paris, p. 8. A letter from Debrie, May 29, 1925, says it is something 'we have not dared to think of'. Instead, he recommends a single lens to enlarge the picture panoramically.
11 Patent no. 11035, Aug. 20, 1926, improved by Patent no. 35.034. This letter is in the collection of the Cinémathèque Française.
12 Oct. 16, 1926, with later improvements. Gance and Debrie hoped to form a company to exploit the triptych.
13 Simon Feldman remembers there were two models — on the second, the cameras fanned out beside each other on an aluminium platform. Magirama later used this principle. See p. 188.
14 *La Cinématographie Française*, Sept. 11, 1926, p. 7.
15 The Admiral was alarmed at the possible effect on his ships of the underwater explosions, not realising they were little more than fireworks.

(Simon Feldman.) Regrettably, one destroyer can just be glimpsed in the scene where Napoleon walks through the wood, and we see the harbour through the trees. Incidentally, this wood was the actual site of the battle for Petit-Gibraltar; a nineteenth-century fort stands there now, called Fort Napoléon.

16 *Le Gaulois*, Feb. 4, 1927.
17 Jean Arroy, *En tournant Napoléon avec Abel Gance — souvenirs et impressions d'un sans-culotte*, Éditions la Renaissance du Livre, Paris, 1927, pp. 130–1.
18 Ibid., pp. 133–4.

14 Flame in the Shadows
1 Contracts with G-M-G and M-G-M, AG/CNC.
2 *Cinéma Spectacles*, Dec. 11, 1926.
3 Ibid.
4 *Hebdo-Film*, Oct. 30, 1926, p. 9.
5 The final figure of the cost of *Napoleon* has been maddeningly elusive. Jacques Deslandes had the account book, and lent it to an accountant to translate the mass of figures into a final and accurate costing. The book was never returned. Jean Arroy, in his book on the making of the film, states that *Napoleon* had 17–18 million francs invested in it (p. 21); this is the most authoritative figure we have. Other references all reflect this figure, except an interview with the Duc d'Ayen which declared *Napoleon* cost 11 million (the figure was probably reduced to emphasise the huge sum spent by Dreyer on *Jeanne d'Arc* — 9 million: Maurice Drouzy, *Carl Th. Dreyer né Nilsson*, Éditions du Cerf, Paris, 1982, pp. 245, 368).
6 *Cinéa-Ciné pour tous*, April 15, 1925, p. 5.
7 Harry Alan Potamkin, *Cinema*, April 1930, p. 24, quoted in Siegfried Kracauer, *From Caligari to Hitler*, Princeton University Press, 1947, p. 126.
8 Notes for *Prisme*, AG/CNC.
9 Interviews, Simon Feldman to author, Paris, 1981/2.
10 Interview, Marguerite Beaugé to André Labarthe and Janine Bazin, ORTF, 1964(?).
11 Interview, Yvonne Martin to author (interpreter Bernard Eisenschitz), Paris, 1982.
12 Roger Icart thinks this occurred on *La Roue*.
13 Int. Yvonne Martin to author.
14 *Le Temps*, March 24, 1926.
15 Int., Yvonne Martin to author.
16 Int., Marguerite Beaugé to Labarthe and Bazin.
17 A. t'Serstevens, *L'Homme qui fut Blaise Cendrars*, Denoël, Paris, n.d. 'It triumphed at the Opéra with the cuts suggested by Blaise.'
18 Etablissements Gaumont to SGF, March 15, 1927, Troussier collection, Paris.

19 *Cinéa-Ciné pour tous*, June 1927.

20 Gance had shot no such closeups for the scene but he apparently agreed with Arroy for he inserted a closeup of Robespierre from the Three Gods sequence.

21 Jean Arroy to AG, dated (by Gance) 1926 but clearly written before the Opéra show as it refers to that in the future tense. Arroy was right about the static eagle; it was severely criticised.

15 The Music of Light

1 Comte de Béarn to AG, Sept. 6, 1927, AG/CNC.

2 *Cinéma*, April 24, 1927.

3 On *La Roue* a speed control had been installed for the conductor, and the same thing was provided for M. Szyfer, the conductor of the Opéra orchestra. It did not prove satisfactory and was replaced by a system of light signals operated from the conductor's podium. *Étude sommaire des conditions à observer pour la projection des scènes triptyques du film* 'Napoléon', par R. Aylmer, chef du service Ciné Matériel aux Établissements Gaumont, courtesy Cinémathèque Française.

4 Interview, Arthur Hoérée to Bambi Ballard, Paris, 1981.

5 A mystery surrounds the presence of Doumergue. Most newspapers reported his arrival as a matter of course. But a scandal erupted when a French reporter, syndicating his story to a German paper, stated that Doumergue had walked out before the end of the film, complaining about deficiencies of technique which made it impossible to sit through any longer. The French papers asserted that this was an outrageous libel. The mystery is further compounded by the fact that the reporter from *Cinémagazine* (April 15, 1927, p. 123) observed that Doumergue's box remained empty throughout the performance. I have not been able to track down any photographs taken at the Opéra première, whereas Doumergue is shown in the magazines posing on the stairs when he attended the Opéra for the première of *Miracle of the Wolves*.

6 Interview, Yvonne Martin to author (interpreter Bernard Eisenschitz), Paris, 1982.

7 Unlike the Army of Italy triptychs, which were panoramic, these pictures were separated by a thin border.

8 Interview, Marguerite Beaugé to André Labarthe and Janine Bazin, ORTF, 1964(?).

9 Int., Yvonne Martin to author.

10 Quoted by Arroy, *Cinéa-Ciné pour tous*, June 1927.

11 Interview, Harry-Krimer to author, Saint-Josse-sur-mer, 1982.

12 *Cinémagazine*, April 15, 1927, p. 122.

13 Interview, Gina Manès to author (interpreter Bernard Eisenschitz), Abitain, 1981.

14 Int., Arthur Hoérée to Bambi Ballard.

15 AG to UFA, Sept. 27, 1927, AG/CNC. For the 1935 version, Gance

used Henri Verdun.

16 *Lanterne*, April 15, 1927.

17 Only eight pieces composed by Honegger survive; these are currently being edited by Adriano of Zurich. Adriano writes, 'I am editing the whole as a score in its original version, and not in the "blown up" one for bigger orchestra, since the manuscript does not have the later version. "Les Ombres", for example, is much better in its original setting for strings, trumpet and percussion, which means without winds, and similar examples are in other pieces too.' (Letter to author, April 28, 1982.) Honegger elaborated the orchestration after complaints that the music at the première was too thin.

18 *Paris-Midi*, April 8, 1927.

19 *Paris-Soir*, April 9, 1927.

20 *Le Petit Journal*, quoted in *Cinémagazine*, Nov. 25, 1927.

21 *Le Gaulois*, quoted, ibid.

22 *Comoedia*, quoted, ibid.

23 *Les Nouvelles Littéraires*, May 21, 1927.

24 *Photo Ciné*, n.d., probably May 1927, pp. 55–7. Gance said to Roger Icart, 'The library mice have gone to a lot of trouble to prove to me that Bonaparte was not in the Cordeliers nor Saint-Just in the Convention on the days when I took them there. Well,' he added cheerfully, 'they are now!' Roger Icart, *Abel Gance*, Institut Pédagogique National, Toulouse, 1960, p. 21.

25 Quoted in *Comoedia*, May 9, 1927.

26 *Mon Ciné*, July 21, 1927. This was written after the screening of the long version, which contained the rapid-cut snowball fight.

27 G. M. Coissac, *Les Coulisses du cinéma*, Pittoresque, Paris, 1929, p. 85.

28 Léon Moussinac, *Panoramique du cinéma*, Au Sans Pareil, Paris, 1929, p. 55. (This comment first appeared in *l'Humanité*.)

29 Denis Mack Smith, *Mussolini*, Weidenfeld and Nicolson, London, 1981, p. 96.

30 Steven Kramer and James Welsh, *Abel Gance*, Twayne, Boston, 1978, p. 164.

31 Brasillach co-authored *The History of Motion Pictures* (with Maurice Bardèche, W. W. Norton & Co. and Museum of Modern Art, New York, 1938). During the German Occupation he edited *Je suis partout* and was shot by the Resistance at the Liberation.

32 *Cinémagazine*, Nov. 25, 1927.

33 AG in letter from Ajaccio, April 27, 1925, in collection Cinémathèque Française, quoted in their brochure for *Napoleon*, May 1982.

16 Ten-day Wonder

1 The first film to be shown at the Opéra was *Miracle of the Wolves*; other films included *Salammbô* and *Croisière noire*, the Citroën expedition to Africa.

2 *Filma*, June 15, 1927.

3 The length of the *version définitive* was an almost unimaginable 12,878 metres, 42 reels—the same length as the original version of *Greed*. It took nine hours to show—four and a half hours on each day. But even though this version was shown elsewhere, it must be regarded as a rough cut. Gance, like Griffith, continued working on the editing of his films, even while they were in release. The Apollo version was immediately shortened. A manuscript page for *Prisme* (typed in 1927) refers to the film being 11,000 metres (36,300 ft): 'I would need eight hours to show it to you.' It *would* take almost eight hours at the correct speed of 20 fps, around which *Napoleon* was photographed. Gance told me that the correct length for the full version was six hours, yet he put the figure of 15,000 metres as the original length on his titles for *Bonaparte and the Revolution*! Roger Icart says that the film was planned to be released in six episodes, but it was subject to further adjustments by exhibitors. (In Toulouse, only three episodes were shown, without triptych.) 'You could have it in twelve episodes, six periods or three chapters!'

The most reliable indication of the length of the full version, as finally edited down by Gance, was the negative sent to M-G-M in 1928, which ran to 38,000 ft. 6,000 ft would have been triptych material for the Entry into Italy, 2,100 ft would have been triptych for the Convention, and alternative, single-screen material covering these scenes would also have been included. So the final length of the full version—confirmed by the receipt of a second version by M-G-M—would have been 29 reels—six hours twenty-eight minutes. The length of the latest reconstructed version is five hours thirteen minutes.

4 *Echo*, May 13, 1927.

5 UFA also acquired the film for Austria, Poland, Finland, Denmark, Sweden and Norway. UFA had recommended Conrad Veidt for the cameo role of the Marquis de Sade. According to Gance's list of the sequences in the long version, a scene of the Marquis de Sade did appear, but there is no evidence that the role was played by Veidt. None of the cast lists includes the role at all.

6 Herr Meydam to AG, Oct. 29, 1927, AG/CNC.

7 Jean de Merly to AG, Sept. 17, 1927, AG/CNC.

8 Henry-Roussell to AG, Oct. 31, 1927, AG/CNC.

9 AG to UFA, Sept. 21, 1927, AG/CNC.

10 AG to Dr Freuner, Oct. 17, 1927, AG/CNC.

11 Quoted in *Cinémagazine*, Nov. 25, 1927.

12 G-M-G were also indulging in the reprehensible American practice known as 'block booking'—offering *Napoleon* to exhibitors only if they accepted other, less attractive titles in the M-G-M programme. If they turned down the offer, they lost the chance of showing *Napoleon*. *Journal*, Nov. 4, 1927.

13 *Rumeur*, Nov. 13, 1927.

14 Programme for *Napoleon*, Marivaux Theatre, Nov. 1927.

15 They were preceded by a subtitle, 'Essais d'une rythmique au triple écran par Abel Gance'. I found this title among Bal des Victimes material selected for *Bonaparte and the Revolution*, proving that Gance had used elements from the triptych dances in that film.

16 Contracts, AG/CNC and M-G-M legal files.

17 *Rumeur*, March 25, 1928.

18 *Information*, March 26, 1928.

19 Jean Toulout to G-M-G, April 7, 1928, AG/CNC.

20 *Information*, July 16, 1928.

21 Gance refers to the Marivaux-Opéra version when Brienne and Toulon were included only at the matinée. See p. 286.

22 *Information*, July 16, 1928.

23 Ibid.

24 Philip Chester, *Cinema World*, quoted in *Paris-Midi*, July 31, 1928.

25 Unidentified press cutting, author's collection.

17 Defeat in America

1 *Information*, July 16, 1928.

2 Louis B. Mayer to J. Robert Rubin, Feb. 7, 1928, M-G-M legal files.

3 Harry M. Geduld, *The Birth of the Talkies*, Indiana Univ. Press, Bloomington, 1975, p. 122.

4 Washington (who was still alive in 1796) was a relic of Gance's plan to provide different versions for different countries, thus making the film truly international.

5 *Variety*, Jan. 23, 1929.

6 *Zit's*, Feb. 26, 1929.

7 *Motion Picture News*, Feb. 16, 1929.

8 *New York Post*, Feb. 12, 1929.

9 Memorandum on distribution of *Napoleon*, n.d., M-G-M legal files.

10 Interview, Comte de Béarn to Bambi Ballard, Paris, 1982.

11 Document, Dec. 9, 1927, AG/CNC.

12 Agreement, Aug. 9, 1928, AG/CNC.

13 The Comte de Béarn said, 'I sued M-G-M, or tried to, using two American lawyers, but I was told that as France had not honoured her war debt I would never get a cent out of America. So I gave up. When G-M-G put it on in Paris, instead of giving me the 50 per cent due to me they gave me nothing at all. I got my lawyer, Suzanne Blum, to sue M-G-M through G-M-G, and I won. However, she wasn't that successful, because G-M-G, instead of giving me the receipts for 1927/28 and 28/29, paid me only those after 1930. We never got hold of the accounts. I believe they disappeared. So I sued again and the court awarded me 500,000 francs against the 5 million I was claiming.' (The amount was actually 100,000 francs and it was his claim which was reduced.) Int., Comte de Béarn to Bambi Ballard.

14 Abel Gance, *Prisme*, Éditions de la NRF, Gallimard, Paris, 1930, p. 355.

15 Philippe Hériat, who played Salicetti in *Napoleon*, also played in this. He was in many important French silents — Cavalcanti's *En Rade* and de Gastyne's *La Merveilleuse Vie de Jeanne d'Arc*. He eventually became a Goncourt Prize-winning novelist. He died in 1971.

16 Such a film was made in Germany in 1931 — Victor Trivas's *No Man's Land*.

Part Two: The Reconstruction
18 Nothing to Declare

1 He did not cut them out, but neglected to print them up and cut them in when they were on separate rolls or included as flash titles.

19 A Gnashing of Teeth

1 The directors were mostly conservative. One of the few to show the flair of the true film-maker was John Krish, a documentary film-maker of extraordinary and neglected talent. He and I became friends and he was one of the earliest supporters of *Napoleon* — including a tribute to Gance in a series of educational film programmes he made for the BBC.

2 One historian, Jean-Michel Martinat, has advanced the thesis that the propagation of 17·5mm Pathé-Rural among the towns and villages of France had a political purpose. His argument is supported by three of the silent films released by Pathé-Rural: *Napoleon*, *Destinée* (Henry-Roussell) and *La Merveilleuse Vie de Jeanne d'Arc*: see IAMHIST Newsletter No. 11, Summer 1981, p. 6.

3 See chapter 1, note 3.

20 Too Good to Last

1 His associates, such as Dagmar Bolin who worked with him at this transitional period, said he could not cope with sound.

21 Vin de l'Empereur

1 *Le Tzar Napoléon* (Éditions Baudinière, Paris, 1928) told the story of a Russian émigré, Alexis, who is obsessed by Napoleon. Hired by a French director to play the lead in a spectacular film of Napoleon, Alexis proves to be the Czarevich — he has survived, after all, cured of haemophilia and ready to liberate his country from the Bolsheviks. Using the film, its international finance, and its Cossack extras — who remain loyal and hail him as 'Czar Napoleon' — he launches an offensive against the Soviets. A British agent outwits Alexis and forces him to abandon his dream. The novel was due to be filmed in 1929, with Dieudonné in the title role. But, like the idea itself, nothing came of it.

2 There was no sign of this material when I examined the Cinémathèque Française's holdings in 1982, so I can only assume their original print was another victim of the great fire.

3 Stuart Byron, *Variety*, Sept. 27, 1967, p. 7.

22 *Somebody Has to Do It*
1 'Un Coeur qui s'appelle Langlois', *Le Monde*, Feb. 21, 1968.
2 *The Times*, May 29, 1968.
3 Henri Langlois to author, Feb. 24, 1969.
4 Author to Langlois, Feb. 26, 1969.

23 *On the Firing Line*
1 'The original negative of *Napoleon* has been destroyed or has disappeared in undetermined circumstances.' Registration, Sept. 8, 1970, for *Bonaparte and the Revolution* between Gance and Films 13.
2 Contracts in the CNC registry.
3 Interview, Claude Lelouch to author, Paris, 1982.
4 This execution sequence was discovered by Gance in 1958 and handed to the Cinémathèque. It has since vanished, presumably another victim of the fire.
5 I have accumulated a number of sequences which do not make sense by themselves and which cannot go into the film until complementary scenes have been rediscovered.
6 Eisenstein describes this scene in *Oeuvres*, Vol. 4, Paris, 1978, pp. 32–3.

25 *A Meeting of Eagles*
1 *Variety*, Sept. 12, 1971.
2 *Hollywood Reporter*, Sept. 27, 1971.
3 *New York Times*, Oct. 24, 1971.
4 Bernard Eisenschitz was once told by Gance that he had been awarded something by Giscard d'Estaing. 'He was shocked they were giving him a decoration and not helping him materially at all.'
5 AG to author, April 5, 1972.
6 *Financial Times*, April 7, 1972.

26 *Fortune Favours the Brave*
1 David Shepard to AG, Feb. 1, 1973.
2 Robert Dellett to David Shepard, April 15, 1973.
3 *Washington Post*, April 15, 1973.
4 AG to author, June 29, 1973.
5 AG to author, July 27, 1973.

27 *Strings Attached*
1 Bob Harris to author, May 5, 1975.
2 I have given up referring to any of this film as 'lost'; a substantial amount of footage has turned up since I began writing this book. See the final chapter.

29 Fortissimo
1 Author to AG, Nov. 30, 1980.
2 *The Times*, Dec. 5, 1980, p. 11.
3 *Guardian*, Dec. 1, 1980, p. 11.
4 *New Standard*, Dec. 4, 1980, p. 25.
5 *New Statesman*, Dec. 5, 1980, p. 32.
6 *Daily Telegraph*, Dec. 5, 1980, p. 5.
7 *Irish Times*, Dec. 10, 1980, p. 10.

30 Cresting the Wave
1 *Evening Outlook*, July 3, 1981.
2 The only other time I have watched a film with 6,000 people was at the Moscow Film Festival, in the vast Palace of Congresses in the Kremlin. Every evening, throughout each Festival, two features are shown in this amazing auditorium.

31 'The Measure for All Other Films, Forever'
1 *Evening Outlook*, July 3, 1981.
2 *Washington Post*, Feb. 1, 1981.
3 *Variety*, Sept. 9, 1981.
4 Ibid., Feb. 2, 1982.

Index